The Doctrines of Jacob Boehme

By

Franz Hartmann

ANODOS
BOOKS

Franz Hartmann (1838-1912)
Originally published in 1891

Anodos Books
1c Kings Road
Whithorn
Newton Stewart
Dumfries & Galloway
DG8 8PP

Contents

Preface

"My writings are only for those who are willing to receive the truth in a simple and childlike state of mind, for it is they who are to possess the kingdom of God. I have written only for those that seek; to the cunning and worldly-wise I have nothing to say." (*Threefold Life*, xv. 65.)

"Neither money nor worldly possessions, neither science nor authority, will bring to you the sweet rest of paradise, at which you can arrive only by the noble knowledge of self. In that you may clothe your soul; it is the pearl which is not eaten by moths, and which no thief takes away. Seek it, and you will find a noble treasure." (*Three Principles*, ix. 1.)

"I write for no other purpose than that man may learn how to know himself." (*Three Principles*, iv. 64.)

THE following is an attempt to present an epitome of the principal doctrines of Jacob Boehme in a certain systematic order, so as to afford a general view of them and to serve as an introduction to the study of Boehme's works. I have herein followed the plan laid down in Dr. J. Hamberger's excellent but now very rare book. The headings of the paragraphs are for the purpose of summarising the quotations that follow. These quotations have in many instances been condensed, and in some cases I have attempted to render them in a more modern and comprehensible phraseology than that of the original text, the latter being very often obscure and untranslatable. This I did because it seemed to me of far more importance that the public, for whom this book is written, should obtain a comprehensive view of the doctrines of Boehme than that merely the learned philologist should find his curiosity gratified by getting the exact form in which Boehme clothed his thoughts. In adding some remarks of my own, my object was not such a presumptuous one as to amend, comment upon, explain, or make clearer the writings of Boehme; for it is self-evident that in order to be able to criticise, amend, or explain the contents of a divinely inspired book, the critic or explainer would have to be divinely inspired himself. I have no such arrogant claims to advance; but I wanted to call the attention of the reader to certain points that may aid in their understanding.

I have carefully compared the doctrines of Boehme with those of the Eastern sages, as laid down in the "Secret Doctrine" and in the religious literature of the East, and I find the most remarkable harmony between them in their esoteric meaning; in fact, the religion of Buddha, Krishna, and that of the Christ seem to me to be one and identical. The greatest obstacle to the understanding of the mysteries of the religion of the living Christ is the very narrow view which we have become accustomed to take of them, according to the merely external and superficial interpretation of the Old and New Testaments, such as is

1

given by the modern churches and by fashionable clericalism, which regards these doctrines from a merely historical or emotional point of view.

A study of Boehme's writings, by means of entering into the spirit in which they were written, is sure to expand the mind and to elevate the heart of the reader, giving him a greater and more sublime conception of God, Nature, and Man, than any other book of which I know.

I am under many obligations to Mrs. E. B. Penny, of Cullompton, for her assistance in this difficult work, and also to Mr. G. W. Medway for valuable suggestions.

The extracts are taken from the 1682 Amsterdam (German) edition of Boehme's Complete Works.

F. H.

Vienna, *September* 1890.

The Life of Jacob Boehme

"The fulness of time has taken place, and the kingdom of God has arrived. Repent and believe in the gospel of truth."—J. B.

JACOB BOEHME was born in the year 1575, at Alt Seidenburg, a place about two miles distant from Goerlitz in Germany. He was the son of poor country people, and in his youth he herded the cattle of his parents. He was then sent to school, where he learned to read and to write, and afterwards he entered as an apprentice a shoemaker's shop.

It seems that even in early youth he was able to enter into an abnormal state of consciousness, and to behold images in the astral light; for once, while herding the cattle and standing on the top of a hill, he suddenly saw an arched opening of a vault, built of large red stones, and surrounded by bushes. He went through that opening into the vault, and in its depths he beheld a vessel filled with money.

He, however, experienced no desire to possess himself of that treasure; but supposing that it was a product of the spirits of darkness made to lead him into temptation, he fled.

On a later occasion, while left alone in the shoemaker's shop, an unknown stranger entered, asking to buy a pair of shoes. Boehme, supposing himself not entitled to make such a bargain in the absence of his master, asked an extraordinary high price, hoping thus to get rid of the person who desired to purchase. Nevertheless, the stranger bought the shoes and left the shop. After leaving, he stopped in front of the shop, and, with a loud and solemn voice called to Boehme: "Jacob, come outside."

Boehme was very much astonished to see that the stranger knew his name. He went out in the street to meet him, and there the stranger, grasping him by the hand, and, with deeply penetrating eyes looking into his eyes, spoke the following words: "Jacob, you are now little; but you will become a great man, and the world will wonder about you. Be pious, live in the fear of God, and honour His word. Especially do I admonish you to read the Bible; herein you will find comfort and consolation; for you will have to suffer a great deal of trouble, poverty, and persecution. Nevertheless, do not fear, but remain firm; for God loves you, and is gracious to you." He then again pressed Boehme's hand, gave him another kind look, and went away.

This remarkable event made a great impression on the mind of Jacob Boehme. He earnestly went through the exercises necessary in the study of practical occultism; that is to say, he practised patience, piety, simplicity of thought and purpose, modesty, resignation of his self-will to divine law, and he kept in mind the promise given in the Bible, that those who earnestly ask the Father in heaven for the communication of the Holy Ghost will have the spirit of sanctity awakened within themselves, and be illuminated with His wisdom.

Such an illumination, indeed, took place within his mind, and for seven days in succession Jacob Boehme was in an ecstatic state, during which he was surrounded by the light of the Spirit, and his consciousness immersed in contemplation and happiness. It is not stated what he saw during those visions, nor would such a statement have the result of gratifying the curiosity of the reader; for the things of the Spirit are inconceivable to the external mind, and can only be realised by those who, rising above the realm of the senses and entering a state of superior consciousness, can perceive them. Such a state does not necessarily exclude the exercise of the external faculties; for while Plato says about Socrates, that the latter once stood immovable for a day and a half upon one spot in a state of such ecstasy, in the case of Jacob Boehme we find that during a similar condition he continued the external occupations of his profession.

Afterwards, in the year 1594, he became master-shoemaker, and married a woman, with whom he lived for thirty years, and there were four sons born to him, who followed a profession like himself.

In the year 1600, in the twenty-fifth year of his age, another divine illumination took place in his mind, and this time he learned to know the innermost foundation of nature, and acquired the capacity to see henceforth with the eyes of the soul into the heart of all things, a faculty which remained with him even in his normal condition.

Ten years afterward, anno 1610, his third illumination took place, and that which in former visions had appeared to him chaotic and multifarious was now recognised by him as a unity, like a harp of many strings, of which each string is a separate instrument, while the whole is only one harp. He now recognised the divine order of nature, and how from the trunk of the tree of life spring different branches, bearing manifold leaves and flowers and fruits, and he became impressed with the necessity of writing down what he saw and preserving the record.

Thus, beginning with the year 1612, and up to his end in the year

1624, he wrote many books about the things which he saw in the light of his own spirit, comprising thirty books full of the deepest mysteries regarding God and the angels, Christ and man, heaven and hell and nature, and the secret things of the world, such as before him no man is known to have communicated to this sinful world, and all this he did, not for the purpose of earthly gain, but for the glorification of God and for the redemption of mankind from ignorance regarding the things of the Spirit.

He taught a conception of God which was far too grand to be grasped by the narrow-minded clergy, who saw their authority weakened by a poor shoemaker, and who therefore became his unrelenting enemies; for the God of whom they conceived was a limited Being, a Person who at the time of His death had given His divine powers into the hands of the clergy, while the God of Jacob Boehme was still living and filling the universe with His glory. He says:—

> "I acknowledge a universal God, being a *Unity*, and the primordial power of Good in the universe; self-existent, independent of forms, needing no locality for its existence, unmeasurable and not subject to the intellectual comprehension of any being. I acknowledge this power to be a *Trinity* in *One*, each of the *Three* being of equal power, being called the *Father*, the *Son*, and the *Holy Ghost*. I acknowledge that this triune principle fills at one and the same time all things; that it has been, and still continues to be, the cause, foundation, and beginning of all things. I believe and acknowledge that the eternal power of this principle caused the existence of the universe; that its power, in a manner comparable to a *breath* or *speech* (the Word, the Son or Christ), radiated from its centre, and produced the germs out of which grow visible forms, and that in this exhaled Breath or Word (the Logos) is contained the inner heaven and the visible world with all things existing within them."

Moreover, he taught that to be a true Christian it was not sufficient to subscribe to a certain set of beliefs; but that only he in whom the Christ is living is a true follower of Christ in spirit and in truth.

> "He alone is a true Christian whose soul and mind has entered again into the original matrix, out of which the life of man has taken its origin; that is to say, the eternal *Word* (λογος). This Word has been revealed in our human nature, which is blind to the presence of God, and he who absorbs this Word with his hungry soul and thereby returns to the original spiritual state in which humanity took its origin, his soul will become a temple of divine love, wherein the Father receives His beloved Son. In him will reside the Holy Ghost.

> "He alone, therefore, in whom *Christ* exists and lives is a Christian, a

man in whom Christ has been raised out of the wasted flesh of Adam. He will be an heir of Christ—not on account of some merit gained by some one else, nor by some favour conferred upon him by some external power, but by inward grace.

"To believe merely in a historical Christ, to be satisfied with the belief that at some time in the past Jesus has died to satisfy the anger of God, does not constitute a Christian. Such a speculative Christian every wicked devil may be, for everyone would like to obtain, without any efforts of his own, something good which he does not deserve. But that which is born from the flesh cannot enter the kingdom of the God. To enter that kingdom one must be reborn in the Spirit.

"Not palaces of stone and costly houses of worship regenerate man; but the divine spiritual sun, existing in the divine heaven, acting through the divine power of the Word of God in the temple of Christ. A true Christian desires nothing else but that which the Christ within his soul desires.

"All our religious systems are only the works of intellectual children. We ought to repudiate all our personal desires, disputes, science, and will, if we want to restore the harmony with the mother which gave us birth at the beginning; for at present our souls are the playgrounds of many hundreds of malicious animals, which we have put there in the place of God, and which we worship for gods. These animals must die before the Christ principle can begin to live therein. Man must return to his natural state (his original purity), before he can become divine.

"There is no other way for *Christ* to live than through the death of old *Adam;* a man cannot become a god and remain an animal still. No one is saved by God as a mark of his gratitude for having attended church and having had the patience to listen to a sermon; but his attendance to external ceremonies can only benefit him if he hears Christ speak within his own heart.

"All our disputations and intellectual speculations in regard to the divine mysteries are useless; because they originate from external sources. God's mysteries can be only known by God, and to know them we must first seek God in our own *centre*. Our reason and will must return to the inner source from which they originated; then will we arrive at a true science of God and His attributes.

"Man's will and imagination have become perverted from their original state. Man has surrounded himself by a world of will and imagination of his own. He has therefore lost sight of God, and can only regain his former state and become wise if he brings the activity of his soul and mind again in harmony with the divine Spirit.

"A Christian is he who lives in Christ, and in whom Christ's power is active. He must feel the divine fire of love burn in his heart. This fire is

6

the Spirit of Christ, who continually crushes the head of the serpent, meaning the desires of the flesh. The flesh is governed by the will of the world; but the spiritual fire in man is kindled by the Spirit. He who wants to become a Christian must not boast and say: 'I am a Christian!' but he should desire to become one, and prepare all the conditions necessary that the Christ may live in him. Such a Christian will perhaps be hated and persecuted by the nominal Christians of his time; but he must bear his cross, and thereby he will become strong.

"The theologians and Christian sectarians keep on continually disputing about the letter and form, while they care nothing for the spirit, without which the form is empty and the letter dead. Each one imagines that he has the truth in his keeping, and wants to be admired by the world as a keeper of the truth. Therefore they denounce and slander and backbite each other, and thus they act against the first principle taught by Christ, and which is brotherly love. Thus the Church of Christ has become a bazaar where vanities are exhibited, and as the Israelites dance around the golden calf, so the modern Christians dance around their self-constructed fetiches, whom they call God, and on account of this fetich-worship they will not be able to enter the promised land.

"The whole Christian religion is based upon a knowledge of our origin, our present condition, our destiny, It shows first how from unity we fell into variety, and how we may return to the former state. Secondly, it shows what we were before we became disunited. Thirdly, it explains the cause of the continuance of our present disunion. Fourthly, it instructs us as to the final destiny of the mortal and immortal elements within our constitution.

"All the teachings of Christ have no other object than to show us the way how we may re-ascend from a, state of variety and differentiation to our original unity; and he who teaches otherwise teaches an error. All the doctrines which have been hung around this fundamental doctrine, and which do not conform with the latter, are merely the products of worldly foolishness, thinking itself wise; they are merely useless ornaments which will create errors, and are calculated to throw dust in the eyes of the ignorant.

"Whoever presumes to set himself up as a spiritual teacher, and has no spiritual power of perceiving the truth, thinking to serve God by teaching the kingdom of God, of which he practically knows nothing, does not serve the true God, but serves his own self, and nurses and feeds his own vanity. He may have been legally appointed to his clerical office, and yet he is not a true shepherd. Christ says: 'He who does not enter the stable of the sheep by the door, but enters by the window, is a thief and a murderer, and the sheep will not follow him, for they do not know his voice.' He is not in possession of the voice of God, but merely of the voice of his learning. But Christ said: 'All plants which have not been planted by my heavenly Father shall be torn out and destroyed.' How, then, can he who is godless attempt to plant heavenly plants, having no spiritual seed and no power? To become a true spiritual teacher, one must teach in the Spirit of God and not in the spirit of selfishness."

In regard to the distinction between faith and mere belief, Boehme says:—

"A historical *belief* is merely an opinion based upon some adopted explanation of the letter of the written word, having been learned in schools, heard by the external ear, and which produces dogmatists, sophists, and opinionated servants of the letter. But *Faith* is the result of the direct perception of the truth, heard and understood by the inner sense, taught by the Holy Ghost, and productive of theosophists and servants of the divine Spirit."

As to the question whether or not sins can be forgiven by a priest, his opinion is not doubtful: "No sin can be taken away by priestly absolution. If Christ is resurrected within the heart, the old Adam will be dead and with him the sins which he has committed. If the sun rises, the night will be swallowed by the day and exist no longer. Dissemble, shout, weep, sing, preach, and teach as much as you please, it will serve to no purpose as long as evil exists in your heart. If I go to confession for 1000 years, and get the priest to absolve me every day, and in addition to that receive the sacrament every four weeks, it will serve me nothing if Christ is not in me. An animal going to church will come out an animal, no matter to what ceremonies it may have been made to submit.

"The modern Christians have a building of stone, wherein they serve the goddess of vanity, where they dissimulate, where the people exhibit their fine clothes and the preacher his learning; but the true Christian has his church within his soul, wherein he teaches and listens. This church is with him and in him wherever he goes, and he is always in his church. His church is the temple of Christ, wherein the Holy Ghost preaches to all beings, and in everything he beholds he hears a sermon of God.

"The true Christian does not belong to any particular sect. He may participate in the ceremonial service of every sect, and still belong to none. He has only one science, which is Christ within him; he has only one desire, namely, to do good. Look at the flowers of the field. Each one has its own particular attributes, nevertheless they do not wrangle and fight with each other. They do not quarrel about the possession of sunshine and rain, or dispute about their colours, odour, and taste. Each one grows according to its nature. Thus it is with the children of God. Each one has his own gifts and attributes, but they all spring from one Spirit. They enjoy their gifts, and praise the wisdom of Him

8

from whom they originated. Why should they dispute about the qualities of Him whose attributes are manifest in themselves?

"We have all only one single order to which we belong, and the only rule of that order is to do the will of God, that is to say, to keep still and serve as instruments through which God may do His will. Whatever God sows and makes manifest in us, we give it back to Him as His own fruit. The kingdom of heaven is not based upon our opinions and authorised beliefs, but roots in its own divine power. Our main object ought to be to have the divine power within ourselves. If we possess that, all scientific pursuit will be a mere play of the intellectual faculties with which to amuse ourselves; for the true science is the revelation of the wisdom of God within our own mind. God manifests His wisdom through His children as the earth manifests her powers through the production of various flowers and fruits. Therefore let each one be glad of his own gifts and enjoy those of the others. Why should all be alike? Who condemns the birds of the forest because they do not all sing the same tune; but each praises its Creator in its own way? Nevertheless, the power which enables them to sing originates in all from only one source."

His first work, entitled "Aurora" (the beginning of the new day), was not quite finished, when, by the indiscretion of a friend, copies of the manuscript came into the hands of the clergy. The head parson of Goerlitz, whose name was Gregorius Richter, a person entirely incapable of conceiving of the depths of that religion which he professed to teach, in ignorance of the divine mysteries of true Christianity, of which he knew nothing but its superficial aspect and form, too vain to bear with toleration that a poor shoemaker should be in possession of any spiritual knowledge which he, the well-fed priest, did not possess, became Jacob Boehme's bitterest enemy, denouncing and cursing the author of that book, and his hate was raised to the utmost degree by the meekness and modesty with which Boehme received the insults and denunciations directed toward him.

Soon the bigoted priest publicly in the pulpit accused Boehme of being a disturber of the peace and an heretic, asking the City Council of Goerlitz to punish the traitor, and threatening that if he were not removed from the town, the anger of God would be awakened and He would cause the whole place to be swallowed up by the earth, in the same manner in which he claimed that Korah, Dathan, and Abiram had perished after resisting Moses, the man of God.

In vain Jacob Boehme attempted to reason personally with the infuriated Doctor of Divinity. New curses and insults were the result of his interview with him, and the parson threatened to have Jacob

Boehme arrested and put into prison. The City Council was afraid of the priest, and, although he could not substantiate any charge against Boehme, nevertheless they ordered him to leave the town for fear of the consequences that might result if they did not comply with the Rev. Richter's request.

Patiently Boehme submitted to the unjust decree. He requested to be permitted to go home and take leave of his family before going into banishment, and even this was refused to him. Then his only answer was: "Very well; if I cannot do otherwise, I will be contented."

Boehme left; but during the following night greater courage entered into the hearts and a better judgment into the heads of the Councilmen. They reproached themselves for having banished an inoffensive man, and the very next day they called Jacob Boehme back, and permitted him to remain, stipulating, however, that he should give up to them the manuscript of the "Aurora," and that henceforth he should abstain from the writing of books.

For seven years Boehme, in obedience to this foolish decree, restrained himself from writing down the experiences which he enjoyed in the realm of the spirit, and, instead of bringing light to mankind, contented himself with mending their shoes. Hard was the battle required to stem the tidal wave of the Spirit, which with overpowering strength descended upon his soul; but at last, encouraged by the advice of his friends, who counselled him not to resist any longer the impulse coming from God for fear of disobeying man-made authorities, he resumed the labour of writing.

The writings of Jacob Boehme soon made their way in the world, and attracted the attention of those who were capable of realising and appreciating their true character. He found many friends and followers among the high and the lowly, the rich and the poor, and it seemed, indeed, as if a new outpouring of the Spirit of Truth was intended to take place in priest-ridden and bigoted Germany.

Jacob Boehme during that time wrote a number of books and pamphlets: "Aurora," "The Three Principles of Divine Being," "The Threefold Life of Man," "The Incarnation of Jesus Christ," "The Six *Theosophical Points*," "The Book of Terrestrial and Celestial Mysteries," "Biblical Calculation Regarding the Duration of the World," "The Four Complexions," his "Defence;" the book about "The Generation and Signature of all Beings," of "True Repentance," "True Regeneration," "The Supersensual Life," "Regeneration and Divine

Contemplation," "The Selection of Grace," "Holy Baptism," "Holy Communion," "Discourse between an Enlightened and an Unilluminated Soul," an essay on "Prayer," "Tables of the Three Principles of Divine Manifestation," "Key to the most Prominent Points," "One Hundred and Seventy-Seven Theosophical Questions," "Theosophical Letters," and other smaller works and articles regarding philosophical matters.

In March, 1624, and shortly before his death, began for Jacob Boehme a time of great suffering. In 1623, Abraham von Frankenburg had some of Boehme's works published under the title of "The Way to Christ," and the appearance of this book, full of divine truth, again inflamed the envy and rage of the angry parson of Goerlitz, being blown into a flame by the observation of the great favour with which the book was received by all truly enlightened minds. With the utmost fury he began again his persecutions of Jacob Boehme, cursing and damning him from the pulpit, and published against him a pasquillo, full of personal insults and vulgar epithets, which contained neither reason nor logic; but in their places innumerable calumnies, such as only the brain of a person made insane by passion could invent or concoct.

This time Boehme did not remain so passive as on a former occasion, but he handed over to the City Council a written defence in justification of what he had done, and he, moreover, wrote a reply to Richter, answering in a quiet and dignified manner every point of the objection raised by Richter, annihilating his arguments by the force of his logic and by the power of truth. This defence was not in an ironical style, but pregnant with love and pity for the misguided man, modest and eloquent to a degree such as rarely can be found even among the greatest orators.

The City Council, however, being once more intimidated by the blustering priest, did not accept Boehme's defence, but expressed a wish that he should voluntarily leave the town; and they expressed their wish to him in the form of a well-meant advice, to save himself from incurring the fate of heretics, which was to be burned alive on a stake by order of the Kurfürst or Emperor, either of whom might have been inclined to lend a willing ear to the representations of the clergy, being supposed to hesitate very little to give the requisite order, if the whim of the priesthood could be gratified by such a comparatively insignificant thing as the execution of a troublesome person who disturbed their peace.

Boehme, in obedience to that advice, which he well knew was a command in disguise, left Goerlitz on the 9th day of May, 1624, and went to Dresden, where he found an asylum in the house of a physician named Dr. Benjamin Hinkelman. There he received many honours and offers of aid, but he remained modest, writing to a friend that he intended to put his trust in no man, but in the living God; and that, as he was doing so, he was full of joy and all was well.

About this time Boehme, by order of the Kurfürst, was invited to take part in a learned discussion which was to take place between him and some of the best theologians of those times, including two professors of mathematics. The discussion took place, and Boehme astonished his opponents by the depths of his ideas and by his extraordinary knowledge in regard to divine and natural things; so that, when asked by the Kurfürst to give their decision, the theologians begged for time to investigate still more the matters which Boehme had represented to them, and which seemed to transcend the limits of what they believed themselves capable of grasping. One of these theologians, Gerhard by name, was heard to say that he would not take the whole world if it were offered to him as a bribe to condemn such a man, and the other, Dr. Meissner, answered that he was of the same opinion, and that they had no right to condemn that which surpassed their understanding; and thus it may be seen that not all the theologians were like Gregorius Richter, but that in the clerical profession, as in any other, there may be wise men and fools. Such theologians, of noble mind and without bigotry, were henceforth to be found among Jacob Boehme's admirers and friends, and whenever he met them he treated them with respect.

Soon afterwards he wrote his last work, entitled "Tables Regarding Divine Manifestation," and, having returned to his home, he was taken sick with a fever. His body began to swell, and he announced to his friends that the time of his death was near, saying: "In three days you will see how God has made an end of me." Then they asked him whether he was willing to die, and he replied: "Yes, according to the will of God." When his friends expressed the hope to find him improved on the following day, he said, "May God help that it shall be as you say. Amen."

This took place on a Friday, but on the next Sunday, on the 20th of November, 1624, before 1 A.M., Boehme called his son, Tobias, to his bedside, and asked him whether he did not hear beautiful music, and then he requested him to open the door of the room so that the celestial songs could better be heard. Later on he asked what time it was, and when he was told that the clock struck two, he said, "This is not yet time for me, in three hours will be my time." After a pause he again spoke, and said, "Thou powerful God Zabaoth, save me according to Thy will." Again he said, "Thou crucified Lord Jesus Christ, have mercy upon me, and take me into Thy kingdom." He then gave to his wife certain directions regarding his books and other temporal matters, telling her also that she would not survive him very long (as, indeed, she did not), and, taking leave from his sons, he said, "Now I shall enter the paradise." He then asked his eldest son, whose loving looks seemed to keep Boehme's soul from severing the bonds of the body, to turn him round, and, giving one deep sigh, his soul gave up the body to the earth to which it belonged, and entered into that higher state which is known to none except those who have experienced it themselves.

Jacob Boehme's enemy, the bigoted head-parson, Gregorius Richter, refused a decent burial to the corpse of the philosopher, and, as the City Council of Goerlitz, again in fear of the priest, were wavering and uncertain what to do, it was already decided to take the body for burial to a country place belonging to one of Boehme's friends, on which occasion, undoubtedly, a row would have taken place, and the ceremony been disturbed by the populace, whose prejudices were aroused by the clergy; but at the appropriate time the Catholic Count Hannibal von Drohna arrived, and ordered the body to be buried in a solemn manner, and in the presence of two of the members of the City Council. This took place accordingly, but the parson pretended to be sick, and took medicine so as to avoid being obliged to hold the funeral sermon, and the clergyman who gave the sermon in his place, although he himself had given absolution and the sacrament to Boehme shortly before the latter died, began his speech by expressing his great disgust at having been forced to do so by order of the Council.

Some friends of Boehme, in Silesia, sent a cross to be put on his grave, but it was soon destroyed by the hands of some bigot, who imagined to please God by insulting the memory of a man who was obnoxious to the priests, but who had done more to bring to mankind a true knowledge of God than priestcraft ever did in modern or ancient times. This cross was very ingeniously cut with occult symbols. On the top there was a flaming cross, with a Hebrew inscription signifying *I H S V H.*, and twelve golden rays. Below this there were the initials of his favourite motto and a picture of a child sleeping and resting upon a skull, signifying the regeneration by means of the mystic death. Then followed an inscription saying, "Here rests the body of Jacob Boehme, born out of God, died in *I H S V H*, and sealed by the Holy Spirit." At the right of that inscription there was a representation of a black eagle upon a mountain, stepping upon a large coiled snake, while holding with its right claw a palm leaf and in its beak the branch of a lily. On this picture was written *Vidi*. On the left side there was the representation of a lion, with a golden cross and crown. With the right hind leg that lion stood upon a stone in the shape of a cube, and with the left upon a globe; but in its right paw it held a flaming sword, and in the other a burning heart with the inscription *Vici*. Below the above-described inscription there was another picture, of oval shape, representing a lamb with a bishop's mitre and staff, standing near a palm tree, next to a flowing spring, in a field covered with various flowers. Below this was inscribed *Veni*. The meaning of these three words is: *In mundum Veni; Satanam descendere Vidi; Infernum Vici. Vivite magnanimi*. Finally, upon the lower part of the cross there were inscribed the last words spoken by Boehme: *Now I shall enter the paradise.*

In his exterior appearance Boehme was little, having a short, thin beard, a feeble voice, and eyes of a greyish tint. He was deficient in physical strength; nevertheless there is nothing known of his having ever had any other disease than the one that caused his death. But, if Jacob Boehme was small in body, he was a giant in intelligence and a powerful spirit. His hands could accomplish no greater works than to write and to make shoes, but the power of God having become manifest in that apparently insignificant organism and compound of elements and spiritual principles which represented the man Jacob Boehme on this terrestrial globe, was strong enough to overthrow, and is still overthrowing, the most petrified and gigantic superstitions existing in his own and subsequent centuries. His "Spirit" is still battling with the powers of darkness, and the Light which was kindled in the soul of poor little Jacob Boehme is still illuminating the world, growing larger and brighter from day to day in proportion as mankind becomes more capable of beholding it and of receiving and grasping his ideas. His spirit, or to speak more correctly, the Spirit of Truth as manifested through the writings of Jacob Boehme, is gradually bringing life into old dry-bone theology, killing clericalism and bigotry, superstition and ignorance, the giant monsters which have been devastating the world for ages past, and to whom more victims have been sacrificed than have died by the hands of the god of war, by pestilence, and drugs. The thinking part of humanity is beginning to see that there is a vast difference between the true spirit of Christian religion, and the external form in which it is represented to the vulgar mind. Even the better class of clergy—that is to say, those who are not fully absorbed in the dogmatic opinions which were engrafted into their minds in their schools, but who dare to seek for self-knowledge in God—know that a clinging to the external forms of religion prevents the mind from penetrating into their depths and grasping the spirit that produced these forms, and which is one and the same in all great religions; for the truth is universal, external, and only one; it is the learned ones who take a multiple aspect of it, and regard it through manifold coloured glasses.

As to the practical application of this doctrine, Jacob Boehme says: "If we allow our mind to brood over earthly desires, our mind will be captivated by them; but if we spiritually rise above the world of earthly desires and sensations, the world of light will captivate our will, the terrestrial world will lose its power of attracting our consciousness, and we will enter the divine state of God. The realm of matter and darkness is the realm of anguish, contention, and suffering; the realm of the Spirit is the kingdom of light, joy, peace, and happiness. There is no human being who would desire to be immersed in material pleasures, if he were able to comprehend and realise the joys of the spiritual state. But if the fire of the soul is not illumined by the divine light, the will of the soul cannot enter that state, but remains in darkness. The superficial reasoner believes that there exists no faculty of seeing except by the exterior eye, and if that sight has departed there is an end of seeing. It is very unfortunate if the soul can only see through the external mirror of the eye. What will such a soul see if that mirror is broken? She will be in darkness, and only perceive the lurid lightnings which are kindled by her own anguish and despair. As long as the soul is connected with the body she may behold the divine light in its modifications as manifested through the intermediate action of the terrestrial sun, and the sun is the source of all her terrestrial joys. Thus the terrestrial sun becomes her God, she mistakes the effect for the cause; she is drawn away from the source of the real and eternal light and sinks into darkness. But if the divine eternal light is received in the soul, it kindles a fire therein which illuminates the whole substance of the soul, so that the latter becomes luminous, and a mirror, or eye, in which the light of God is reflected. Let, therefore, each man examine himself, and see which of the three worlds is master over him, the world of light, the world of illusions, or the world of darkness. Let him search his own soul, to see whether the four elements of evil, ambition, anger, envy, and avarice, are the rulers therein, or whether universal charity, benevolence, kindness, meekness, and good will prevail, and let him not grow weak in his battle with the lower elements, so that the Spirit of God may be victorious in him. He who consciously carries the divine image of God will not die when his physical body dies, nor will he lose any of the attributes which his soul

15

has acquired during its life in the physical body. The world of good and the world of evil are both contained within the world of man. Whatever we make of ourselves, that must we be in the future; whatever we awaken within ourselves will live in ourselves; in whatever direction we struggle, there shall we receive our guide."

Jacob Boehme was in possession of remarkable occult powers. He is known to have spoken several languages, although no one ever knew where he had acquired them, they having probably been learned by him in a previous life. He also knew the language of nature, and could call plants and animals by their own proper names. He was endowed with psychic faculties, which enabled him to "psychometrically" see the past and "clairvoyantly" look into the future. Many anecdotes are told of him in regard to these powers, of which the following may serve as a specimen: One day a dissolute nobleman railed at Boehme, calling him a false prophet and daring him to tell anything which he had not learned in the ordinary way. Boehme asked to be left in peace; but as the nobleman continued his offensive language, Boehme at last told him his own past private history, mentioning a great many villanous things which that nobleman had done in secret. He also predicted that this person would soon come to an untimely end. Thereupon that nobleman flew into a rage, and while he admitted that what Boehme said was true, he bestrode his horse and hurried away. On the next morning he was found dead in the road, having been thrown from his horse and broken his neck.

Boehme's favourite motto was—"*Our salvation is in the life of Jesus Christ in us.*"

This alone is sufficient to show the true character of the Christianity of Boehme, who did not look for salvation from a dead and historical person, but from the living Jesus, made alive by the Christ within himself; or to express it in other terms, by the higher *Manas* (the mind) becoming self-conscious in the light of the *Atma-Buddhi* (the spiritual soul).

When asked for his autograph, he frequently used to write the following—

> "He to whom time is the same as eternity,
> And eternity the same as time,
> Is free from all contention."

A similar saying is—

"He to whom sorrow is the same as joy,
And joy the same as sorrow,
May thank God for his equanimity."

Among the most prominent followers and successors of Jacob Boehme might be named many celebrated theologians and philosophers, such as Dr. Balthasar Walther, Abraham Frankenberg, Friedrich Krause, and even the son of Boehme's worst enemy, Richter of Goerlitz, who published eight books containing extracts of Boehme's works.

Boehme's works were translated into different languages, and attracted the attention of Charles I. of England, who, after reading his "Answers to Forty Questions," exclaimed, "God be praised that there are still men in existence who are able to give from their own experience a living testimony of God and His Word." Johannes Sparrow, in the years 1646–1662, produced a translation in English of Boehme's works, and Edward Taylor another during the reign of James II. A third translation was published in 1755 by William Law, and many authors (the great Newton included) are said to have drawn largely from Boehme's works. His prominent disciples, however, and the ones most capable of grasping his ideas, seem to have been Thomas Bromley (1691) and Jane Leade (died 1703), the founder of the society of Philadelphians (if comprising under that name all persons who have entered a certain stage of development can be called the founding of a society).

Henry Moore, Professor at Cambridge, was requested to examine the books of Jacob Boehme, and to *report against them*. He examined them; but his report turned out differently from what had been expected; for even if he, on account of his own engrafted theological ideas, was not fully able to comprehend Jacob Boehme, and misunderstood him in many ways, nevertheless, he pronounced himself in his favour, and said that he who treated Boehme with contempt could not be otherwise but ignorant and mentally blind; adding that Jacob Boehme had undoubtedly been spiritually wakened for the purpose of correcting those false Christians who believed merely in an external Christ without regard whether or not they had the Spirit of Christ within themselves.

For the instruction of those who believe that the present may learn a lesson from the experience of the past, we must prominently mention the name of Johann George Gichtel, a pious man, and one of the greatest disciples of Boehme, a man of great insight and power.

He was a deep thinker, leading a blameless life. In 1682 he republished

Boehme's writings, and added to them many valuable engravings, with explanations, showing great profundity of thought and spiritual knowledge. By exposing the faults of the clergy, he made them his enemies. He wanted to reform them by force. Several times he was put into prison, and once he was even publicly exposed in the pillory in consequence of his sincerity. He established a society called the "Angelic Brothers," and in which every member was supposed to have actually renounced the world and entered into a state of angelic perfection. These "Angelic Brothers" were to be free from all human imperfections, and so situated as not be pestered with terrestrial cares. They were supposed not to be inclined to marry, and not to do any manual labour; but to live in continual contemplation and prayer, and by penetrating to the centre of good to abolish all evil, so that the wrath of God might be extinguished within the souls of all men, and universal love and harmony prevail everywhere. They were to depose the clergy, and in their place to be true priests, after the order of Melchisedec, taking upon themselves the Karma of all men and the sin of the world for expiation and redemption. Thus, this otherwise well-meaning man forgot that the organisation of an angelic brotherhood would require, above all, the acquisition of angels to constitute its membership. Such angels are not easily to be found, and if they were to be found, they would require no external organisation. Nevertheless, Gichtel's society, although being presumably neither angelic nor divinely wise, is said to have done a great deal of good, and Henke, a church historian, writes that they especially were tolerant, and never condemned any person on account of his belief or opinions, and that they never boasted, but silently accomplished many good works.

The followers of Jacob Boehme were not always left in peace. There will be theological and other bigots as long as ignorance exists in the world. Such persons, incapable of understanding the spirit of Boehme's teachings, imagined them to contain heresies, and, in 1689, Quirinus Kuhlmann, a follower of Boehme, was burned alive at the stake at Moscow, because he had been too free in expressing his opinions regarding the iniquities of the clergy of those times.

All the arguments which the enemies of Jacob Boehme have ever put forward consist merely in the application of vile epithets, such as "Fool! Atheist! Swine! Shoe-patcher! Crank! Hypocrite!" and phrases such as the following:—

> "Boehme's sect is truly devilish, and the vilest excrement of the devil; it has the father of lies for its origin; the devil had possession of Boehme, and grunted out of his mouth." (*Johann Trick.*)

"We have no desire to climb up the ladder of dreams created by Boehme. To do so would be to tempt God and lead us down to perdition." (*Deutsch.*)

"The writings of Jacob Boehme contain as many blasphemies as there are lines. They have a fearful odour of shoemaker's pitch and blacking." (*Richter.*)

"The shoemaker is the Antichrist." (*Richter.*)

"We ask who deserves belief? The word of Christ or the prejudiced shoemaker with his dirt?" (*Richter.*)

"The Holy Ghost has anointed Christ with oil, but the villain of a shoemaker has been daubed over with dirt by the devil." (*Richter.*)

"Christ spake about important things; but the shoemaker speaks about things that are vile." (*Richter.*)

"Christ taught publicly; but the shoemaker sits in a corner." (*Richter.*)

Christ used to drink good wine; but shoemakers drink whisky." (*Rev. Gregorius Richter.*)

The above will be sufficient as specimens of the theological arguments of those times. However laughable they may appear at the present time, there was a serious aspect attached to them for Jacob Boehme and his successors. Hobius, of Hamburg, a follower of Boehme, had to leave the city for fear of being assassinated by the rabble, whose fury was excited against him by the bigoted parson, Rev. J. Frederic Mayer; and Abraham Hinkelman, from the same cause, died of grief; while Joh. Winkler, a theologian, who had refused to express a contempt for Jacob Boehme, was saved from his persecutors by the protection offered him by the king.

On the other hand, there were many of the more enlightened theologians who stood up in defence of Boehme and his doctrines; foremost of all John Winkler, John Mathaei, Frederick Brenkling and Spencer, and especially so Gottfried Arnold, the author of a history of churches and heretics. The wise can find wisdom in everything, even in the prattle of a child; but the fool sees his own image in everything, and therefore the great historian Mozhof (1688) sees in Jacob Boehme a saint and a sage; while F. T. Adelung, who wrote a book on human folly, denounces him and Theophrastus Paracelsus as fools. The so-called "Rationalists," and the great bulk of the theologians, combined with each other to fight against that which they were unable to understand, while Johann Salomo Samler, a self-thinking man and

19

capable of entering into the spirit of Boehme, calls the writings of Boehme "a fountain of happiness and spiritual knowledge, from which everyone may drink without having the order of his external life disturbed thereby."

Among those who were pre-eminently capable of grasping Jacob Boehme's ideas, we will only mention the great theologian, Frederic Christop Oetinger, Pastor Oberlin and Louis Claude de St. Martin, the "Unknown philosopher," who translated some of his works into French. Many other persons, whose names are well known in history, and who had more or less penetrated to the fountain of truth, such as Henry Jung Stilling, Friederich von Hardenberg, Friederich von Schlegel, Novalis, Heinrich Jacobi, Schelling, Goethe, Franz Baader, Hegel, and many others might be named; but all this proves nothing. The value of the truth cannot be made to depend on the recommendation or certificate of any person, however great an authority he may be; it is beyond all praise. The reason why men have so much difficulty in seeing the truth is because it is so simple that even a child can behold it; but the minds of the worldly-wise are complicated, and they seek for complexity in the truth. Let, therefore, those who wish to enter the spirit of the doctrines of Jacob Boehme dismiss their own prejudices, and open their eyes to the light. Those who are able to see it will see it; while to those whose eyes are closed the writings of Jacob Boehme will be a sealed book, and it will be advisable for them to learn first the lesson taught by terrestrial life before they attempt to judge about the mysteries of the life in the Spirit of God.

From the fountain of the interior life in man springs that mysterious power to see and to feel the truth which is called "intuition." It is the power to perceive at once by the sense of touch and interior sight things that belong to the spirit. It is not the understanding, and there is no sense in speaking of the "reliability" or the "fallibility" of the intuition; it is spiritual perception, and as in outward life we must be able to see a thing, and to feel it by means of the touch, before we can have any true knowledge about its external qualities, likewise in the contemplation of spiritual things we must be able interiorly to perceive the object of our investigation before we can understand what it is.

The writings of Jacob Boehme are all in accordance with the statements contained in the Christian Bible, and this circumstance will at once prove to be an obstacle in the way of those who have no understanding for the internal meaning of the Bible accounts, and may frighten them away from giving any attention to his works. The Bible, which, in an external sense, was formerly credulously believed and accepted by the pious and ignorant, is now universally disbelieved and laughed at by the "enlightened" portions of rationalistic humanity; and very naturally so, because the rationalistic specimens of mankind are not enlightened enough to see the delicious fruit within the indigestible shell; they do not know that behind these tales, full of absurdity, there is hidden more wisdom than in all the philosophical books of the world. They know nothing about the inner life, the Soul-life of this world, and that the personalities, which are as dramatic actors introduced to us in the Bible, represent actual living and conscious powers, which may or may not have become objectified and represented in terrestrial forms on the terrestrial plane. If, departing from the pseudo-scientific standpoint, which regards the world as being made up of a conglomeration of self-existent, individual entities, we look at the world, and especially at our solar system, as being unity, indivisible in its essential nature, but manifesting itself in a multitude of appearances and forms of life, the history of the Bible will cease to appear to us as the history of persons that lived in olden times, and whose lives and adventures can have no serious interest for us at the present time; but the history of the evolution as contained in the Bible will be understood to mean the history of the evolution of Man—*i.e.*, *Adam*, the king of the earth, whose body is as great as our solar system; the history of the universal Man, in whom we all exist; who has become material and degraded; but was again redeemed and spiritualised by the awakening within him of the immortal life and light of the Christ.

When or at what time a descent of divine Logos took place is a question which may be left to the decision of the historian and theologian; to me it is sufficient to know that there is a divine element in humanity, by means of which humanity may be redeemed from materialism and ignorance and be brought to realise again its originally divine state. Moreover, each human individual constitutes for itself a little world wherein are contained all the powers, principles, and essences that are said to exist in the great world, the solar system wherein we live. In each of these little worlds the great work of redemption which is described in the Bible as having taken place in the great world is continually going on. For ever the divine Spirit descends into the depths of matter within our corporeal being, and, by the power of light and love of Christ within the soul, overcomes the lurid fire of the wrathful will within for the purpose of re-establishing in man the divine image of God. For ever the Christ is born amidst the animal elements in the constitution of man, teaching the intellectual powers therein; crucified on the cross, in the centre of the four elements, and resurrected in those who do not resist the process of their own

21

regeneration, whereby they may attain life in the Christ. It is a process eternally repeating itself; but that in regard to our world it had a beginning in time, as it has a timely beginning in every individual being upon the earth, seems to be self-evident, for if "Adam had never fallen in sin"—that is to say, if the universal consciousness constituting the foundation of our solar system had never sunk into a material state— there would have been no occasion for redeeming it by awaking within it a consciousness of a higher kind; neither can it be supposed that the world is perfect now, and has always been and remained perfect, because we see that it is not perfect, and if it were so, the work of evolution would be useless and come to an end.

This work of evolution and redemption is going on continually everywhere. Downwards shines the light of the sun and upwards spring the fountains that come gushing from the womb of the earth. Thus the light of the Spirit comes from the sun of divine wisdom, the sacred Trinity of Will and Intelligence and its manifestation; and from the depths of the human heart up-wells the light of love, overruling the arguments of the intellect that has been misguided by external appearances. The seed is put into the earth, not for the purpose of finding its final object in enjoying itself in the earth, but to gradually die and become transformed while it lives; to die as a seed, while developing into a plant, whose body is raised out of the dark earth into the light and air, and whose form bears no trace of the original form of the seed; nor has the seed been put into the ground to die and to rot before becoming a plant. Thus the spiritual regeneration of man is to be effected now, and while he lives in the body, and not after that body, which is necessary for such a transformation to take place, has died and is eaten up by worms or destroyed by fire.

When the seed ceases to be a seed, it becomes a plant. When man, the medium between an intellectual animal and a god, ceases to be an animal, he becomes a god. This takes place when the universal God, the Christ, begins to live in him. Then the illusions end, and the interior truth becomes revealed. Not in books, nor in opinions, nor in the vagaries of metaphysical speculations, but in the living Truth itself is the Light to be found.

Thus prepared, we may take up the study of Boehme's doctrines. These doctrines all culminate in the one point that man should. accomplish the will of God, and the question therefore arises, "What is the will of God?" To this Jacob Boehme answers: "We ourselves are God's will for evil and good. Whatsoever of these is manifested in us, we are that ourselves, whether it be in hell or in heaven." The life of man is a form of the divine will, and to do the will of God means, therefore, to become godlike and divine, by trying to realise one's own highest ideal in thoughts, words, and deeds. "God must become man, and man must become God. Heaven must become one with the earth, and the earth must become a heaven, so that her will may become the will of heaven."—(*Signature*, x. 48.) To express this in other words, we may say, "The universal will in its action in man must become divine, so that man may become conscious of being in possession of divine powers. The earthly mind of man must have awakened within itself the divine light of the spirit, so that a heaven may be created within the mind." The doctrines of Jacob Boehme, therefore, are not so much intended to teach us what we should know or what we should do, but they are to aid us to realise the all-important fact what we must be.

He himself says in the introduction to one of his books as follows:—

> "God-loving reader! If it is your earnest and serious will and desire to devote yourself to that which is divine and eternal, the reading of this book will be very useful to you; but if you are not fully determined to enter the way of holiness, it would be better for you to let alone the sacred names of God, wherein His supreme sanctity is invoked, because the wrath of God may become ignited within your soul. This book is written only for those who desire to be sanctified and united with the Supreme Power from which they have originated. Such persons will understand the true meaning of the words contained therein, and they will also recognise the source from which these thoughts have come."

One of the most enlightened critics of Jacob Boehme says, in regard to his book on divine mysteries:—

> "This book is a treasure-box wherein all wisdom has been hidden from the eyes of the fool; but to the children of light it is always open. No one will clearly understand it unless he has the key necessary for that purpose, and that key is the Holy Ghost. He who is in possession of that key will be able to open the door and to enter and see the mysteries of divinity, divine magic, angelic cabala, and natural philosophy. That key opens the door of divinity, and, like a lightning flash, it illuminates the darkness of material conditions; for its imperishable spirit is contained within all things. The Spirit alone can teach the soul of man from what depths the truths contained in this book have originated, for the purpose of glorifying the divinity in nature and man."

And, again, he says:—

> "The spirit of man is rooted in God; the soul of man in the angelic world. The spirit is divine, the soul angelic. The body of man is rooted in the material plane; it is of an earthly nature. The pure body is a Salt;

the soul a Fire; the spirit is Light. Spirit and soul have been eternally in God and breathed by God into a pure body. This pure body is a precious treasure hidden within the rock. It is contained in matter doomed to perish; but it is neither material nor mortal itself. It is the immortal body spoken of by St. Paul. These things are mysterious, sealed with the seal of the Spirit, and he who desires to know them must be in possession of the Spirit of God. It is this Spirit that illuminates those minds who are His own, and wherever it is to be found, there will the eagles—the souls and the spirits—collect. No animal man, living according to his sensual attractions and animal reasoning, will understand it; because it is above the reach of the senses, and above the reach of the semi-animal intellect; it belongs to the holy mountain of God, and the animal touching that mountain must die. Even the sanctified soul rising up to that mountain must bare her feet and leave behind that which is attached to her as a creature. She must forget her personality, and not know whether she is in or out of the body. God knows it. These things are sacred. They are written for children; to animals we have nothing to say."

Let, then, the reader pray; not with his mouth nor with mere words, but with his spirit—that is to say, let him open his heart to the influence of the power of God, and by the power of the Divine Will rise up to that universal realm of Light from which Jacob Boehme received his illuminations. It is the realm of the living Word which was in the beginning, and by whose power the world was created; the Christ that continually whispers consolation to the despairing and dying soul; the heart and centre of God, of which the material sun that fills our terrestrial world with light and life is merely a symbol, an outward representation. Then shall we see the internal world filled with a supernal and living light, incomparably superior to that of the physical world, and in that world we shall find God and the Christ and the holy Spirit of Truth revealed, together with all the angels and mysteries, truly and satisfactorily beyond the possibility of being disputed away; because we shall not then need to be taught by mere letters or words, but by the truth itself, and learn what it is, and not what it appeared to be to another, because we shall then ourselves be one with the Truth, and know it by the knowledge of self.

In the year 1705 the saintly Gichtel wrote: "Whoever in our time wishes to bring forth anything fundamental and imperishable, must borrow it from Boehme. Boehme's writings are a gift of God, and, therefore, not every kind of reason can apprehend them; therefore, you must not be satisfied with mere reading and rational speculation, but beseech God to give you His Holy Spirit, that shall lead you into all truth."

These prophetic words, quoted in Mrs. A. J. Penny's excellent essay on the way how to study Jacob Boehme's writings, have been fully verified by the succeeding events; for every great philosopher that has come before the public since that time seems to have received his inspiration from Boehme's books. Even the great Arthur Schopenhauer, one of the most admired modern philosophers, whose works are praised by many who would treat with contempt the works of Boehme, which they have never studied, was a follower of Boehme, and his writings are fundamentally nothing but an exposition of Boehme's doctrines from the point of view of Mr. Schopenhauer, who misunderstood Boehme in many respects. Schopenhauer likewise says about Schelling's works

> "They are almost nothing except a remodelling of Jacob Boehme's '*Mysterium Magnum*,' in which almost every sentence of Hegel's book is represented. But why are in Hegel's writings the same figures and forms insupportable and ridiculous to me, which in Boehme's works fill me with admiration and awe? It is because in Boehme's writings the recognition of eternal truth speaks from every page, whilst Schelling takes from him what he is able to grasp. He uses the same figures of speech, but he evidently mistakes the shell for the fruit, or at least he does not know how to separate them from each other." (*Handschriften, Nachlass*, p. 261.)

It would be too tedious to produce a collection of what the various modern philosophers in different nations have said about the writings of Jacob Boehme; the only way to form a correct estimate about him is to enter into his spirit and to see as he saw. We will, therefore, in conclusion, merely quote the words of Claude de Saint Martin: "I am not young, being now near my fiftieth year; nevertheless, I have begun to learn German merely for the purpose of reading this incomparable author." . . . . " I am not worthy to unloose the shoestrings of this wonderful man, whom I regard as the greatest light that has ever appeared upon the earth, second only to Him who was the Light itself." . . . " I advise you by all means to throw yourself in this abyss of knowledge of the profoundest of all truths." . . . " I find in his works such a profundity and exaltation of thought, and such a simple and delicious nutriment, that I would consider it a waste of time to seek for such things in any other place." (*Letters to Kirchberger*.)

If we once become acquainted with the writings of Jacob Boehme, we shall be filled with surprise that not every lover of truth knows these books, and considers them his most valuable and useful treasure in spiritual literature.

The Doctrines of Jacob Boehme
Chapter I
Introduction

"Our whole doctrine is nothing else but an instruction to show how man may create a kingdom of light within himself. . . . He in whom this spring of divine power flows, carries within himself the divine image and the celestial substantiality. In him is Jesus born from the Virgin, and he will not die in eternity." (*Six Points*, vii. 33.)

"Not I, the I that I am, know these things; but God knows them in me." (*Apology, Tilken*, ii. 72.)

"Science cannot abolish faith in the all-seeing God, without worshipping in His place the blind intellect."

"The true faith is that the spirit of the soul enters with its will and desire into that which it does neither see nor feel." (*Four Complexions*, 85.)

It is self-evident that if we wish to attempt a contemplation of that which is divine and eternal, we must first of all not refuse to believe in the possibility that something divine and eternal exists or may reveal itself in the constitution of man. This spiritual principle in man is superior to the animal and reasoning man; superior to the material body, and superior to the arguing intellect; it does not need to reason and guess; it perceives and knows. Being superior to the intellect, it cannot be conceived intellectually; but it can be perceived by man if he rises above the animal and intellectual plane to the consciousness of his own divine spirit; or to express it in the language of Boehme, if he attains self-knowledge in Christ. The animal instincts in man belong to the animal nature in man, his intellectual faculties belong to his intellectual nature, but that which is divine in him belongs to his God, his own true and real and permanent self.

Merely theoretical speculation in regard to the things that belong to the Spirit in man is therefore entirely inadequate for their true understanding, and is not divine wisdom; it can only lead to the formation of theories and opinions about it, which may or may not be true, but which do not constitute real knowledge, while true wisdom is the result of practical experience, attainable in no other way than by entering the divine state. In other words, it is the knowledge by which God in "man" knows His own self.

Most surely the attainment of this divine state is not the result of fancy's flights, of pious dreaming, or of allowing the imagination to run away with one's self. There is nothing more positive, real, and practical than the consciousness of being a man, and to find one's centre of gravity in the dignity which arises from true manhood; or in other words, from the knowledge of being a living temple wherein resides the power of one's own immortal self.

Every state of knowledge has its uses in the sphere to which it belongs and not to any other. Jacob Boehme says:—

> "I do not say that man should not investigate natural sciences, and gain experience in regard to external things. Such a study is certainly useful to him; but man's own reasoning should not be the basis of his knowledge. Man should not have his conduct guided merely by the light of external reasoning, but he should, with all his reasoning and with his whole being, bow in deep humility before God." (*Calmness*, i. 3 5.)

As long as a man does not recognise the existence of a divine principle within his own self, it will be of little use for him to philosophise and speculate about the attributes of the Divinity in the universe; he cannot know the Holy Ghost as long as the Spirit of Holiness is not active within himself.

> "Natural man knows nothing about the mystery of the kingdom of God, because he is outside and not within the state of divinity, as is daily proved by the action of the philosophisers who are disputing about the attributes and the will of God, and who nevertheless do not know God, because they do not listen to the word of God within their own souls." (*Letters*, xxxv. 5.)

External man judges according to his external reasoning. Man, depending entirely on his external perceptions, and having neither belief nor confidence in anything except what he sees with his bodily eyes, knows only that which he sees with those eyes, and is not aware that there is anything superior to that.

> "When external reason beholds the things of this world, and how misfortunes befall the pious as well as the godless, and that all things are doomed to death and destruction—if it moreover perceives that there seems to be none to save the virtuous from trouble and grief, but that he, like the wicked, sorrowfully enters the valley of death, then man's reason thinks that all things are due to hap-hazard, and that there is no God to take care of those that are suffering." (*Contemplation*, i. 1.)

If there is no proof of the existence of a benevolent God to be found within the world of phenomena, there is likewise no divine self-knowledge to be obtained by the superficial reading of Holy Writ, nor by an external study of the Bible, or conceiving of its contents from a merely historical point of view. Neither will listening to sermons be productive of self-knowledge, if he who preaches or he who listens has not the living Spirit of Truth within himself.

> "All those who desire to speak of or teach divine mysteries ought to be in possession of the Spirit of God. Man should recognise within himself the divine light of the truth, and in that light the things which he desires to represent as being true. He should never be without such a divine self-knowledge, and not make the force of his arguments to depend merely on external reasonings or literal interpretations of the Bible." (*Menschwerdung*, i. 1, 3.)

> "What would it benefit me if I were continually quoting the Bible, and knew the whole book by heart, but did not know the Spirit that inspired the holy men who wrote that book, nor the source from which they received their knowledge? How can I expect to understand them in truth, if I have not the same spirit as they? "(*Tilk.* ii. 55.)

Spiritual truths are above and beyond intellectual reasoning, and can, therefore, not be intellectually explained. They can at best be represented by allegories and pictures such as may induce men to give way to exalted thoughts, and thus to acquire a higher state of perception.

> "The children of God spake as they were made to speak by the Holy Spirit. Therefore their words remain a mystery to the men of earth; and even if the latter imagine that they understand them, nevertheless they see only the external meaning." (*Letters*, xi. 40.)

> "In all things received by mere hearsay, without self-perception, there still remains a doubt as to whether that which one has heard is actually true; but that which is seen by the eye and understood by the heart carries conviction with it." (*Three Principles*, x. 26.)

It should never be forgotten that speculative philosophy and theosophy are two entirely different, if not opposite things, and those who clamour for intellectual explanations of spiritual truths that are beyond intellectual reasoning have an entirely wrong conception of the meaning of the term "Theosophy."

> "The true understanding must come from the interior fountain and enter the mind from the living Word of God within the soul. Unless this takes place, all teaching about divine things is useless and worthless." (*Letters*, xxxv. 7.)

> "I do not wish to divert men from the Word as it is written and taught; but my writings are intended to lead them from a merely historical belief to a living faith, even to Jesus Christ (the Light and Truth) Himself. All preaching and teaching is in vain if it is mere talk, and if

29

the preacher or teacher has not the power of Christ, if not Christ Himself by means of the Word acts within those that teach and within those that listen." (*Richter*, 45.)

By studying a book we may at best imagine what the author believed; but such an imaginary knowledge is not self-knowledge. Real spiritual knowledge comes only from the awakening of the spirit.

"I am not collecting my knowledge from letters and books, but I have it within my own self; because heaven and earth with all their inhabitants, and moreover, God Himself, is in man." (*Tilk.* ii. 297.)

The essential man is not limited by the visible physical form of his material body; his spiritual substance extends as far as the stars. His true self is the Spirit of God, wherein are existing all worlds.

"The spirit of man has not merely come from the stars and the elements, but there is hidden within him a spark of the light and the power of God. It is not empty talk if Moses (Genesis i.) says God created man in His own image. To be His own image created He him." (*Aurora*, Preface, 96.)

The divine Spirit, once awakened in the consciousness of man, knows all things by the knowledge of its own self.

"The soul searches into the Godhead, and also into the depths of nature; for she has her fountain and origin in the whole of the divine Being." (*Aurora*, Preface, 98.)

"As the eye of man reaches the stars wherefrom it has its primitive origin, likewise the soul penetrates and sees even within the divine state of being wherein she lives." (*Aurora*, Preface, 99.)

"Oh, how near is God to all things. Nevertheless, no thing can comprehend Him unless it be tranquil and surrenders to Him its own self-will. If this is accomplished, then will God be acting through the instrumentality of everything, like the sun that acts throughout the whole world." (*Mystery*, 45.)

"Why is it that we cannot see God? This world and the devil (perverted good) within the wrath of God are the cause that we cannot see with the eyes of God. There is no other impediment. If any one says, 'I can see nothing divine,' let him understand that flesh and blood and the craftiness of the devil (perverted desires) are to him an obstacle and an impediment. If he were to enter the new life, if he were to step below the cross of Christ, he would then be sure to see the Father and his Redeemer the Christ, and also the Holy Ghost." (*Menschwerdung*, ii. 7.)

Let those would-be philosophers who reject God and that which is divine remember that there can be no divine wisdom without something divine, and that man can become divine in no other way than through the power of Divinity.

> "There is no spark of divine life in him who is without God. For this it is not God who is to blame, but the person himself. Such persons have themselves, and by their own will, entered into that state, and have themselves drowned their higher consciousness, while the precious jewel, although unknown to them, is still hidden within the centre. Let them, therefore, again go out with their will from their wilful ignorance or malignity and enter again into the will of God." (*Menschwerdung*, 3, 5.)

All this goes to show that it is useless and vain to seek for divine wisdom, meaning a true realisation of eternal truth in outward things, in external observations, in the reading of books, or in the sayings of the sages, if we do not recognise the truth that exists within our own self. All dependence placed upon external things and persons or gods outside of our own true self, is merely idol-worship and deceptive if we do not recognise the God that exists within ourselves. The words, "Thou shalt worship no strange gods or idols, but have only one God," mean, Thou shalt have faith and confidence and trust in no other God than in the one whose temple you are, and who resides within your own self.

"God," according to Boehme, is "the will of eternal wisdom." To become strong in God is to become strong in that will which renders one wise. This is the true faith, of which Boehme says that "it is not merely a certain method of thinking, or a belief in certain historical occurrences, but the receiving of the spirit and the power of Christ within one's self." (*Letters*, xlvi. 39.)

> "This light and this power of Christ arises in His children within their interior foundation, and illumines the whole of their life. Within that foundation is the kingdom of God in man." (*Communion*, v. 18.)

But what is it that prevents man from recognising God within his own self? What hinders him from seeing the light of the truth, and hearing the voice of the Divinity? To this Jacob Boehme answers, "Thy own hearing, willing, and seeing prevents thee from seeing and hearing God. By the exercise of your own will you separate yourself from the will of God, and by the exercise of your own seeing you see only within your own desires, while your desiring obstructs your sense of hearing by closing your ears with that which belongs to terrestrial and material things. It overshadows you so that you cannot see that which is beyond your own human nature and supersensual. But if you keep quiet, and

31

desist from thinking and feeling with your own personal selfhood, then will the eternal hearing, seeing, and speaking become revealed to you, and God will see and hear and perceive through you."—(*Supersensual Life*, 1–5.)

Here it may be asked by some, "Is it then necessary for us, if we want to attain divine wisdom, that we should sit down, and think, and feel, and do nothing at all?" Those who ask such a question do not realise that, as there is a region below all feeling and thought, in which man resembles an animal, if not a corpse, there is also another state, beyond all speculative thought, a state of divine being. Not a state in which man imagines himself to be divine, but a condition in which the will of man, having stripped off all that is earthly, becomes divine and absorbed in the self-consciousness of divinity.

"The only true way by which God may be perceived in His word, His essence, and His will, is that man arrives at the state of unity with himself, and that—not merely in his imagination, but in his *will*—he should leave everything that is his personal self, or that belongs to that self, money and goods, father and mother, brother and sister, wife and child, body and life, and that his own self should become as nothing to him. He must surrender everything and become poorer than a bird in the air that owns a nest. Man must have no nest for his heart in this world. ' Not that a person should run away from his home, and desert his wife, child, or relatives, commit suicide, or throw away his property, so that he may not be therein corporeally; but he should kill and annihilate his self-will, the will that claims all these things as its possessions. He should surrender all this to his Creator, and say with the full consent of his heart, Lord, all is Thine! I am unworthy to govern it, but as You have placed me therein, I shall do my duty by surrendering my will wholly and entirely to You. Act through me in what manlier You will, so that Thy will shall be done in all things, and that all that I am called upon to do may be done for the benefit of my brothers, to whom I am serving according to Thy command. He who enters into such a state of supreme resignation enters into divine union with Christ, so that he sees God Himself. He speaks with God and God speaks with him, and he thus knows what is the Word, the Essence, and the Will of God." (*Mysterium*, xli. 54–63.)

"Follow my advice, and leave off your difficult seeking for the knowledge of God by means of your selfish will and reasoning; throw away that imaginary reason, which your mortal self thinks to possess, and your will shall then be the will of God. If He finds His will to be your will in His, then will His will become manifest in your will as in His own property. He is All, and whatever you wish to know in the All is in Him. There is nothing hidden before Him, and you will see in His own light." (*Forty Questions*, i. 36.)

All of one's own seeking and investigating of divine mysteries in a spirit of selfishness is useless and vain. The self-will cannot comprehend anything of God, because that will is not in God but external to Him. The will in a state of divine tranquillity comprehends the divine, because it is an instrument of the Spirit, and it is the spirit wherein the will is tranquil that has the faculty of such a comprehension. There are many things, undoubtedly, that may be investigated and learned and comprehended in a spirit of selfishness, but the conception thus formed by the mind is merely an external appearance, and there is no understanding of the essential foundation." (*Signature* 15, 33.)

To express the above in other words, we might say that the selfish will of man, being limited, cannot conceive the universal will of God; it must give up its selfishness and limitation, to become one in the Spirit of God and understand its own self. Neither can the self-will know even a part of God, because God is one and a Unity, and cannot be conceived in parts.

"The will should strive after or desire nothing but the mercy of God in the Christ; it should continually enter into the love of God, and not permit anything whatever to turn it away from that object. If external reason triumphs and says, 'I have the true knowledge,' then should the will make that carnal reason bow down to the earth, and cause it to enter into the highest state of humility, and always repeat to it the words, 'You are foolish. You have nothing whatever except the mercy of God.' Into that mercy you must seek to penetrate and to become entirely nothing within yourself, and step out of all of your own selfish knowing and desiring, regarding it as an entirely impotent thing. Then will the natural self-will enter into a state of helplessness, and the Holy Spirit of God will take a living form within yourself and ignite the soul with its flame of divine love. Thus the high knowledge and the science of the Centre of all being will arise and appear. The human selfhood will then follow in its perceptions the Spirit of God, tremblingly and in the joy of humility, and become able to see what is contained in time and in eternity. Everything is near to a soul in that state, for the soul is then no longer her own property, but an instrument of God. In such a state of calmness and humility should the soul then remain, like a fountain remains at its own origin, and she should without ceasing draw and drink from that well, and nevermore desire to leave the way of God." (*Calmness*, i. 24.)

As the worm, crawling in the dust of the earth, cannot rise like the eagle above the clouds, so the self-willing thought of man, wandering in the labyrinth of conflicting opinions, does not enter the realm of eternal truth. But when man attains freedom by giving up self-will and selfish desires—or, to express it in other words, when by means of the Christ (eternal Light and Truth) he arrives at that state of oneness (at-one-ment) with God, which renders his soul godlike and divine, he then also receives in the Christ a true and essential knowledge of God and of Nature.

> "As soon as the newly-regenerated man becomes manifest, will he attain real knowledge. As the external man sees the external world, likewise the regenerated man sees the divine world wherein he dwells." (*Letters*, xxvii. 3.)

This spiritual world, wherein the regenerated ones consciously live, is not an imaginary or illusive world, but perfectly real; neither has it anything in common with the vulgar conceptions of heaven, which are merely the products of fancy.

> "It is to be regretted that men are led so blindly by those that are blind, and that the truth is stopped from manifesting itself to us in its glory and purity by our conceptions of external pictures and forms; for when the divine power in all its splendour becomes manifest and active within the interior foundation of the soul to such a degree that man earnestly desires to depart from his godless ways and to sacrifice his whole being to God, then will the whole of the triune Deity be present within the life and the will of the soul, and the heaven, wherein God resides, will be open to her." (*Mystery*, lx. 43.)

This is the only way in which a knowledge of God can be attained, and there is no other way.

> "Christ says: The Son of Man does nothing except what he sees that the Father is doing. If the Son of Man has become our body and His spirit our own, shall we then not be able to know God? If we live in the Christ the Spirit of Christ will see through us and in us whatever it desires, and that which the Christ desires we will see and know in Him. The world of the angels is easier and more clearly comprehensible to the regenerated man than the terrestrial world. He also sees into heaven, and beholds God and eternity." (*Menschwerdung*, ii. 7, 3.)

> "Our seeing and knowing is in God. He reveals to every one in this world as much as He wills, and as much as He knows will be useful to him. We are not in possession of our own selves. We know nothing of God.

> God Himself is our knowing and seeing. We are nothing, so that He may be All in us. We should be blind and deaf and mute, and know nothing and know of no life of our own, so that He may be our life and our soul, and that our work may be His." (*Menschwerdung*, ii. 7, 9.)

Seen in this true light, how foolish appear the practices of those who seek to obtain spiritual power and greatness by their speculations and mental efforts, without the light of God. It is well known that the light of the sun does not shine upon the earth because we desire it to shine, neither can we attract the sunlight to us. All we do is to step out of the darkness, or climb to the top of the mountain which rises above the clouds. Likewise the sunlight of divine wisdom does not enter the mind because the mind wills it to enter; but if our soul rises up to the mountain of the true faith, whose top reaches above the clouds of fear and superstition, and idle speculations and conflicting opinions, then will that light come to us by its own sweet grace, and without any merit or effort on our part to attract it.

The low cannot produce the high; neither can anything give birth to something higher than that which it contains. Neither animal nor reasoning man can create God, but the lily-bud of divinity unfolds itself in man by its own power. The divine man creates himself outside of man's willing. He is a god, and therefore self-created and self-existent; he does neither grow greater nor lesser; he is what he is; all that he requires is the conditions necessary for his revealing himself, and this condition is a pure will and a mind undisturbed by passions and idle thoughts, a heart full of calmness and peace.

Few indeed are the persons capable of entering into such a state of humility that divine and eternal truth can manifest itself in them without being distorted by selfish thoughts and desires. Not that not all human beings have not within themselves the inherent capacity for seeing the divine image that exists within themselves; but the truth is so simple and uncomplicated that it will not be accepted by those whose ways are complicated, and who therefore seek for complexity everywhere.

Jacob Boehme was of a simple and unsophisticated nature. Having received but little external education, there was not for him the necessity of unlearning ingrafted errors, and erasing misconceptions and acquired prejudices from his mind. Leading a pure life, his soul was like a clear mirror, in which he could perceive the image of the Godhead reflected therein, and his mind was like an unsoiled page, whereon the word of truth was plainly written. Nevertheless he, like all other persons similarly situated, had to overcome a certain amount of illusion arising from external observation, and from the reflections of the generally prevailing ideas within his own mind. He says:—

> "Before I knew that which I deeply know now, I, like others, thought that there was no other true heaven than that which as a blue circle encloses the world high above the stars; thinking that God had a separate existence therein, and that He was ruling this world by means of His Holy Spirit. But after I had met with many a hard obstacle in

following out this theory, I fell into a state of deep melancholy and grief in beholding the great depth of this world, the sun and the stars, the clouds, rain and snow, and in fact the whole of creation. I compared all that with the little speck called 'man,' and how insignificant he is before God, if compared with this great work of heaven and earth.[1] Finding, moreover, that there is good and evil in all things, in the elements as well as in creatures, and that in this world the wicked meets with the same fate as the pious, having good and ill luck; furthermore, that barbarous people occupy the best countries of the world, and are more favoured by fortune than those that are pious, I became very melancholy and dejected, and could find no consolation in Holy Writ, although I knew the Bible from beginning to the end. Perhaps it may be that the devil played a part in all that, for I often had heathenish thoughts, of which I will, however, say nothing at present.[2]

"When my spirit, full of sorrow, earnestly, and as if moving in a great storm, arose in God, carrying with it my whole heart and mind, with all my thoughts and with the whole of my will, and when I would not cease to wrestle with the love and mercy of God unless His blessing descended upon me—that is to say, unless He illumined my mind with His Holy Spirit, so that I could understand His will and get rid of my sorrow, then the light of the Spirit broke through the clouds. While in my zeal I powerfully stormed against the portals of hell, as if I had more strength than was in my possession, and willing to risk even my life (all of which would have been impossible to me without the aid of God); then after some hard fights with the powers of darkness, my spirit broke through the doors of hell, and penetrated even into the innermost essence of the newly-born Divinity, where it was received with great love, such as is offered by a bridegroom welcoming his beloved bride.

"No words can express the great joy and triumph which I then experienced, neither can I compare this gladness to anything except to a state in which life is born in the midst of death, or with a resurrection of the dead. While in that state, my spirit immediately saw through everything, and recognised God in all things, even in herbs and grasses, and it knew what is God and what is His will. Then very soon my will grew in this light, and received a strong impulse to describe the divine state." (*Aurora*, xix. 4.)[3]

Truly, none can enter the kingdom of heaven (meaning spiritual self-

---

[1]At that time Boehme, like other persons, mistook his terrestrial personality for his real self, because he had not yet learned to know the God within his own heart, and therefore he felt the insignificance of the former, if compared with the grandeur of the universal power of God manifested in nature, until at last he awoke to a realisation of the fact that the universal God and the God within his heart were one, and that his own personality was merely one of millions of similar instruments or organisms through which God is manifesting His power.

[2]The "devil" and the "powers of darkness" are the perverted fiery will, with his evil productions, originating from Lucifer, the "*Dhyan-Chohan*" of evil; the greatest angel before he fell.

[3]"Rejoice and be glad, and praise the Lord above all; for His name arises in glory above all the mountains and hills. It grows up like a sprout and performs great miracles. Who will hinder it?" (*Apologia*.)

knowledge and unspeakable joy) than he who is reborn in the Spirit; but no one can be reborn unless he dies entirely to all sense of self-will, and he then ceases to be a person and becomes pure joy, pure knowledge itself.

If this truth is once realised, if it is known that a limited personality, subject to the conditions of time and space, cannot embrace infinite wisdom and joy, then it appears self-evident that all the attempts for the attainment of divine wisdom, as long as one clings to self, must necessarily be unsuccessful. In fact no one should seek for spiritual knowledge for the purpose of rendering himself knowing and wise, but he should strive after dying within the Christ—that is to say, to become entirely one with divine truth, so that it is not any longer "he" who lives, but the truth living in him. He should not wish to become celebrated or renowned or self-satisfied, but rather pray that his knowledge should be taken away from him, unless it would lead to the glorification of God in him. In short, he should not wish to *become* anything, but he should *be* all knowledge, all joy, wisdom, and glory itself. Boehme says—

> "I have never desired to know anything about divine mysteries, neither did I understand how I might seek or find them. I sought for nothing except the heart of Jesus Christ (the centre of truth), wherein I might hide myself and find protection from the fearful wrath of God, and I asked God earnestly for His Holy Spirit and mercy, that He might bless and conduct me, and take away from me all that could avert me from Him, so that I might not live in my own will but in His. While engaged in such an earnest seeking and desiring, the door was opened to me, so that in one quarter of an hour I saw and learned more than if I had studied for many years at the universities." (*Letters*, xii. 6, 7.)

> "I am not a master of literature nor of arts, such as belong to this world, but a foolish and simple-minded man. I have never desired to learn any sciences, but from early youth I strove after the salvation of my soul, and thought how I might inherit or possess the kingdom of heaven. Finding within myself a powerful *contrarium*, namely, the desires that belong to the flesh and blood, I began to fight a hard battle against my corrupted nature, and with the aid of God, I made up my mind to overcome the inherited evil will, to break it, and to enter wholly into the love of God in the Christ. I therefore then and there resolved to regard myself as one dead in my inherited form, until the Spirit of God would take form in me, so that in and through Him I might conduct my life. This, however, was not possible for me to accomplish, but I stood firmly by my earnest resolution, and fought a hard battle with myself. Now while I was wrestling and battling, being aided by God, a wonderful light arose within my soul. It was a light entirely foreign to my unruly nature, but in it I recognised the true

nature of God and man, and the relation existing between them, a thing which heretofore I had never understood, and for which I would never have sought." (*Tilk.* 20–26.)

The realisation of the truth that we are nothing, but that God is all, constitutes the beginning of the true faith, which forms the basis of true knowledge and the first step on the road to spiritual unfoldment.

To wish, to will, to desire, to know, to do nothing except what God desires, wills, wishes, knows, or does in and through man is true resignation; it is the deepest humility for the carnal mind, while at the same time it is the glorification of God in man, and therefore the highest attainable state.

> "I am continually waiting for my Redeemer, willing to submit myself entirely to Him, whatever He may do. If He wants me to know a certain thing, then do I want to know it; but if He does not, then am I not desirous of knowing it. In Him I have put my will, my knowledge, my science, my desiring and doing." (*Letters*, viii. 60.)

> "Hundreds of times have I prayed to God, begging Him to take away from me all knowledge, if it did not serve for His glorification and for the amelioration of the condition of my brothers, and that He should only retain me within His love. But the more I prayed the more the internal fire within myself became ignited, and in such a state of ignition did I execute my writings." (*Letters*, xii. 60.)

This interior illumination of the mind by the light of eternal Truth alone, and not any other state or condition, is that which constitutes the true theosophy. Therefore true theosophy does not consist in intellectual learning of any kind, nor in morality, nor in being pious or virtuous, nor in belonging to any Church or society, nor in humanitarianism, or in anything that can be accomplished by man, but *theosophy is the self-knowledge of God in man*, the illumination of the mind by the light of the Christ, the eternal Truth itself. Such theosophy is not as some have claimed, "a branch of theology," nor any system of thought, nor a certain school, in which heretofore unknown secrets are divulged, but it is *divine wisdom* itself, without any other qualification. It is beyond all merely human conception, inconceivable to the reasoning intellect, and can therefore not be explained. It is itself the most secret thing, which can be known by no one except by him who has experienced it; neither do those that live entirely within the realm of animality, or within that of the speculating intellect, believe that such a state is possible, and in fact it is unattainable for any person; because he who enters into it, ceases to be a person, except in regard to his external appearance and form—that is to say, all sense of personality is lost to him, and has ceased to exist in the field of his inner consciousness.

It is therefore unnecessary to repeat that this state cannot be entered by the exercise of the self-will of animal man; neither can it be produced by him by means of any intellectual study; nor is it dependent on his social condition, or education, profession, or external qualifications in life, but it comes to man solely and alone by the *mercy and grace of God*. It means the presence of the divine light, and that presence depends on nothing else than on that presence itself. Boehme says—

> "It pleases the Supreme to reveal His secrets by means of the foolish, who are looked upon by the world as being nothing; so that it may be seen that their knowledge does not come from these fools, but from Him. Therefore I ask you to regard my writings as being those of a child in which the Supreme has manifested His power. There is in them so much, that no kind or amount of argumentation and reasoning can comprehend or grasp it; but to those that are illumined by the Spirit their understanding is easy and merely child's play." (*Letters*, xv. 10.)

> "The understanding is born of God. It is not the product of the schools in which human science is taught. I do not treat intellectual learning with contempt, and if I had obtained a more elaborate education, it would surely have been an advantage to me, while my mind received the divine gift; but it pleases God to turn the wisdom of this world into foolishness, and to give His strength to the weak, so that all may bow down before Him." (*Forty Questions*, xxxvii. 20.)

The reasoning intellect has nothing to do with originating perceptions, but is used for the purpose of bringing the ideas received from the clear perception of truth into a requisite form; and as the mind is then in a higher than the normal condition, it often happens that on returning to the lower state it does not understand, and perhaps not even remember, the ideas which it expressed during that time.

> "I say it before God, and testify before His judgment-seat, where everything must appear, that I in my human self do not know what I shall have to write; but whenever I am writing the Spirit dictates to me what to write, and shows me all in such a wonderful clearness, that I often do not know whether or not I am with my consciousness in this world. The more I seek the more I find, and I am continually penetrating deeper; so that it often seems to me as if my sinful person were too low and too unworthy for the reception of knowledge of such high and exalted mysteries; but in such moments the Spirit unfolds His banner and says to me, 'Behold! in this shalt thou live eternally, and be crowned therewith. Why art thou terrified?'" (*Letters*, ii. 10.)

"I might sometimes perhaps write more elegantly, and in a better style, but the fire burning within me is driving me on. My hand and my pen must then seek to follow the thoughts as well as they can. The inspiration comes like a shower of rain. That which I catch I have. If it were possible to grasp and describe all that I perceive, then would my writings be more explicit." (*Letters*, X. 45.)

From this it appears that truly inspired writings are quite different from those produced by ordinary mediumship; because in the former instance the seer perceives the truths which he is to express, while in the latter case the medium is either an unconscious machine, or feels an inspiration without knowing the nature of the source from which that inspiration comes.

It is also not to be supposed that any person, as long as he inhabits a physical body, and is to a certain extent dependent on external conditions, should be at all times in that superior spiritual state necessary to realise fully the eternal glory of the kingdom of God; but that there must necessarily be a return of the lower state of consciousness. Boehme says—

"As the lightning-flash arises within the centre, and disappears again in a moment, so it is with the soul. When during her battle she penetrates through the clouds, she sees the Godhead like a flash of light; but the clouds of sin soon gather again around her and cover her sight." (*Aurora*, xi. 76.)

"The soul has her origin partly from nature and partly from God. There is good and evil in nature; and man, by means of his sinful tendencies, has become subject to that which is fiery in nature, so that his soul becomes daily and hourly spotted with sin. Therefore the power of the soul to recognise eternal truth is not perfect." (*Aurora*, Preface, 100)

"As long as God watches over me with His protecting hand, I understand that which I have written; but whenever He becomes hidden before me, I then no longer recognise my own work, and this proves to me the impossibility of penetrating into the mysteries of God unless by the aid of His Spirit." (*Letters*, x. 29.)

If the carnal mind cannot understand the language of the Spirit, how then could that mind arrive at a true recognition of the truth by its own reasoning, that reasoning leading at best only to an opinion of what the truth cannot be, but not to a perception of what it is? Those who wish to understand such writings must enter into the spirit of the author. Mere reasoning will not serve the purpose.

"These writings transcend the horizon of intellectual reasoning, and their interior meaning cannot be grasped by speculation and

40

argumentation; but it requires the mind to be in a godlike state, and illumined by the Spirit of Truth." (*Letters*, xviii. 9.) 1

"If any one desires to follow me in the science of the things whereof I write, let him follow rather the flights of my soul than those of my pen." (*Three Principles*, xxiv. 2.)

This flight into the regions of eternal freedom is impossible for him who is bound by the chains that are forged by the illusion of "self," and is therefore unattainable to those who seek for a knowledge of God with the object of gratifying their curiosity, or with any other selfish object in view.

"Above all, examine yourself for what purpose you desire to know the mysteries of God, and whether you are prepared to employ that which will be received for the glorification of God and to the benefit of your neighbour. Are you ready to die entirely to your own selfish and earthly will, and do you earnestly desire to become one with the Spirit? He who has no such high purposes, and merely seeks for knowledge for the gratification of self, or that he may be looked upon as something great by the world, is not fit to receive such knowledge." (*Clavis*, ii. 3.)

1 "If you once understand the true meaning of what I have written, you will then be released from the conflict of opinions and possess self-knowledge; but, as a matter of course, this is not to be accomplished by the mere reading of the letters, but by the living power of the Spirit of Christ." (*Apologia*.)

Neither is such a state attained without a hard fight against the powers of darkness.

"If any one desires to follow me, let him not be intoxicated by terrestrial thoughts and desires, but girded with the sword of the Spirit, because he will have to descend into a terrible depth, even into the midst of the kingdom of hell. It indeed requires hard labour to fight with the devil between heaven and hell, as he is a powerful lord. During such battles I have often made many bitter experiences, which filled my heart with sorrow. Often the sun has disappeared from my sight, but then he rose again, and the oftener the sunset occurred, the more beautiful, clear, and magnificent was the sunrise." (*Aurora*, xiii. 20.)

He who desires nothing for himself, to him everything shall be given. The infinite cannot be made to contract, to be comprehended by the finite mind of man; but let the mind of man expand by the power of the Spirit, and become conscious of its infinity, and it will then conceive of infinite truth.

"Spiritual knowledge cannot be communicated from one intellect to

41

another, but must be sought for in the Spirit of God. Truly theosophical writings will even to the intellect convey here and there a ray of recognition; but if the reader is found worthy by God to have the divine light kindled within his own soul, then will the inexpressible words of God be heard by him." (*Letters*, lv. 8.)

"He who reads these writings and cannot understand them, should not throw them aside, imagining that they can never be understood. He should seek to change his will, and elevate his soul to God, asking Him for grace and understanding, and then read again. He will then perceive more truth than he did before, until at last the power of God will manifest itself in him, and he will be drawn down into the depths, into the supernatural foundation—that is to say, into the eternal unity of God. Then will he hear actual but inexpressible words of God, which will conduct him through the divine radiation of the celestial light, even within the grossest forms of terrestrial matter, and from thence back again unto God; and the Spirit of God will search all things in and with him." (*Clavis*, Preface, 5.)[4]

---

[4]This may perhaps be also expressed in the following words:—It is not the mortal intellect, but the divinity in man, which is in possession of divine knowledge.... A man knowing nothing of God, and having no faith in the power of anything divine, which may become revealed in him, cannot be in possession of divine self-knowledge; but if man, by being obedient to the law, enters into a state of harmony and union with God, then may God become revealed in him, and the mind being penetrated by the light of the divine spirit, man may partake of the knowledge of divinity. In this way he may learn all about everything in the three kingdoms; for the Spirit of God pervades the All. Occult knowledge, therefore, does not consist in gathering information or opinions from books and authorities, but its foundation is the recognition of the divine will in man.

Chapter II
The Unity of the All

"We are all one body in Christ, and have all the Spirit of Christ within our reach. If, then, we enter into the Christ, we may see and know everything by the power of His Spirit." (*Forty Questions*, xxvi. 5.)

THAT which is finite cannot conceive of the infinite; that which has a beginning cannot conceive of that which is without beginning and without an end. Who has measured space? Has it an end? and if so, what is there beyond the utmost limits of space? But if, there is no end to space, does not thought lose itself in seeking to penetrate into its depths? We cannot conceive of infinite space, but we can conceive of limited forms, which are space rendered objective; and in describing a form we describe space in a certain state or condition. Likewise, we cannot describe that which exists eternally in God, nor the eternal processes continually taking place within the divine life, in any other way than by speaking of them as if they had a beginning in time, and by using terrestrial terms, all of which are necessarily inadequate to produce a conception of that which cannot be conceived by the terrestrial mind, because it is infinitely above all terrestrial things.

"I cannot describe to you the whole of divinity as it were in a circle, because God is immeasurable; nevertheless the Godhead is not inconceivable to the spirit resting in the love of God. Such a spirit may grasp eternal truth, one part after another, and in this way it may end in perceiving the whole." (*Aurora*, x. 26.)

"If I am to make comprehensible the eternal generation, unfolding, or evolution of God out of His own self, I cannot speak otherwise than in a devilish (knowingly erroneous) manner, making it appear as if the eternal Light had ignited itself in the darkness, and as if the Godhead had a beginning. In no other way can I instruct you, so that you may form an approximate conception of it. There is nothing first and nothing last in this generation and evolution, nevertheless in describing it I have to put one thing after another." (*Aurora*, xxiii. 17–33.)

"We do not mean to say that the Deity had a beginning; we merely wish to show the way in which the Godhead has revealed itself by means of nature. God has no beginning in time; He has an eternal beginning and an eternal end." (*Signature*, iii. i.)

"The Godhead is an eternal band, which cannot perish. It generates itself from eternity to eternity, and the first therein is always the last, and the last the first." (*Three Principles*, vii. 14.).[5]

[5]God is unchangeable, and has no beginning in time; the "beginning" refers only to the manifestation of His power in nature. Nature resembles a continually revolving wheel, wherein forms in which the power of

43

That which is subject to the conditions of time may conceive of temporal things; only that which is eternal in man can realise the existence of the eternal.

> "We cannot speak the language of the angels, and even if we were to speak it everything would appear to the inhabitants of this world as if it did refer to created beings, and before the terrestrial mind it would represent itself as terrestrial. We are ourselves only parts of the whole, and we can conceive and speak only of parts, but not of the whole." (*Threefold Life*, ii. 66.)

> "I advise the reader, whenever I am speaking of the Godhead and its great mystery, not to conceive of what I say as if it were intended to be understood in a terrestrial sense, but to regard it from a higher point of view, in a supernatural aspect. I am often forced to give terrestrial names to that which is celestial, so that the reader may form a conception, and by meditating about it penetrate within the inner foundation." (*Grace*, iii. 19.)

God is self-existent, self-sufficient, infinite Will, having no origin. That Will, by conceiving of its own self, thereby creates a mirror within its own self. The same takes place in the microcosm of man. By conceiving of his own self man creates a mirror in which he " feels " his own self, and thereby he becomes self-conscious and realises his existence as an individual being.

> "Within the groundlessness (that which by some writers is called the 'Non-Being '—a term without any meaning) there is nothing but eternal tranquillity, an eternal rest without beginning and without an end. It is true that even there God has a will, but this will can be no object for our investigation, as to attempt to investigate it would merely produce a confusion in our mind. We conceive of this will as constituting the foundation of the Godhead. It has no origin, but conceives itself within itself." (*Menschwerdung*, xxi. 1.)

> "Divine Intelligence is a free will. It never originated from or by the power of anything. It is itself, and resides only and solely within itself, unaffected by anything, because there is nothing outside or previous to it." (*Mysterium*, xxix. 1.)

> "Eternal Freedom has the will, and is itself the will. In the will there is a desire to do or an impulse to wish something. There is nothing besides that will towards which that impulse could be directed. The will therefore sees within itself as within eternity; it sees what it is itself, and thereby creates within itself a mirror." (*Forty Questions*, i. 13.)

By this eternal mirroring, or God seeing Himself within Himself,

God becomes manifest are born and die. The death of one form is the birth of another. Thus life is born out of death; but that which produces life and causes death is eternal.

44

divine self-consciousness—that is to say, the self-knowledge of God, or in other words, divine wisdom, exists. The eternal Will, in its aspect as the Father, eternally conceives of itself as the Son, and, so to say, re-expands as the Holy Spirit. The same process on a minor scale takes place in the microcosm of man: for if he finds himself within himself by penetrating to the boundless abyss within himself, he then finds in the self-consciousness of his own manhood that power and strength by whose expansion his will and thought become powerful to act even at unmeasured distances.

Therefore it is said, that the deeper we lower ourselves and enter within our own centre, diving down into the groundless foundation of our own soul, even so deep that the sense of our own personality is completely lost, the higher shall we be exalted into the realm of divine and universal being.

> "God is the will of eternal wisdom, and the wisdom eternally generated from Him is His revelation. This revelation takes place through a threefold spirit. First, by means of the eternal Will, as such, in its aspect as the Father; next, by means of the eternal Will in its aspect as divine love, the centre or the heart of the Father; and finally, by means of the Spirit, the power issuing from the will and the love." (*Mysterium*, i. 2, 4.)

> "The Father Himself is the will of the groundlessness (the Absolute). This will conceives within itself the desire to manifest itself to itself. This love or desire is the power conceived by the will or Father within itself—that is to say, the Son, heart, or seat (the first foundation within the non-foundation or groundlessness), the first beginning within the will. The will is outspoken by means of this conceiving itself, and this issuing of the will in speaking or breathing is the Spirit of the Divinity." (*Mysterium*, i. 2.)[6]

> "The first inconceivable will without any origin generates within itself the one eternal God—a conceivable will, it being the son of the causeless will, but equally eternal with the former. This other will is the sensitivity and conceivability of the primordial will, by means of which that which is nothing finds itself to be something. By so doing the inconceivable causeless will issues by means of that which it has eternally found, and enters into a state of eternal meditation about its own self. The first causeless will is called the eternal Father; the conceived and generated will of the groundlessness is its inborn Son; the issue of the fathomless will by means of the conceived Son is the Spirit. Thus the one will of the Absolute, by means of the first eternal and beginningless conception, manifests a threefold activity, but nevertheless remains only one undifferentiated will." (*Grace*, i. 5–12.)

[6]The possibility of a being conceiving of its own self is experienced by its awakening to a consciousness of its own self.

This eternal mirroring, or God beholding Himself within Himself, may be called divine imagination. It is as infinite as the triune Spirit, beholding itself in that infinite mirror of divine wisdom, but it remains a merely passive power in regard to the active will. In the same sense the mind of a man is not the man himself, and the imagination of a man is or should be subject to his will; while a man without the power to think or imagine is unthinkable, and could not exist as a human being.

> "The first activity in God is divine contemplation or wisdom, by means of which the Spirit of God, with the outbreathed powers, plays as with one uniform power. This internal imagination is neither great nor little; it has neither beginning nor an end, but it is infinite, and its formative power is without limits." (*Grace*, i. 14.)

God, in His aspect as the father or creative will, is therefore the active or male element in creation; while divine wisdom, the mother, is the passive productive principle, having no will whatever of her own, but acting entirely according to the will of the father in her. It is true that the will of the father could produce nothing if it were not for the presence of the mother in whom the forms are evolved—or, to express it in other words, He could not create anything if He had not the wisdom to do so; but all the wisdom in the world creates nothing unless it is made active by the will.

> "Wisdom stands before God like a mirror or reflection, wherein the Godhead sees its own self and all the great wonders of eternity, which have neither a beginning nor an end in time, but whose beginning and end is eternal. Wisdom is a revelation of the holy Trinity; but this is not to be understood as if she were revealing herself to God by her own power or choice, but the divine centre, the heart and essence of God, becomes revealed in her. She is like a mirror of the Godhead, and like any other mirror, she merely holds still; she does not produce an image, but merely conceives it." (*Menschwerdung*, i. 1, 12.)

That which the father eternally desires to give, the mother eternally desires to receive.

Life is male, the earth, or "matter," is female. The earth does not cause a seed to grow, but the seed planted into the earth carries within itself the power to grow; the earth merely furnishes the material which the life in the seed extracts from the earth. Likewise the mother does not create the child, but merely furnishes the materials required by the creative spirit existing within the child, and which, before it is born, attracts from the organism of the mother that which it needs, comparable to the way in which, after the child is born, it draws its nutriment from the mother's breast.[7]

> "Wisdom is the outspoken word of divine power, knowledge, and sanctity, an antithesis of the unfathomable unity in essentiality, wherein the Holy Spirit forms and imagines. She is passive, but the Spirit of God is active, like the soul in the body." (*Clavis*, v. 18.)

This eternal Trinity is inconceivable in its aspect as a spiritual potentiality, in the same sense as a fire is inconceivable if it does not burn; but as the burning fire reveals itself by means of the light and the heat, likewise the divine power reveals itself in a threefold aspect in eternal nature.

> "The threefold Spirit is a unity, an only being; or to speak more correctly, not a being, but eternal Reason; consequently a mystery comparable to the intelligence of man, which is also incomprehensible." (Mysterium., i. 5.)

> "God in His primitive aspect is not to be conceived of as a being, but merely as the power or the intelligence constituting the potentiality for being—as an unfathomable, eternal will, wherein everything is contained, and which, although being itself everything, is nevertheless only one, but desirous of revealing itself and to enter into a state of spiritual being. This takes place by means of the fire in the desire of love, *i.e.*, in the power of the light." (*Mysterium*, vi. 1.)

> "Here we have not yet cause to say that God is three persons, but He is threefold in His eternal evolution. He gives birth to Himself in trinity; and in this eternal unfoldment He is nevertheless an only being, neither Father, nor Son, nor Spirit, but only the eternal Life or God. The Trinity will become comprehensible in His eternal revelation only when He reveals Himself by means of eternal nature—that is to say, in the light by means of the fire." (*Mysterium*, vii. 9–12.)

> "Within the stillness of eternal freedom the Father does not yet appear as a father. He appears as such only when He is desirous to create, and conceives within Himself the will to generate nature, within Himself." (*Threefold Life*, iv. 64.)

We cannot conceive of a man without a body of some kind, nor of a universal God without a universal nature. The very essence which constitutes "man" is will and intelligence manifesting itself in a human form. God begins to exist as a being only when He is manifesting

[7]Terrestrial men and women are male and female organisms, in which the active and passive elements of creation are manifesting themselves in their external expression. Each man has in him male and female elements. A woman in whom merely the principle of will were active, without the presence of thought, would be nothing but an accumulation of blind force. A man without any female element, *i.e.*, without any will, would be like a mirror full of images, but incapable to produce anything. The true woman, in the ideal marriage of the soul, has no other thought than that of her husband; neither does the true man will any thing that is not compatible with the desire of his wife.

Himself in nature. From all eternity has God thus been revealing Himself to Himself; and the cause of this self-revelation rests first of all in the will of God in the Trinity and in the longing of eternal wisdom.

> "Of eternity we cannot speak otherwise than as of a spirit, for everything was spirit in the beginning; but it has also from all eternity evolved itself into being." (*Menschwerdung*, i. 2.)

> "That which is tranquil and without being, resting within itself, does not contain darkness, but is a calm, clear, lucid happiness. This then is eternity without anything else, and means above all God. But as God cannot be without being, He conceives within Himself a will, and this will is love." (*Threefold Life*, ii. 75.)

> "The whole of the divine Being is in a state of continual and eternal generation comparable to the mind of a man, but immutable. There are continually thoughts born from the mind of man, and from them arises desire and will. From desire and will originates action, and the hands do their work, so as to render it substantial., Thus it is with eternal evolution." (*Three Principles*, ix. 3 5.)

> "At first the will is as thin as a nothing, and therefore it desires and longs to be something, and to become manifest to itself. This nothingness causes the will to enter into a state of desire, and this desire is an imagination. The will beholding itself in the mirror of wisdom causes its own image to appear within the groundlessness, and thus it creates a foundation in its own imagination." (*Menschwerdung*, ii. 1.)

> "Wisdom, the eternal virgin, the playmate of God to His honour and joy, becomes full of desire to behold the wonders of God that are contained within herself. Owing to this desire, the divine essences within her become active and attract the holy power, and thus, she enters into a state of permanent being. By this she does not conceive of anything within herself; her inclination is resting in the Holy Spirit. She merely moves before God for the purpose of revealing the wonders of God." (*Three Principles*, xiv. 87.)[8]

The possibility of such an "external" or corporeal revelation of God rests in the divine magic power, which exists within the divine life itself. It is the power of the magic will to produce that which it desires.

> "The magic power is the Spirit desirous for being. It is essentially nothing but will, but it enters into existence. It is the greatest mystery; it is above nature, and forces nature to assume forms according to the form of its will. It introduces the foundation into the abyss of the groundlessness, and changes nothing into something. It is the mother

---

[8]Thus divine wisdom in man does not speculate or "draw logical conclusions," neither is it dependent for knowledge on communications received from anybody; but it is the power of the true living faith, *i.e.*, the power of the spirit of man to grasp spiritual truths existing within its own self.

of eternity and of the essentiality of all beings. In it are contained all the forms of the latter. It is not the intellect, but it acts according to the will of the intellect. It is not majesty, neither the power itself, but a desire entering into the dark nature (matter) and proceeding by means of that dark nature into the fire, and through the fire into light. Through this magic power the wonders of the number Three become revealed by means of nature." (*Six Mystical Points*, v. 1–11.)

"The corporeity of God results from His essentiality. This essentiality is not spirit, but it appears like impotency if compared with the power wherein the Three resides. This essentiality is the element of God, wherein is life but no intelligence." (*Threefold Life*, v. 53.)

A thesis presupposes the antithesis. In the One there exists no relation. There can be no consciousness manifest without something to be conscious of, and without that which is to be conscious. Without nature there could be no freedom of nature; without the positive there could be no negative; without the dark basis of fire there could be no light.

"The One has nothing within itself which it could possibly desire, neither can such a unity feel its own self. This is possible only in a state of duality." (*Theosophical Questions*, iii. 3.)

"If everything were only one, that one could not become manifest to itself. If there were no anguish joy could not be known." (*Mysterium*, iv. 22.)

"God introduces His will into nature for the purpose of revealing His power in light and in majesty, to constitute a kingdom of joy. If there were no nature originating within the eternal unity, there would be nothing else but eternal tranquillity. Nature entering into a state of pain, the tranquillity becomes changed into motion, and the powers become audible as the word." (*Grace*, ii. 16.)

"The One, the 'Yes,' is pure power, and the life and the truth of God, or God Himself; but God would be unknowable to Himself, and there would be in Him no joy or perception, if it were not for the presence of the 'No.' The latter is the antithesis or the opposite to the positive or the truth; it causes the latter to become revealed, and this is only possible by its being the opposite wherein eternal love may become active and perceptible." (*Theosophical Questions*, iii. 2.)

"If there is to be a light, there must be a fire. The fire produces the light, and the light renders the fire manifest; it receives the nature of the fire within itself and resides in the fire." (*Mysterium*, xl. 2.)

"Joy enters the state of desire for the purpose of producing a fiery love, a realm of happiness, which could not exist in the tranquillity." (*Signature*, vi. 2.)

"The majesty of God could not become revealed in power, joy, and magnificence, if it were not for the attraction caused by desire. Likewise there could be no light, if desire were not entering and overshadowing, and thereby creating a state of darkness, which grows until the ignition of the fire takes place." (*Grace*, ii. 14.)

Relative good cannot exist without relative evil, and evil cannot exist without good. The fire can no more exist without the light than the light without the fire. No multiplicity is possible without the unity. Each requires and therefore desires the other.

"Light and darkness are opposed to each other, but there is between them a link, so that neither of them could exist without the other." (*Threefold Life*, ii. 86.)

"In God there are two states, eternally and without end—namely, the eternal light and eternal darkness. The light is God, and in the darkness there would be no pain if it were not for the presence of the light. The light causes the darkness to long for the light and to suffer anguish therefor." (*Three Principles*, ix. 30.)

"The will having issued from the state of unity (by assuming a position, as it were, against the unity in desiring its own self), enters as a state of desire, and this desire is magnetic—that is to say, indrawing; but the unity as such is outflowing; it seeks to issue outwardly, so as to become revealed. The will having issued from the state of unity, desires to enter within itself, so as to attain sensation in the unity, and that thereby the unity may attain sensation in the will." (*Theosophical Questions*, iii. 9.)

"The light-life has its own motion and impulse, and likewise the fire-life; but the latter generates the former and the former is the lord of the latter. If there were no fire, there would be no light and no spirit; and if there were no spirit to breathe upon the fire, the latter would be extinguished and darkness would rule. Each of the two would be nothing without the other; both are mutually dependent upon each other." (*Forty Questions*, i. 62.)

There is, however, no equality between this duality, for the unity is superior to the multiplicity, freedom to nature, light to fire; the higher always rules the lower.

"The will as such is an insensible life, but it finds the desire, and in willing to desire it constitutes itself in a being. The will is superior to the desire, for although the desire is an exciting cause for the will, the will is a life without a cause and it is also intelligence. It is therefore, lord over desire. It rules the life of the desire and uses it as it pleases. This eternal will-spirit we know to be God, but the active life of the desire is eternal nature." (*Inner Mystery*, i. 1; iii. 2.)

"God is from eternity Power and Light, and is therefore called God according to that, but not according to the fire-spirit. In regard to the latter, we speak of it not as God, but as 'the *wrath of God*' and the consuming part of His power. The light of God has also the quality of the fire, but in it the wrath is changed into love; hate and bitter pain into mild beneficence and sweet desire or satisfaction." (*Menschwerdung*, i. 5–16.)

"The fountain of love is a clasping and keeping of the stern wrathfulness, an overcoming of the harsh power, because meekness takes away the rule of the acrid and hard power of the fire. The light of peacefulness keeps the darkness imprisoned and resides in the darkness. The stern power desires only wrathfulness and imprisonment in death; but the mildness issues like a sweet growth, it blossoms out and overcomes death, giving eternal life." (*Threefold Life*, ii. 92.)

"When love becomes revealed in light by means of the fire, it streams over nature and penetrates her, like the sunshine penetrating an herb or fire penetrating through iron." (*Clavis*, viii. 36.)

To understand the above it is only necessary to realise these things within one's own being. To the speculating intellect they will for ever remain a mystery.

Not in the trunk, the root, the branches, or the leaves, but only in the flower of a plant, can be found the germ that produces the fruit or seed from which a new plant of a similar kind may grow. Likewise, not in the passions of man, nor in his intellectual acquisitions, but only in the spiritual efflorescence of his soul, exists the germ for the new-born being capable of obtaining consciousness of its own immortality.

Chapter III
The Seven Properties or Qualities of Eternal Nature[9]

I. ♄ ☽ II. ☿ ♃ III. ♂ ♀

IV. ☉

V. ♀ ♂ VI. ♃ ☿ VII. ☽ ♄

WHEN the Eternal One, in its aspect as a Trinity and with reference to divine wisdom, reveals itself on the seven planes of existence, this revelation constitutes seven different rays or states of eternal nature, comparable to the sevenfold scale of colours, tunes, chemical substances, &c., all of which are seven different forms in which the fundamental one is manifesting itself. Of these seven forms or sourcive states of eternal nature, the first and the seventh refer to the Father, the second and sixth to the Son, the third and fifth to the Holy Spirit, while the fourth represents the balance in which exists the division between spirit and matter.

> "The eternal Essence, being desirous of revealing itself to itself (to attain self-consciousness), had to conceive within itself a will; but as within itself there was no object for its will or desire, except the powerful Word, which in the tranquil eternity did not exist, the seven states of eternal nature had to be born from within. From these, then, proceeded, from eternity to eternity, the powerful Word, the power, the heart, and the life of the tranquil eternity and its eternal wisdom." (*Threefold Life*, iii. 21.)

> "The first and the seventh quality must be regarded as one, likewise the second and sixth, and also the third and the fifth; but the fourth is the object of division. The first then refers to the Father, the second to the Son, the third to the, Holy Spirit." (*Clavis*, ix. 75.)

By means of the manifestation of these seven qualities of eternal nature the infinity of divine being does not become limited; they are merely seven different forms in which the power of God is manifesting itself, and the existence of each of these seven properties depends on that of the rest.

---

[9] If it is asked how it is possible that Jacob Boehme knew anything about the invisible spiritual processes taking place in the universe, the answer is that the spirit of man is one and universal, and he who knows his own divine self knows the whole of the universe. Seen from the spiritual point of view, the universal cosmic processes in the body of universal nature are internal processes taking place within the organism of macrocosmic man, mirrored forth and eternally repeated in the microcosm of the individual. The history of the universe is the history of a man.

> "If I speak of the seven states of eternal nature, it is not to be understood as if there were a limitation of the Godhead in regard to object and measure. Its power and wisdom is without end, without measure and unspeakable." (*Mysterium*, vii. 17.)

> "Do not imagine these seven spirits to be standing one by the side of the other, comparable to the stars, which are seen side by side in the sky; they are all seven like only one spirit. Likewise the body of man has many organs, but each organ partakes of the power of the rest. (*Aurora*, x. 40.)

In the same sense we speak of the bones and flesh, the arteries and veins and nerves of a body, all of which go to make up only one organism. Likewise a picture is made up of many different colours, of which each has a certain individuality of its own, while the sum total is necessary to form one individual picture.

> "As the organs of a man's body love one another, so do the spirits in divine power. There is nothing but longing, desiring, and fulfilling, and each triumphs and rejoices in the other." (*Aurora*, ix. 37.)

They are like seven living and conscious rays contained within the original colourless ray, and broken into seven different tints by their passage through "matter."

> "You must know that one spirit alone cannot generate another, but the birth of one spirit results from the cooperation of all the seven. Six of them always generate the seventh, and if one of them were absent the others could not be there." (*Aurora*, x. 21.)

> "All the seven spirits of God are born one in another. One gives birth to the other; there is neither first nor last. The last generates the first, as well as the first the second, the third the fourth, up to the last. They are all seven equally eternal." (*Aurora*, x. 2.)

> "If I am sometimes describing only two or three as being active in the generation of another spirit, I am doing so on account of my weakness, because in my degenerate mind I cannot retain the impression of the action of all the seven in their perfection. I see all the seven; but when I begin to analyse what I see, I then cannot grasp all the seven at once, but only one after another." (*Aurora*, x. 22.)

These seven properties *are never transformed one into another;* each retains eternally its own specific essentiality. The relations into which they enter with each other serve for the purpose of their mutual glorification; so that they, when they meet each other like strains of sweet harmonies in God's eternal nature, appear like flaming lights of life and joy. Thus matter is never transformed into spirit, but illumined and glorified by the latter, while the spirit obtains its corporification from matter, and, is thus enabled to become manifest.

Likewise ignorance is never transformed into knowledge, nor death into life.; but an ignorant person may become wise if illuminated by the light of wisdom, and a body in which life is inactive may be made living if the activity of life is aroused therein.

> "Each of these principles is strongly defined in regard to its nature, nevertheless there is no antipathy between them. They are all rejoicing in God as one only spirit. Each loves the other, and there is nothing among them but joy and happiness. Their evolution is an eternal one and never any other." (*Aurora*, x. 51.)

> "The higher they become exalted, and the more they become ignited, the greater will be their joy in the kingdom of light." (*Mysterium*, v. 6.)

> "Each quality of the spirit desires the other, and when it acquires its object it becomes as it were changed into that other; but its own quality is thereby not lost, it merely adapts itself to the other, and manifests another kind of anguish (consciousness), but both retain their own special qualities." (*Threefold Life*, iv. 8.)

Thus the darkness is illumined by the light, but it never becomes light itself, nor can the light become darkness. The light shineth eternally into darkness, but the darkness comprehendeth it not.

> "Each of these divine forms of life desires to govern; each has a will of its own. Without that there could be no sensibility nor perceptibility, but only eternal tranquillity. Neither, however, of them is pressing forward to make itself manifest more than the rest, but all are in perfect harmony with each other." (*Stiefel*, ii. 348.)

> "When the fourth principle enters into the first, all the spirits intermingle their light, triumph, and rejoice. They then arise all one within the other, and evolve each other as if moving in circular motion; and the light in the midst of them begins to shine and renders them luminous. Their harsh quality then remains hidden like a kernel in a fruit. As a sour or bitter unripe apple by ripening in the sun becomes changed, so that it acquires an agreeable taste, but nevertheless retains the qualities that constitute it an apple, likewise the Godhead retains its own essential qualities, but they become manifest in a sweet and agreeable manner." (*Aurora*, xiii. 80.)

> "All the seven principles are spiritual within eternal nature, and appear there in a clear, crystalline, translucent substantiality." (*Grace*, iii. 40.)

> "The seven candlesticks in Saint John's Revelation refer to the seven spirits in the Godhead, also the seven stars. The seven spirits are in the

centre of the Father—that is to say, in the power of the Word. The Word changes the wrathfulness into sweet joy and shapes it into a crystalline ocean; therein the seven spirits appear in a burning form, like seven luminous torches." (*Threefold Life*, iii. 46.)

A variety of colours is necessary to make up a picture, to represent an idea, and although the idea represented by the various colours is only one, nevertheless each colour retains its essential qualities. The various organs of the human body manifest various powers, nevertheless they all go to make up one manifestation of life. The various planets have each one its own special qualities, nevertheless they go to make up one world. Likewise each of the seven forms remains what it is, but their manifestations differ widely according to the planes and conditions under which they are manifesting themselves.

The First Quality begins when God, for the purpose of revealing His majesty, allows His eternal nature to contract within herself, whereby a state of darkness and corporeity is created.

"The first quality is the desire. It is comparable to magnetic attraction, and therefore the comprehensibility of the will. The will conceives of itself as something. By this act of impressing or contracting it overshadows itself and causes itself to become darkness." (*Clavis*, viii. 38.)

"In this state there is no active life or intelligence; it is merely the first principle of substantiality, or the first beginning of the becoming." (*Three Principles*, vii. 11.)

"In eternity beyond nature there can be no darkness, because there is nothing that could produce it. The will by desiring contracts and becomes substantial. Thus darkness is created within the will, while without that desire there would be nothing but eternal stillness without substantiality." (*Forty Questions*.)

"Desire is an acrid, astringent, attracting (contracting) quality. It is an active power, and without it there would be nothing but tranquillity. It contracts and fills itself with itself; but that which it attracts constitutes nothing but darkness, a state which is more compact than the original will, the latter being thin as nothing, but it then becomes full and substantial." (*Threefold Life*, ii. 12.)

The fact of this contractive power of desire, by which the will is rendered substantial, corporeal, and heavy, is experienced by every one who feels the weight of sorrow caused by some unfulfilled desire weighing upon his soul, while freedom from desire, and consequently from care, renders the heart (the will) light and ethereal.

56

Simultaneously with the appearance of the first enters *the Second Form*, namely, motion. Matter and motion are co-eternal, and neither of them can exist without the other. There could be no contraction without motion, neither would there be any expansion if there were no desire to contract. With the beginning of action reaction begins. There is then a duality of manifestation of the eternal One. From this duality of action, having its source in the One, results the manifestation of relative life.

> "Motion divides the attracted desire and causes differentiation, thereby awakening the true life." (*Clavis*, viii. 30.)

> "From this results sensitiveness in nature, and herein is the cause of differentiation. Hardness (solidity) and the motion of life are opposed to each other. Motion breaks up the solidity (expands), and by means of attraction it also causes hardness (contracts)." (*Tabulæ Princip.*, i. 34.)

> "Desire, being a strong attraction, causes the ethereal freedom, which is comparable to a nothing, to contract and enter into a state of darkness. The primitive will desires to be free of that darkness, for it desires the light. The will cannot attain this light, and the more it desires for freedom the greater will be the attraction caused by the desire." (*Six Theosophical Points*, i, 38.)

> "There must be an opposition, for the will desires not to be dark, and this very desire causes the darkness: The will loves the excitement caused by the desire, but it does not love the contraction and darkening. The will itself does not become dark, but only the desire existing in it. The desire is in darkness, and therefore a great anguish results within the will, as its desire for freedom is strong, but by this desire it causes itself to become still more harsh and dark." (*Forty Questions.*)

Eliphas Levi expressed a corresponding truth by saying; "The will accomplishes that which it does not desire." A selfish desire for heaven defeats its own object.

The Third Quality, called into existence by the action and reaction of the absolute One, calls sensation into existence; or, to express it in other words, absolute consciousness, by manifesting itself, becomes relative. Nothing new is thereby created, only that which already was begins to exist. This relative consciousness is called " anguish " by Boehme.

> "The third quality, the anguish, is evolved in the following manner:— The hardness is fixed, the motion is fugitive; the one is centripetal, the other centrifugal; but as they are one, and cannot separate from each

other (nor from their centre) they become like a turning wheel, in which one part strives upwards and the other one in a downward direction. The hardness furnishes substantiality and weight, while the 'sting' (desire in motion) supplies spirit (will for freedom) and fugitive life. All this causes a turning around and within and outwardly, having nevertheless no destination where to arrive. That which the attraction of the desire causes to become fixed is again rendered volatile by the aspiring for freedom. There then results the greatest disquietude, comparable to a furious madness, from which results a terrible anguish." (*Mysterium*, iii. 5.)

The truth of this every one experiences within his own self, because as long as man is nailed to the cross of terrestrial life, there is a continual battle raging in him between his higher and lower impulses, or between his ideal aspirations and his material self-interests.

"The more the first principle gathers its hardness for the purpose of arresting the second principle, the stronger does the action of that principle grow, and the stronger is the raging and breaking. The sting refuses to be subdued, but the will (from which it originates) holds on to it with great strength, and it cannot follow its impulse. It strives upwards and the will strives downwards, for the acerbity indraws, rendering itself heavy. Thus the one strives to rise upwards, and the other to sink downwards, while neither of them can accomplish its object, and thus eternal nature becomes like a revolving wheel." (*Menschwerdung*, ii. 4.)

This macrocosmic battle leads its counterpart in the microcosm of man. There is in him also the continual fight between matter and spirit, between desire and renunciation, between the desire for existence and the will for that freedom which cannot be found before even the desire for freedom itself is at rest.

These three first forms or qualities, wherein the activity of the Father, the Son, and the Holy Spirit are represented, or to express it in other words, through which the quality of will and intelligence becomes revealed, are sometimes alluded to under the names of "salt," "sulphur," and "mercury."

"The first three principles are not God Himself, but only His revelation. The first of these three states, being a beginning of all power and strength, originates from the quality of the Father; the second, being the source of all activity and differentiation, comes from the quality of the Son; and the third, being the root of all life, originates in the quality of the Holy Spirit." (*Grace*, vi. 9.)

"The ancients said that in sulphur, mercury, and salt are contained all things. This refers not so much to the material as to the spiritual aspect of things, namely, to the spirit of the qualities wherefrom material things grow. By the term 'salt' they understood the sharp metallic desire in nature; 'mercury' symbolised to them the motion and differentiation of the former, by means of which each thing becomes objective and enters into formation. 'Sulphur,' the third quality, signified the anguish of nature." (*Clavis*, 46.)

The true divine life wherein the substantiality of divine Trinity is revealed is rendered possible only by means of the *Fourth Quality*, called the lightning-flash, whose ignition is caused by the desire of eternal nature and by the longing of eternal freedom.

"The fire is originally darkness, hardness, eternal coldness and dryness, and there is nothing in it except an eternal hunger. How then does it become actual fire? The Spirit of God, in its aspect as the eternal light, comes to the aid of the fire-hunger. The hunger itself originates from the light, because when the divine power mirrors itself in the darkness, the latter becomes full of desire after the light, and this desire is the will (of eternal nature). But the will or the desire in the dryness cannot reach the light, and therein consists the anguish and the craving for light. This anguish and craving continues until the Spirit of God enters like a flash of lightning." (*Three Principles*, xi. 45.)

This ever-turning "wheel of Ixion" is represented by the Cross, the "Tree of Life." Free is the spirit of man before he enters this valley of suffering, but after he enters he is nailed to the cross of his own personal desires. Man himself is the "Cross," and he creates a cross for himself, from which there is no liberation until he discovers the true spiritual Cross by entering into the realm of light through the power of the fire, which means that his spirit breaks through the bonds of matter and becomes again free.

"Freedom by means of the eternal will grasps the darkness, and the latter reaches out for the light of freedom but cannot attain it. It imprisons itself by means of its own desire within itself, and causes itself to be darkness. From these two—namely, the dark impression and the desire for light or freedom which is directed towards the former, there results then in the former darkness the lightning-flash, the primitive condition of the fire. But freedom being a nothing, and therefore inapprehensible, it cannot retain the impression. Therefore the impression surrenders to freedom, and the latter devours the dark nature of the former. Thus freedom governs within the darkness, and is not comprehended by it." (*Signature*, xiv. 22.)

"Eternal unity or freedom, *per se*, is of infinite loveliness and mildness, but the three qualities are sharp, painful, and even terrible. The will of the three qualities longs for the mild unity, and the unity longs for the fiery foundation and sensibility. Thus one enters into the other, and when this takes place the lightning-flash appears, comparable to a spark produced by the friction of flint and steel. Thereby the unity attains sensibility, and the will of nature receives the mild unity. Thus the unity becomes a fountain of fire, and the fire penetrated by desire, like a fountain of love." (*Clavis*, ix. 49.)

Thus the light conquers the darkness, but does not destroy it; it merely becomes victorious over it and consumes it in a manner comparable to that of the assimilation of food by the organism which conquers and consumes that food by means of the fire of life.

"When the spiritual fire and light has become ignited in the darkness (it having, however, burned from all eternity), the great mystery of divine power and knowledge becomes eternally revealed therein, because in the fire all the qualities of nature appear exalted into spirituality. Nature herself remains what she is, but her issue—namely, that which she produces, becomes spiritualised. In the fire the dark will is consumed, and thereby issues the pure fire-spirit, penetrated by the light-spirit." (*Clavis*, ix. 64.)

When this great internal revelation 'takes place, the internal senses are then opened to the direct perception of spiritual truth. There will then be no more necessity for drawing conclusions of any kind in regard to such unknown things, because the spirit perceives that which belongs to its sphere in the same sense as a seeing person sees external things.

"Behold how all life in the external world attracts its food to itself. Thus you may recognise how life originates from death. There can be no life unless that from which life is to issue is broken up in its form. Everything has to enter into the state of anguish to attain the lightning-flash, and without this there will be no ignition." (*Menschwerdung*, ii. 5.)

This, then, is the beginning of the manifestation of God as the principle of fire and the principle of light. The Godhead, as such, the will of the Trinity willing to enter from the groundlessness into Trinity, is not yet a principle, and has no beginning, but is the beginning itself of itself.

"If a thing becomes that which it has not been before, this does not constitute a principle; a principle is there where a form of life and motion begins, such as has not existed before. Thus the fire is a principle, and also the light which is born from the fire, but which, nevertheless is not a quality of the fire, but has a life of its own." (*Six Theosophical Points*, ii. 1.)

In the fire there is represented the division of the two aspects in which God is manifesting Himself—namely, as God and as Nature; also the division between the sweet life in love and the life in wrath.

"As the sun in the terrestrial plane transforms acerbity into concord, so acts the light of God in the forms of eternal nature; This light shines into them and out of them; it ignites them so that they obtain its will and surrender themselves to it entirely. They then give up their own will and become as if they had no power at all of themselves, and are desirous only for the power of the light." (*Six Theosophical Points*, v. 3.)

By the union of fire and light the third principle attains substantiality.

"If the Godhead according to the first and second principle is to be regarded only as a spirit and without any conceivable essentiality, there is in it nevertheless the desire to evolve a third principle, wherein rests the spirit of the two first principles, and wherein it will become manifest as an image." (*Six Theosophical Points*, i. 25.)

"The fire receiving within itself the essence of desire as its food, so that it may burn, renders a joyful spirit and opens the power of the mild essentiality in the light." (*Six Theosophical Points*, i. 57.)

"The fire, drawing within itself the mild essentiality of the light, there issues from it, by means of the wrath of death, the mild spirit that was enclosed therein, and which has within itself the quality of nature." (*Tilk.*, i. 171.)

When the power of the light becomes revealed it manifests its activity first of all in the *Fifth Quality*, which is evolved by means of the preceding four as sweet love, or a luminous water-spirit.

"The first three principles are merely qualities conducive to life, the fourth is life itself, but the fifth is the true Spirit. Whenever this power has been evolved from the fire, it lives within all the others and changes them all into its own sweet nature, so that painfulness and enmity cannot be found therein in any shape whatever." (*Tabulæ Principæ*, i. 46.)

"The fifth quality is the true love-fire, which in the light separates from the painful fire, and wherein divine love appears as a substantial being. It has within itself all the powers of divine wisdom; it is the trunk or the centre of the tree of eternal life, wherein God the Father becomes revealed in His Son by means of the speaking Word." (*Grace*, iii. 26.)

In the *Sixth Quality* the divine powers, still united, and therefore undifferentiated and not manifest in the fifth, become differentiated and audible.

"The sixth form of eternal nature is intelligent life or sound. The qualities being all in a state of equilibrium in the light (the fifth), they now rejoice and acquire audibility. Thereby the desire of the unity enters into a state of (conscious) willing and acting, perceiving and feeling." (*Tabulæ Principæ*, i. 48.)

"To constitute audible life, or the sound of the powers, hardness and softness, compactness and thinness and motion are required. To constitute the sixth principle there are therefore required all the other qualities of nature. The first form furnishes hardness, the second motion; by means of the third division takes place. The fire changes the harshness of the conceived essence by consuming it into a spiritual being, representing mildness and softness, and this becomes formed into sound, according to the qualities which it contains." (*Mysterium*, v. 11.)

This sound of course is not to be compared to terrestrial audible sound.

"In the light of God the kingdom of heaven (the consciousness of the spirit), sound is very subtle, sweet, and lovely, so that if compared with terrestrial noise, it is like a perfect stillness. Nevertheless in the realm of glory it is indeed comprehensible sound, and there is a language which is heard by the angels—a language which is, however, only partaking of the nature of their world." (*Mysterium*, v. 19.)

The third principle reappears in the seventh, and therein consists the "resurrection of the flesh."

"*The Seventh Principle* is the corporeal comprehension of the other qualities. It is called '*Essential Wisdom*' or the '*Body of God.*' The third principle appears in the seven forms of nature in so far as they have been brought into comprehensibility in the seventh. This principle or state of being is holy, pure, and good. It is called the eternal untreated heaven or the kingdom of God, and it is outspoken from the first principle, of the dark fire-world and from the holy light-flaming love-world." (*Grace*, iv. 10.)

"The seventh form is the state of being wherein all the others manifest their activity, like the soul in the body. It is called Nature, and also the eternal essential wisdom of God." (*Tabulæ Principæ*, i. 49.)

"The seventh spirit of God is the body, being born from the other six spirits, and in it all the celestial figures are taking form. From it arises all beauty, all joy. If this spirit did not exist God would be imperceptible." (*Aurora*, xi. 1.)

"Wisdom is the substantiality of the spirit. The spirit wears it as a garment, and becomes revealed thereby. Without it the form of the spirit would not be knowable; it is the corporeity of the spirit. To be sure, it is not a bodily, tangible substance, like the bodies of men, but has nevertheless substantial and visible qualities which the spirit *per se* does not possess." (*Threefold Life*, v. 50.)

There is no language to describe the beauty and splendour of divine wisdom. Whatever there is of magnificence perceptible in this terrestrial world exists in the celestial world in a far superior state, in eternal spiritual perfection.

"Earthly language is entirely insufficient to describe what there is of joy, happiness, and loveliness contained in the inner wonders of God. Even if the eternal Virgin pictures them to our minds, man's constitution is too cold and dark to be able to express even a spark of it in his language." (*Three Principles*, xiv. 90.)

Neither are these superterrestrial pictures mere shadows or creations of fancy.

"Just as the earth continually produces plants and flowers, trees and metals, and beings of various kinds, one always more glorious, stronger, and more beautiful than the rest; and as on our terrestrial plane one form appears while others perish, there being a continual working and evolving of forms, likewise the eternal generation within the holy mystery continually takes place in great power; so that, in consequence of this perpetual wrestling of spiritual powers, one after another divine fruits appear by the side of each other, all and each of them in the radiance of beautiful colours. All that whereof the terrestrial world by which we are surrounded is merely an earthly symbol, exists in the celestial realm in exquisite perfection in a spiritual state. It does not exist there merely as a spirit, a will, or a thought, but in corporeal substantiality, in essence and power, and appears inconceivable merely in comparison with the external material world." (*Signature*, xvi. 18.)

This beauty the divine and essential wisdom, the eternal Virgin, does not produce by her own power; but by the power of God that acts within her. She herself is without any will of her own.

"Not wisdom, but the Spirit of God, is the centre, or the discloser. As the soul is manifesting herself in the body by means of the flesh, and as the latter would have no power if it were not inhabited by a living spirit, likewise the wisdom of God is the corporeity of the Holy Spirit, by means of which He assumes substantiality, so as to manifest Himself to Himself. Wisdom gives birth, but she would not do so if the Spirit were not acting within her. She brings forth without the power of the fire-life; she has no ardent desire, but her joy finds its perfection in the manifestation of the Godhead, and therefore she is called a virgin in chastity and purity before God." (*Tilk.*, ii. 64.)

Divine wisdom exists only by means of the Trinity, and the latter can be revealed only by forming eternal nature within its own body.

"The light and the power of the sun disclose the mysteries of the external world by the production and growth of various beings. Likewise God, representing the eternal Sun, or the one eternal and only Good, would not reveal Himself without the presence of His eternal spiritual nature, wherein alone He can manifest His power. Only when the power of God becomes differentiated and relatively conscious, so that there are individual powers to wrestle with each other during their love-play, will be opened in Him the great and immeasurable fire of love by means of the forthcoming of the Holy Trinity." (*Grace*, ii. 28.)

The Father, ruling the first principle, the fire, generates eternally the Son, the light, by means of the seven forms of eternal nature; and the Son, revealing Himself in the second principle as the light, for ever glorifies the Father.

"The eternal will, the Father, conducts His heart, His eternal Son, by means of the fire into great triumph, into His kingdom of joy." (*Grace*, ii. 21.)

"When the Father speaks His Word—that is to say, when He generates His Son—which is done continually and eternally, that Word first of all takes its origin in the first or acrid quality, where it becomes conceived. In the second or the sweet quality it receives its activity; in the third it moves; in the heat it arises and ignites the sweet flow of power and the fire. Now all the qualities are made to burn by the kindled fire, and the tire is fed by them; but this fire is only one and not many. This fire is the true Son of God Himself, who is continuing to be born from eternity to eternity." (*Aurora*, viii. 81.)

"The Father is the first of all conceivable beings, but if the second principle were not becoming manifest in the birth of the Son, He would not be revealed. Thus the Son, being the heart, light, love, and the beautiful and sweet beneficence of the Father, but being distinct from Him in His individual aspect, renders the Father reconciled, loving, and merciful. His birth takes place in the fire, but He obtains His personality and name by the ignition of the soft, white, and clear light, which He is Himself." (*Three Principles*, iv. 58.)

"The Son is perpetually born from eternity to eternity, and shines perpetually into the powers of the Father while these powers are continually generating the Son." (*Aurora*, vii. 33.)

The Holy Spirit, manifesting Himself in the third principle, issues eternally from the Father and the Son, and in and with Him issues the splendour of God's majesty.

"The Eternal Father becomes manifest in the fire, the Son in the light of the fire, and the Holy Spirit in the power of the life and the motion that issues front the fire and the light." (*Signature*, xiv. 34.)

"The Holy Spirit reveals the Godhead in nature. He extends the splendour of the majesty, so that it may be recognised in the wonders of nature. He is not that splendour itself, but its power, and He introduces the splendour of the majesty into the substantiality wherein the Godhead is revealed." (*Threefold Life*, iv. 82; v. 39.)

Thus the holy Trinity is everywhere, manifesting itself in and through the seven qualities of eternal nature.

"We Christians say that God is threefold, but one in essence, and this is misunderstood by the ignorant as well as by the half learned, for God is not a person except in Christ. He is an eternally generating power and the kingdom with all beings." (*Myst. magn.*, vii. 5.)

"He is generating Himself in a threefold aspect, and in this eternal generation there is nevertheless to be understood only one essence and generation; neither Father, nor Son, nor Spirit but only the one eternal Life, or Good." (*Myst. magn.*, vii. 11.)

Chapter IV
Creation

Everything we see in nature is manifested truth; only we are not able to recognise it as such, unless the truth is manifest within ourselves.

GOD is the supreme, fundamental, universal, self-existent eternal cause; absolute and unimaginable glory, perfection, goodness, beauty, magnificence, and splendour. He created everything out of His own self, as there was nothing but Himself to create from. It is, therefore, logical to suppose that the first powers which He created and which were nearest to Him must have been divine and spiritual, all lower existences being more remote from His supreme state, belonging to a more " material " condition of creation. The same may be observed in man. His thoughts are nearer to his divine centre and self than his muscles and bones, and the realm of his soul is nearer to his spirit than his material body, and the more holy his thoughts the more will they be capable to communicate with the God in him. Boehme says:—

> "God has created the holy angels, not by means of any substance foreign to His own self, but out of His own self, out of His power and eternal wisdom." (*Aurora*, iv. 26.)

Truly, if there was or is nothing but God, it follows that God is the All, and that there is nothing which is not God. Nevertheless, those creations of God which are in a certain sense remote from the divine centre are not divine, and therefore not God.

> "It is said that God is everything, that He is in heaven and earth, and also the external world, and such an assertion is true in a certain sense; because everything originates in and from God. But of what use is such a doctrine, which is not a religion? Such a doctrine was accepted by the devil, who wanted to be manifest and powerful in everything." (*Tilk.*, ii. 140.)

Such a system of Pantheism may satisfy the rationalistic reasoner, who has no power of spiritual perception, but true divine knowledge has nothing to do with such a Pantheism nor with rationalistic Theism. It does not admit of a confounding of the terms "God" and the "world." The universe is not identical with God, neither is the spirit of man identical with his body. Not even the Christ is identical with God, in so far as He has become human.

> "The external world is not God, and will not be God in all eternity. The world is merely a state of existence wherein God is manifesting

67

Himself." (*Stief.*, ii. 316.)

God is not man.

> "There will always a distinction have to be made between the Godhead and humanity, between the human will and the will of God." (*Stief.*, ii. 95.)

The moon has no light of her own; she merely reflects the light of the sun. Nevertheless the light coming from the moon is not equal to sunlight. Likewise man's will and consciousness is derived from God; but for all that it is only human, and not divine.

> "If a man says of himself, 'I, the living word of God in this my holy flesh and bone, say and do this or that,' he then dishonours the sacred name of God. This is also against the doctrines of the Bible; for whenever the intellect of a man was selected for the purpose of prophecy, the prophet did not say, 'I, Mr. So-and-So, say this or that,' but he said, 'Thus speaks the Lord!' This means that the Lord speaks in and through such a man, and the latter is His medium and instrument." (*Stief.*, i. 84.)

A man can never be God; not even Christ in His human aspect made ever any such claims.

> "Christ never said, 'I, in my human selfhood, am the voice of God, I am speaking as God, in or with God,' &c.; but He said, 'The words which I speak are the Father's, who lives in me '—that is to say, who lives in my human or natural self." (*Stief.*, i. 94.)

To the blind reasoner God is an universal blind and unconscious power; the god existing within the imagination of the narrow-minded sectarian is equally narrow; but to the enlightened, God is a personal (individual) God and all-loving Father, residing within His own holy omnipotence, superior to all that can be conceived.

> "Do not imagine God to be a blind power, existing and moving in, or beyond, or above heaven, having neither reason nor knowledge, comparable to the sun, who runs around in his orbit, sending out light and heat regardless whether it benefits or harms the earth and her creatures. No! Not thus is the Father; but He is an omnipotent, all-wise, and all-knowing God, in Himself good, kind, and merciful, joyful, and even joy itself." (*Aurora*, iii. 11.)

> "If you consider the depth of heaven, the stars, the elements, and the earth, you will, of course, not grasp with your eyes the pure and clear Godhead, although God is there and within it; but if you rise up in your thoughts and direct your mind to God, who in His holiness rules within the All, you are then penetrating through heaven and grasping

the very sacred heart of God Himself." (*Aurora*, xxiii. 11.)

God is not subject to the law of evolution, but the law has its foundation in Him. God as a Spirit, eternally perfected within Himself, did not need to create for the purpose of perfecting Himself. There is no being who can perfect itself by its own power, or give to itself anything which is not within its reach. The growth of a plant and the unfoldment of the human soul requires the presence of a superior power. A God capable to grow would presuppose the presence of a superior God from which to draw power. Only that which descends from above can rise again upwards, as is symbolised by the double interlaced triangle.

> "Before the time of the creation of heaven, the stars, the elements, and also before the creation of the angels, there was nothing but Deity, reproducing itself for ever sweetly and lovely, and conceiving of its own image." (*Aurora*, xxiii. 15.)

> "God did not create for the purpose of perfecting Himself, but to reveal Himself to Himself in great joy and magnificence. This joy did not begin with the beginning of creation, but it has been from all eternity a subjective state in God." (*Signature*, xvi. 2.)

God did not make the world out of something intellectually conceivable or out of something that was not Himself; neither does a man create the images which constitute his thoughts out of anything outside of his own mind. Before creation took place it was resting (subjectively) like a seed in His own completion and perfection, comparable to the imagination of a marl whose mind rests in a peaceful slumber, while for all that the divine spirit in him is self-conscious.

> "We cannot truly say that this world has been made out of something." (*Signature*, xiv. 7.)

> "We cannot reasonably suppose any formation or differentiation to have existed in the eternal *One* from which, or according to which (formation) something could have been made; for if such a form, or predisposition to making a form, had existed, there would have been another cause, besides God, from which the form would have resulted, and then there would have been something else (another god), and not the one only and eternal God." (Baptism, i. 1.)

> "Creation is nothing else but a revelation of the all-essential, unfathomable God, and whatever exists in His own eternal evolution, which is without a beginning, is also in that creation. But the latter is in regard to God what an apple that grows upon a tree is to the tree. The apple is not the tree, but grows out of the power of the tree. Likewise all things have their origin in divine desire, and that desire

caused them to enter into being. In the beginning there was nothing to produce them, except the mystery of eternal generation (evolution)." (*Signature*, xvi. 1.)

"Imagine a mother (a womb) having the seed within herself. As long as she contains the seed as such, it belongs to herself, but when it becomes a child then is the seed not hers, but it is the property of the child. Thus it is with the angels. They have all been configured out of the divine seed; but after this has been done, each one has its own corporeal being to itself." (*Aurora*, iv. 34.)

"The reason why the eternal and unchangeable God has created the world is an unfathomable mystery; it can only be said that He did it in His love." (*Hamberger.*)

God, being pure knowledge, does not require to have recourse to reasoning, for the purpose of attaining an object; He being Himself His own subject and object, self-sufficient and eternal. We can, therefore, only say that He creates; because He is an ever-flowing fountain of love, in the same sense as the sun shines; because he is an everlasting source of light.

"How it came to happen that God stirred to produce creation, while He Himself is unchangeable, cannot be discovered, and an attempt to do so would merely produce a confusion of mind." (*Menschwerdung*, i. 2, 5.)

"We cannot tell how it happened that that which stood eternally in the essentiality of God entered into motion, because there is nothing that could have caused God to move, and the will of God is eternal and unchangeable. We can only say that the *Three* was desirous of having children of its own kind." (*Forty Questions*, i. 273.)

The world could not have been made as it exists now, directly out of the purely divine state of being. In its material aspect it is material and not spiritual. God is unchangeable and independent of external conditions (which do not exist for Him); but the manifestations of His power change according to the conditions that are caused by their mutual relations. Thus the light of the sun remains always the same; but it gives various hues to the flowers, according to their own individual qualities.

"No creature can issue from the purely divine state of being, because this state has neither cause nor beginning, nor can it be brought into a beginning." (*Grace*, viii. 45.)

"Within the light and the heart of God, as such, there can be nothing created; because the light is the end of nature and has no quality.

70

Therefore it cannot change or be made into anything, but remains for ever the same in eternity." (*Three Principles*, x. 41.)

Nevertheless it is the Triune God that created all things out of eternal nature. We may say that the world, as we know it, is constituted entirely of forms of heat, or of motion, or of electric conditions, or light, &c., &c. All this is true in so far as it refers to the relations which it bears towards ourselves. All these powers are only modes of manifestation of one primordial and originally divine power, namely, the will of God acting in His own eternal wisdom.

> "The eternal Triune God created all things by and through the eternal Word out of His own self, namely, out of His two aspects or qualities; out of eternal nature, the fury or *wrath*, and out of His *love;* by means of which the wrath or "nature" was pacified. Thus He created them, and caused them to enter into existence." (*Stief.*, ii. 33.)

> "The Father, being primordial Will, speaks out all things by means of the Word, out of the centre of freedom; but the issue from the Father by means of the Word is the spirit of the power, and this spirit gives form to that which has been outspoken, so that it appears as a spirit." (*Threefold Life*, ii. 63).

This magic power, or "Word," has been in God from all eternity, and as such it is God and the "Christ" in its purely divine aspect.

There is not any time during which "God goes to sleep" or loses His self-consciousness; neither does the idea to create come to Him from some outside influence; but God beholds the universe from all eternity in His wisdom as a mirror, and by the act of creation He projects into objectivity (so to say) the image existing subjectively in Him. It is, therefore, Nature and not God that goes to rest during the "nights of creation," in the same sense as the body of a man goes to sleep, while his spirit remains self-conscious in its own sphere.

> "Wisdom is a divine imagination, wherein the ideas of the angels and souls have been seen from eternity; not as substantial, actual creatures, but non-essential, like the images in a mirror." (*Clavis*, x. 5.)

> "The likeness of God, having been seen in the wisdom of God from all eternity, and in which God created Man, was without life and substantiality before the beginning of the time of this world. It was merely a reflection of the image wherein God saw how He would be in an image." (*Stief.*, ii. 123).

> "Man has not been from eternity; but only like a shadow stood the image, wherein God in His wisdom knew all things from eternity, in the mirror of His own wisdom." (*Stief.*, ii. 143.)

The will of God is only *one;* but by its action within eternal nature a great many divine powers are produced.

The ideas existing in the universal mind are innumerable, and therefore there is the possibility of innumerable different forms coming into existence by the action of the divine will. There is, however, nothing fully perfect besides the Godhead, and consequently there exist on all planes beings of different states of perfection, and capable to become more perfect by means of the will of God, which is the law of evolution.

> "The kinds of creatures are as varied as are the eternal thoughts in the wisdom of God." (*Three Principles*, ix, 37.)

> "As the divine powers are manifold, even innumerable, so there is a differentiation of ideas and a difference among the angels; in consequence of which some appear like kings or rulers and others as servants." (*Theosophic Questions*, v. 9–12.)

> "There being nothing perfect except the divine Three, consequently all things differ from one another, and likewise the angels have different qualities." (*Threefold Life*, v. 90.)

These "angels" (good or evil) are living and conscious powers existing in nature. Neither the power of God nor any angel, or devil or creature of any kind, can have any existence outside of Nature, *i.e.,* outside of the dark fire-ground, the will of God, out of which everything is born.

> "No created spirit can exist without the fire-world. Even the love of God could not exist, if not the wrath of God, or the world of fire, were existing in Him; for the wrath or the fire of God is a cause of light, strength, power, and omnipotence." (Stief. ii. 4.)

> "The wrath (the fire) is the root of all things and the origin of all life; in it is the cause of all strength and power, and from it are issuing all the wonders (manifestations of power). Without that fire there would be no consciousness, but everywhere a mere nothing." (*Three Principles*, xxi. 14.)

> "No being can be born unless it has within itself the fiery triangle, *i.e.,* the first three natural forms." (*Grace*, ii. 38.)

Every form is the product or manifestation of a power which is building up such forms. Without the presence of such a power there could be no manifestation of it; neither can any form exercise or know any power except that which resides therein.

Therefore a being incapable of any emotion would be unable to rise above the sphere of emotions; a being without any energy to commit evil would have no energy to accomplish anything good.

The foundation from which all powers and ideas spring is eternal; but the created beings as such have a beginning in time.

> "Everything has been from all eternity, but merely as ideas, and not as corporeally existing things. Only incorporeal spirits existed (as ideas) in eternity, as in a world of magic, where one thing contains the other in potentiality." (*Forty Questions*, xix. 7.)

> "The creation of the angels has a beginning, but not that of the powers whereof they have been created. The latter are co-eternal with the eternal beginning." (*Mysterium*, viii. 1.)

> "In eternity, in eternal Will, there was a nature, but it existed therein only as a spirit, and its essentiality was not manifested except in the mirror of that Will, *i.e.*, in eternal *wisdom*." (*Signature*, xiv. 8.)

> "The *mysterium magnum* is the *chaos* wherefrom originates good and evil, light and darkness, life and death. It is the foundation or womb wherefrom are issuing souls and angels and all other kinds of beings, and wherein they are contained as in one common cause, comparable to an image that is contained in a piece of wood before the artist has cut it out." (*Clavis*, vi. 23.)

In the soul of man exists potentially the whole of the universe—heaven and hell, God and the devil, angels and spirits, the whole of the celestial, terrestrial, and infernal kingdoms, with all their powers and essences; but unless these powers become manifested as forms (created beings on the spiritual, astral, or terrestrial plane), they can have no existence recognisable to his internal senses.

Creation was an act of the free will of God, and not induced by any inferior cause. The will of God would not be divine if it were not free. It is itself the law, and therefore not subject to " natural law," or the law of mechanics. Creation took place by means of God unfolding His eternal nature, whereby through His active love or desire He caused that which heretofore had been in Him merely as a spirit (subjectively) to become substantial and corporeal (objective).

> "The created world was before the mysterium magnum, for all things were then in a spiritual condition in wisdom, as in a continual play or wrestle of love. The one only Will conceived this spiritual form into the Word, and permitted the intelligence (the separate consciousness—*i.e.*, the acrid and astringent quality), to act without restraint, so that each power could enter or build itself a form according to its own specific quality." (*Grace*, iv. 12.)

> "The eternal Mind is always desirous for the power, and the power is the astringency, and the astringency is the contraction, attraction, or the eternal *fiat*, which creates and renders corporeal that which the eternal Will desires in its own benevolence. The Will desires by means of the keen *fiat* to bring into substantiality (render objective) that which it beholds in eternal Wisdom." (*Three Principles*, xiv. 74.)

Thus the divine spirit in man, by means of the thoughts of the latter, brings the powers which exist in his microcosm into shapes which are objective to him, and which form the soul world wherein he resides.

Creation could, however, become actually complete only by means of the activity of all the seven divine spirits. It is therefore true that in one sense it was not God, the primordial Cause, that directly created the world, but the *elohims* or "powers" that created it by means of the power received from the fundamental causation.

> "The universe with all its beings has been created out of eternal nature, out of the seven spirits of eternal nature." (*Threefold Life*, iii. 40.)

> "Whenever anything is born out of the divine Essence, it is brought into form, not merely by one spirit, but by all the seven." (*Aurora*, x. 4.)

> "When the Godhead stirred for the purpose of creating a world, it softly moved within the acrid quality and contracted the latter within the divine *sal-nitre*." (*Aurora*, xiii. 94.)

In the formation of beings, their own spirit co-operates with the universal Spirit. The universal Life could not produce a tree out of the four elements if there were not a seed containing the qualities necessary to grow into a tree. Nevertheless, by the expression "their own spirit," it is not to be understood as if these spirits were anything essentially different from God. They are merely individual centres, receiving their power from the universal Fountain of love.

> "Originally the spirit is a magic gush or outburst of fire and desires for substantiality—that is to say, 'form.' This is then caused by that desire, and constitutes the corporeity of the spirit, and the spirit is then called a created being." (*Tilk.* i. 186.)

Every human being has within himself the capacity to create, but not every one has that power developed. Everybody can imagine, but not every one is artist enough to bring the objects of his imagination into an external objective form by painting or sculpture. Likewise every one has good and evil powers within himself, but not every one has his spiritual strength sufficiently developed to create of them living and

74

conscious forms.

"The centre of each thing is spirit, co-existing with the Word. The separation (differentiation) of a thing (by which it distinguishes itself from other things) is in the quality of its will, by means of which it assumes a form or state of being according to its own essential (predominating) desire." (*Letters*, xlvii. 5.)

"Even to-day the act of creation still continues, and it will not end until the judgment of God arrives. Then will that which has grown in the holy tree of life become separated from the unholy thistles and thorns." (*Three Principles*, xxiii. 25.)

"Whether or not God will create something more out of His will after the end of this time is not perceptible to my spirit, for it does not penetrate deeper than within its own centre wherein it lives, and therein is the paradise and the kingdom of heaven." (Principles, ix. 41.)

Chapter V
The Angels

"If you wish to hear the Holy Ghost speak out of the mouth of another you must first enter yourself with your will into the spirit of holiness."—JACOB BOEHME.

IT is perfectly useless to attempt to enter into theoretical speculations for the purpose of trying to find out whether or not the doctrines of Jacob Boehme in regard to that which transcends the reasoning power of man are true or not. Logic can never supply the place of perception; it can only teach us what a thing cannot be, but it does not enable us to see what it is. The only way to convince ourselves whether there is a divine state of existence and celestial powers is, by the aid of God, to seek within ourselves for these powers which Jacob Boehme describes. If we succeed we shall then know the Holy Trinity and the archangels; in the meantime a consideration of Boehme's doctrines may serve -to destroy the erroneous conceptions which hinder us from seeing the truth as it exists in ourselves.

God (the divine primordial Will) by becoming objective to Himself, and thereby constituting Himself a created being, assumed a threefold aspect, which gave rise to three different self-conscious divine powers, called "archangels," representing the three types of the Holy Trinity. The angels or powers are called Michael, Lucifer, and Uriel.[10]

> "God, constituting Himself a created being, assumed the aspect of such a being in regard to His trinity; and as this trinity is the greatest and highest in God, also He created three princes of angels (divine reflections of His own image) which are superior to all others." (*Aurora*, xii. 88.)

> "Michael represents God the Father.[11] This is not to be understood as if he were God the Father Himself; but there is among the created beings (the angels) one who represents God the Father. The circle or space wherein he with his angels is created is his kingdom, and he is a beloved son of God, a joy for his Father. You ought not to compare him with the heart or the light of God, which is in the totality of the Father, and which, like the Father Himself, has neither beginning nor end. This prince is a created being, and has (as such) a beginning; but he is in God the Father, and bound to Him in love. Therefore he wears upon his head the crown of honour, power, and strength, and except God Himself in His trinity, there can be nothing found in heaven that

---

[10]Whether we call them by those names, or whether we adopt the names by which they are called in other theologies, will be of no consequence, and not alter the fact that such powers exist.

[11]Jehovah.

77

is higher, or more beautiful or powerful, than he." (*Aurora*, xii. 86.)

"As Michael has been created after the type and beauty of God the Father, so was Lucifer created after the type and beauty of God the Son, bound to Him in love, and his heart was resting in the centre of light, as if he were God Himself." (*Aurora*, xii. 101.)

> "The third king, Uriel, is formed after the type and character of the Holy Spirit. He is a magnificent and beautiful prince of God, and also bound up in love with the other princes, as in one heart." (*Aurora*, xii. 111.)

From the three result the seven, according to a law that is manifesting itself eternally on all planes of existence. There are seven qualities or properties revealed in the life of God; there are seven natural qualities, and there are likewise seven high angels besides the former three, after which follow innumerable subdivisions of angels and spirits, occupying different ranks on the ladder of eternal progression.

These "angels," "thrones," and "dominions" we find also in the Hindu mythology, although under different names. It ought to be kept in mind that "myths" are not "fables." Myths are representations of actualities clothed in a fabulous form. Their kernel is true, even if the shell in which it is clothed is an illusion.

> "There are seven principal qualities in the divine Power, wherefrom the centre of God is born, and likewise there are some powerful princes of angels created, each one, according to his main quality, being a ruler in the army to which he belongs. Each of them, is next to his king or archangel, the chieftain of other subordinate angels." (*Aurora*, xii. 7.)

> "God has also called into existence other princes of angels, corresponding to the seven spirits, such as Gabriel, Raphael, &c." (*Aurora*, xii. 88.)

> "We have to consider especially seven high princely divisions in three hierarchies, according to the fountain of the seven qualities of nature, each of these forms ultimating in one throne." (*Grace*, x. 24.)

Although these self-conscious powers or angels are differentiated, each class and each individual having its own special characteristics, nevertheless they originate all from one common root, and in so far as they have remained faithful to their Creator, they are united by the most powerful love and harmony, and mingle with each other like the individual tones constituting one grand accord in creation.

> "The angels have among themselves only one love-will. Neither of them envies the other on account of his beauty, but they are in regard

to each other like the spirits of God. They love each other, and neither of them imagines himself to surpass another in beauty; but each rejoices in the beauty and loveliness of the rest." (*Aurora*, xii. 17).

"When the spirits of God arise in their divine glory, they cannot be bound in such a manner as would prevent them from intermingling with each other, and the angels are not limited by the locality in which they reside. The spirits of God perpetually rise within each other, and in their eternal generation they enjoy a continual exchange of love. Thus the holy angels move within each other and go with each other in all the three kingdoms, whereby each one receives from the other beauty of form, loveliness and virtue, and supreme happiness; but each one retains the position belonging to hire (his centre of gravitation) which in his aspect as a created being has: been assigned to him as his own special property." (*Aurora*, xii. 57.)

All the angels have been created out of the fire and the light; each of them is therefore a complete being, having within himself all the seven qualities in various stages of unfoldment. In the evolution of the seventh the corporeal body is formed, because the third quality reappears in the form of the seventh. This reappearance of the third within the seventh constitutes the "resurrection of the flesh." Not in a dead and putrefied corpse, but in the living soul, does that resurrection take place.

"When God created the angels, the principle of fire and light became manifest. Their spirit or life-anguish (consciousness) has its origin in the fire. From thence it passed through the light, and became there the anguish of love, by which the wrath was extinguished." (*Menschwerdung*, i. 3–10.)

"The angels have all been created in the first principle, formed and corporified by the moving Spirit, and illumined by the light of God." (*Three Principles*, iv. 67.)

"From all eternity the light of God was lovely, sweet, and clear; but when God moved to create, the matrix (the foundation), with its fiery, dark, acrid and bitter qualities, became manifest; for the angels have been created out of that matrix into the light, and rendered corporeal by the moving Spirit." (*Aurora*, v. 24.)

"Each angel has the power of the seven primitive spirits within himself." (*Aurora*, xii. 8.)

"The body of the angels—that is to say, its apprehensibility, originates from the seventh spirit, and the generating powers in that body are the seven spirits." (*Aurora*, xvi. 15.)

The body of the angels is the incorporated spirit of nature, and it encloses the seven other spirits. They generate themselves in that body, as is also the case in the Godhead." (*Aurora*, iii. 30.)

If the terrestrial world which we know is corporeal to us, having been thrown into objectivity by the power of the divine Will acting upon the images existing in the bosom of eternal Wisdom, there is no reason why the same Will should not have called into existence in the same way a superterrestrial, supersensual, and celestial world, whose subjects will be as real and corporeal to its inhabitants as the objects in our world are corporeal to us.

> "There is a life superior to life in this world in eternity. The spirit of this world (the terrestrial mind) cannot conceive of its nature. It has within itself all the qualities of this terrestrial life, but not in such inflamed essences as the latter. Truly, it also has a fire, and a very powerful one, but it burns in a different way; it is sweet, mild, and without pain; it does not consume, but causes majesty and living splendour, and its spirit is pure love and joy." (*Threefold Life*, viii. 1.)

> "In heaven, in the spiritual world, are the same qualities as there are in the terrestrial world; but they are there not manifested in such a furious (gross) form, but in a superior state, like darkness that is absorbed by light." (*Mysterium*, x. 7.)

As the eyes of the blind are unable to see the objects of the external world, so those whose spiritual perceptions have not been opened will be unable to. perceive the objects existing within the inner world.

There are objective products in that celestial world which appear there as "natural" as ours appear on the terrestrial plane; but as the celestial world is far more refined, glorious, and beautiful than the terrestrial world, those products must also be superior to any that can be found upon this earth.

> "The celestial powers, by their interaction, generate trees and bushes, whereon grows the beautiful and lovely fruit of life. Likewise, by means of these powers, there arise various flowers of beautiful celestial colours and exquisite odour, in a similar manner as in this perverted and dark terrestrial valley various kinds of trees, shrubs, flowers, and fruits grow, and as the earth produces beautiful stones, silver, and gold. All these external forms are symbols of the celestial generation. Nature labours very diligently with the degenerated and inert earth, for the purpose of producing celestial forms and kinds; but she produces only dead, dark, bitter, cold, and evil fruits. In heaven there are no such dead, hard, wooden trees as in the terrestrial sphere, but spiritual growths. Nevertheless we speak, not symbolically, but of real, actual plants, and this is to be taken in no other than in a literal sense." (*Aurora*, iv. 10.)

The objects existing in the ideal, but nevertheless perfectly real world, are as far above those existing in the external world as tile ideal conceptions of a great genius are above what he can possibly execute by his hands.

The realm which formerly was governed by Lucifer embraced our earth and the whole depth of the starry sky. The realms of Michael and Uriel are equal in extent to the former, and exist beyond the starry sky.

> "What Boehme says about the extent of the kingdoms of Michael and Uriel is not to be taken in an external terrestrial sense. The realm of Lucifer before his rebellion was immaterial like the others, and only afterwards descended into materiality and terrestrial relations to space." (*Hamberger.*)

> "The whole locality of this world, the depth of the earth and above the earth, up to the sky and the created heaven itself, which we see with our eyes, but which, nevertheless, we cannot comprehend with our senses—all this space is one kingdom, wherein Lucifer was the ruler before his fall; but the other two kingdoms, that of Michael and Uriel, exist beyond the created heaven (space) and are equal to the former realm." (*Aurora*, vii. 7.)

"The angels are God's instruments in governing the world, and as such they not only glorify the celestial nature wherein they rule, but they also dominate over the terrestrial world and its individual regions."

They rule the world according to the principle of divine wisdom which is manifested in and through them, and not, like man, according to their notions or smartness or policy. They execute the will of God, and not any will of their own.

> "God the eternal *One* rules all things by means of the activity of the angels. The power and the action is of God; but they are His instruments." (*Theosophical Questions*, vi. 7.)

> "That which the angels will and desire is brought into images and forms by means of their thoughts." (*Theosophical Questions*, vi. 9.)

They are full of the will of divinity, and therefore their thoughts are rendered effective by that will, and do not vanish like the superficial fancies of man, fed by his imaginary self-will.

> "Whenever the celestial melody of the angels begins to sound, there are arising within the divine sal-nitre various worlds of growths, figures, and magnificent colours." (*Aurora*, xii. 24.)

> "Each country has its princely guardian spirit, with its legions. Likewise

there are angels governing the four elements—fire, water, air, and earth." (*Mysterium*, viii. 9.)

If man knew the beauties of the spiritual world by which he is surrounded, and which he may see when he awakens from the dream of external life by becoming self-conscious in the spirit, his interest in the affairs of this mundane existence would be diminished to a considerable extent. Such a knowledge, however, is only attainable to those who are capable of entering the interior state, and has nothing to do with the dreams of the visionary who revels among the products of his own fancy.

St. Martin says: "There" (in the higher world) "it is not like in our dark dwelling-place, wherein sounds can only be compared with sounds, colours with colours, and a substance only with that which is directly related to it. There all things are more closely related with each other. There the light is sounding; melody produces light; colours have motions, because they are living, and the objects are all at once sounding, transparent, moving, and can penetrate each other."

The belief in guardian angels is not a fable. Man is surrounded by good and by evil, self-conscious and invisible powers, which may influence him for good or for evil. His soul is the battle-field where the combat between devils and angels takes place, and he is free to side with the one or the other, as is beautifully described in the "Bhagavad Gita." The evil influences are easily attracted if we merely remain passive to their power; but the spirit of holiness cannot enter unless unholiness is chased away. In this battle against evil the angels are always ready to assist man in an invisible manner against the temptations of the "devils," provided that he is willing to receive such an aid.

> "The external nature of this world cannot comprehend the nature of heaven: Both are compared with each other, like death compared with life. We cannot see the angels according to our external nature, neither can they be with us externally; but they reside internally with us. Whenever we battle with the devil they ward off his blows, and thus they take under their protection the soul that aspires for that which is holy." (*Aurora*, xix. 30.)

> "Know that the devil often fights with the angels. When the soul of man is secure in God, then the devil desires to enter; but he is stopped, so that he cannot do what he wills. Whenever the soul imagines, and lustful desires begin to arise, then is the devil victorious."[12] (*Threefold Life*, xiv. 13.)

---

[12]Therefore no man can resist, successfully resist the devil by fighting him on the same level, nor can any one overcome temptations in the end except by rising above them.

> "Each principle is attracted by, knows, and loves that which is like unto its own self. The principles existing within the periphery are acting upon their corresponding principles in the centre. Love acts upon love, hate upon hate; good is attracted by good, and evil by evil. If there is no evil desire active in man, evil influences cannot take root in his soul. The devil is the poorest of all creatures. He cannot move a leaf upon a tree unless the wrath is contained therein." (*Theosophical Points*, v. 18.)

Man without any principle could know nothing; it is always a certain principle in him that recognises its corresponding principle in nature. A man without love cannot know what love is. Neither can any one recognise the Christ, or be recognised by Him, unless he has the Christ within his own soul.

The self-will, *i.e.*, the will of God perverted in a created being, is the "fire-life" of the latter and the cause of its anguish. All the angels have originally been created out of the light; but for the purpose of remaining therein they had to give up to God their fire-life, and not rise up in their self-will against the Lord.

> "Each angel who wishes to live in the light and power of God must give up the selfhood of the dominion of the fire within the desire; he must surrender himself and all that belongs to him to the will of God; he must die in regard to his self-will, and unfold in the light of love as a fruit of divine love, so that the will-spirit (the spiritual will) of God shall rule his life." (Stief. ii. 49.)

> "The devil was an angel, and it would have been his duty to put his imagination (faith) into the light of God. In that case he would have received the divine substantiality in his imagination, and his light would have remained luminous. The fire-fountain would have remained in that essence and quality, and he would have remained an angel." (*Tilk.* i. 187.)

Thus those who crave for intellectual knowledge, while deserting the basis of the true knowledge of God, will ultimately become the victims of their own conceit, and turn into devils.

In the recognition of good and evil rests the freedom of choice. This knowledge is attained by means of the fourth form. If that quality has awakened in a being, then may the latter go ahead in a forward direction either toward absolute good or evil until the orbit is reached, where the attraction of one or the other ceases to act. As long as this limit is not reached, a being may either enter the divine love-will, or turn in the opposite direction, and sink within the lower qualities of nature.

"In the lightning flash, the fourth form of nature, is the origin of life, and it attains perfection in the constancy of the fire. Here, in the object of division, is the spirit born, and this spirit can either go backwards and enter with his imagination into his mother, the dark world, or move forward, and by means of death sink into the anguish of the fire, and then bloom out into life. He is free, and therefore either of these two ways is within his choice." (*Theosophical Points*, vii. 2.)

Every being is free and responsible only according to the degree of its knowledge; not its intellectual knowledge, but according to that which is the result of the experiences of its spirit—its "conscience."

"In the principle of fire is the turning-point. There the will may move in whatever direction he chooses. If it desires the "Nothing," *i.e.*, freedom, it must sacrifice itself to the fire, and sink in the death of that principle.[13] Then the Father, the eternal Will to nature, will put it into the will of the Son; where for the great deal which that being has given, it will receive all; but not to its own honour, but for the glorification and power of God. When this is accomplished, God in such a man is his will and his doing, and his fire becomes a light and a clear mirror; but if he does not will to do so, but wishes to be himself a master, and to possess multiplicity for his own self; then must he enter into the severe astringency, into the world of darkness, and cannot conduct himself in his principles higher than up to the fire, or rather only up to the lightning flash. He remains in darkness, because only freedom outside of nature can supply the light and the clearness." (*Theosophical Points*, vii. 6).

The fourth form is the object of division after the death of the body, and the centre of consciousness will be either with the higher part or the lower, according to the preponderance of either good or evil. The higher consciousness enters the light; the lower consciousness continues to exist in its own hell-fire and self-created suffering. God "redeems" man by redeeming Himself from man's animal elements, to which he is tied during the terrestrial life of the personality.

Lucifer could have retained his state of celestial life; it was by his own will that he surrendered himself to the wrath of nature.

"The life of the eternal creature was in its beginning entirely free, because it was in the appropriate harmonious temperature. The angels were created for heaven, and even if the world of darkness with the realm of phantasy was contained therein, it was in latent condition, and not manifest. By the action of the free will in the fallen angels the world of darkness became objective in them; because they were

---

[13]To "desire the Nothing" does not mean to become unconscious of everything, like a man when he goes to sleep, but it means "contentment," and a state of perfect rest and happiness found in the self-consciousness of being and possessing the All.

inclined towards phantastry (speculation), and consequently the latter took possession of them and arose in their essence." (*Grace*, iv. 45.)

"One should not think that King Lucifer could not have remained that which he was. He had before him the light of the majesty, just like the other throne angels. If he had contemplated therein, he would have remained an angel; but because he acted according to his own selfish will, he is now an enemy of the love of God, and of all holy angels." (*Menschwerdung*, i. 217.)

He knew the will of God, and nevertheless acted in opposition to it, and therefore he did not become merely an idiot, but a devil.

"The realm of illusion has been from eternity, and gave cause to the angels' fall; it presented the conditions without which such a fall from the angelic state could not have taken place; but Lucifer entered into it by his own free will, and without any coercion." (*Grace*, Vi. 2.)

"Lucifer had within himself the fire and the light. He was free. Why then did he imagine (project his consciousness) into the fire? The light and the power of God did not draw him into the fire, but the wrath of nature. Why did his spirit consent?" (*Menschwerdung*, i. 5.)

"The fiery lust, which was strong in Lucifer, incited him. Likewise the darkness (matter) wanted to become created (objective) in him." (*Mysterium Magnum*, ix. 9.)

The very divine beauty, and the high power and authority with which Lucifer was invested, incited him to attempt to rise above God, instead of surrendering himself to Him in humility,[14] and thus he stimulated the activity of his sourcive spirits (latent principles) in an unnatural manner.

"When the kingly body of Lucifer became corporified (organised), and his spirits (principles or qualities) began to become qualified and generated (unfolded), the lightning flash of life arose in his heart, and the spirit went from the heart back again into all the veins of his (organising) body, inflaming all the seven spirits. Thus he stood, a divine king, in transcendent clearness." (*Aurora*, xiv. 4.)

His condition may be compared to that of a man who uses the powers which are given him for the purpose of enabling him to rise up to the kingdom of God to feed his own passions.

- "When Lucifer saw that he was so very beautiful, and when he realised his high birth and great power, the spirit which he had generated in himself (*i.e.*, his own free will) arose and became desirous to triumph

---

[14] True humility does not consist in self-abasement, but in the entire sacrifice of one's lower self, whereby the power and the majesty of God become revealed in man.

85

over the divine birth, and to exalt itself above the heart of God." (*Aurora*, xiv. 13, 32.)

"When Lucifer was in such a kingly form, and placed in such high glory, he ought to have moved in God as God moved in him; but this he did not do, for after his sourcive spirits were endowed with such a glorious light, they were filled with so much joy that they revolted against the natural right (the law), and desired a still higher, prouder, and more magnificent qualification than God Himself. Then it happened that the acrid quality contracted her essence to such a state of hardness that the sweet water therein became exsiccated. Simultaneously (with that) the lightning flash was so glaring that it became intolerable to the rising spirits, because it went into the acrid quality in such a terrible manner, as if it wanted to burst them asunder with great joy." (*Aurora*, xiii. 116.)

It must not be supposed that God created an especial pain for the purpose of punishing Lucifer for his sinful conceit; but Lucifer himself inaugurated a hell for himself by turning away from God and exciting the lower natural qualities.

"God did not create a hell or a special state of suffering wherein to torment the creatures that deserted Him; but as soon as the devils went out of the light and attempted to rule by the power of fire over the beatitude in the heart of God, in the same moment they were outside of God and in the four lower qualities of eternal nature. Thereby they were kept imprisoned in the abyss of hell." (*Threefold Life*, ii. 5 3)[15]

"The devil is not affected with any pain coming from the outside, but (the cause of all suffering) is in himself. This is the bell wherefrom he is created, and the light of God is his eternal dishonour, because he is the enemy of God, and no longer in the light of God." (*Three Principles*, iv. 36.)

"The foundation of hell was from eternity; however, it was not manifest, but hidden until it became awakened." (*Theosophical Questions*, xv. i.)

"The four lower principles without the eternal light are the abyss, the wrath of God, and hell. Their light is the terrible lightning-flash, wherein they must awaken themselves." (*Threefold Life*, ii. 50.)

"The acrid and stern desire moved in Lucifer, awakening the sting and the desire of anguish. Thus the beautiful star overshadowed its own light and perished, and its legions acted as he did." (*Mysterium*, ix. 10.)

Neither could Lucifer's legions have acted in any other way, because it

---

[15]Hell is created in man by the awakening of his lower qualities, whereby they attain self-consciousness and self-will, and refuse to obey the divine will in man.

was his will acting in them. They are parts of himself.

All the forms of nature are warring furiously against each other in Lucifer, being in a state of implacable animosity towards each other. They generate in him a proud and dark monster, instead of a son of God, united with Him in love.

"If the spirits arising (in Lucifer) would have interacted peacefully and according to the will of God, they would have generated a son within themselves who would have been like the Son of God and His beloved brother; but when they arose in a state of keen ignition, they generated a self-conceited, triumphant son, who, according to the first quality, was hard, harsh, cold, and dark; and according to the second, of a bitter, burning, fiery appearance. The sound in him was a hard fire-sound, and in the place of love there was proud enmity. Thus in the seventh form of nature there appeared a proud monster which fancied to be above God and that there was no equal to it. Love was grown cold; the heart of God could not touch this perverted being. Whenever that heart, full of benevolence and loveliness, moved to meet it, the heart of the monster appeared dark, cold, hard, and fiery." [16] (*Aurora*, xiii. 40–47.)

"The acrid quality was the first murderer, for seeing that he was generating a beautiful light, he contracted still harder than God had created him. The second quality, as the second murderer, went with great strength into the acrid one, as if he wanted to rend its body to pieces. The heat, being the third murderous spirit, killed its mother, the sweet water. The sound arose so furiously that it sounded like a clap of thunder; it intended thereby to prove its own new divinity, and the fire arose like a terrible glare of lightning. Thus the whole body became a dark valley, and there was no comfort nor help. Love turned into enmity, and the angel of light became a black and dark devil." (*Aurora*, xiv. 19–25.)

As the saint becomes identified with God, so the wicked may become identified with the devil. Either of the two is an "incarnation" of that principle which has attained self-consciousness in him.

Lucifer having conceived a will entirely opposed to the divine, and intending to put his own products in the place of the formations of God, not only God, but also the pure angels, especially Michael with his legions, separated from him.

"Lucifer saw creation and knew its foundation. Thereupon he also wanted to be a god, and to rule in all things by the power of fire. He wanted to bring into form his own thoughts, and not that which the

---

[16] The same is the case with every one who turns away from the light and seeks the darkness, until at last he becomes identified with the darkness, and can no longer separate himself from it.

Creator desired. Thus he became an enemy of God, and desired to destroy what was formed by the action of God for the purpose of putting in its place his own effects and figurations." (*Theosophical Questions*, x. 1.)

"Lucifer having left the harmony of God, the holy name of God separated from him and remained in its own unity; but Lucifer remained in the qualities of the central fire which he had awakened within himself." (*Theosophical Questions*, x. 6.)

"The dark realm of phantasy and the creature which is constituted by the fallen angels is only one thing, one will, one being; and as this rebellious will did not want to reside and rule solely in the phantasy, but wanted to rule also in the holy power wherein it stood at first, the holy power repelled it out of itself and hid itself away before it—that is to say, the inner heaven shut it out of its own state, so that it could not see God. Thus it died to the kingdom of goodwill." (*Grace*, iv. 46.)

"When Lucifer proved to be such a tyrant and corrupter of all that is good, the whole army of heaven turned against him, and he likewise turned against everything. Then the battle began, and the arch-prince Michael with his legions fought against him, and the devil with his legions conquered not; but was driven away from his position as one who has been conquered."[17] (*Aurora*, xvi. 9.)

The separation of Lucifer from the world of light was a total separation, but not a local one in the ordinary sense of this word.

"The world of light knows nothing of the devils, and the devils know nothing about the world of light except that they once belonged to it." (*Theosophical Points*, v. 2.)

"Heaven is in hell, and hell is in heaven, and nevertheless there is neither of them revealed to the other. Even if the devil were travelling for many hundred thousands of miles, for the purpose of going to heaven, he would nevertheless always remain in hell. Thus the angels do not see the darkness; they see only the light of divine power; but the devils see only the darkness of the wrath of God." (*Mysterium*, viii. 28).

Every being is in that state which constitutes its own consciousness.

The hellish being has not yet attained completion in its development. The existence of the terrestrial world, in whose evil parts the evil spirits reside and work, is an obstacle to that.

As man loses his knowledge of God, he correspondingly loses his power for evil A man cannot become a complete devil until he attains Godlike

---

[17]It must not be supposed that the good angels "made up their minds" to fight Lucifer, but this separation was according to natural laws, in the same sense as water is opposed to fire.

knowledge and corresponding powers.

> "As the devils, led by conceit and wantonness, ignited themselves, they have now been entirely cast out from the generation of light, and cannot conceive or comprehend it in all eternity. Nevertheless the dwelling of Lucifer is not yet completed, because in all things in this world there are love and wrath still residing together, and wrestling and battling with each other. Still those things or beings realise not the wrestling of light, but merely the wrestle of wrath."[18] (*Aurora*, xviii. 32.)

> "The hellish being is not yet fully manifest; the devils will have to wait for a still greater judgment. The sun and the water keep their kingdom still hidden unto the day of reckoning, and therefore the devils have so much fear of the judgment day." (*Theosophical Questions*, xiii. 5.)

> "There are always two kingdoms (states) to be distinguished in the elements. In one of these rules the love that issued from God, and in the other His wrath. The devils reside only in the realm of wrath, where they are enclosed within eternal night, and they cannot come in contact with the good powers of the elements." (*Theosophical Questions*, xiii. 7.)

The evil spirits are especially inimical to man; but they cannot injure him if his will is directed towards the divine, and if he does not permit himself to be captured by evil desire.

No man, except he who is regenerated in the spirit, is free and his own master. It is always either divine or diabolical influences acting through him; but he is endowed with a certain amount of divine reason to choose either the one or follow the other.

> "If we leap into earthly desire, we shall be captured by it, and then will the anguish of the abyss be lord over us. But if by the power of our will we ascend beyond this world, then will the world of life capture our will, and God will be our Lord." (*Theosophical Points*, vi. 5.)

> "Let no man think that it is in the power of the devil to tear from his heart the works produced by the light. He can neither see them nor understand what they are. Therefore, even if in the most external generation the devil rages and storms, as long as you do not yourself transfer the products of wrath into the light of your heart, your soul will be safe from being injured by the devil, he being deaf and blind in the light." (*Aurora*, xix. 97.)

Lucifer anticipated the misery which he was bringing upon himself; but

---

[18]The good which we receive is not recognised, because it causes no pain. No one complains about receiving more blessings than he merits; but the deserved evil which we receive causes suffering, and the unmerited evil is keenly resented.

his knowledge was only a "science"—that is to say, it was not a condition fully realised by his experience; it was rather of a theoretical character than actual self-knowledge, and having lost the spiritual power of faith to aid him to maintain his position, this "science" was not sufficient to keep him from his fall. Moreover, He was curious to attain something entirely new.

> "Did then Lucifer not know of the judgment of God and the fall? Yes, he knew it well; but he had this knowledge not in his *feeling* (he did not realise it as an actual experience); it was with him merely a science, an intellectual conception." (*Mysterium*, ix. 9.)

> "Lucifer knew that he was not God, and he also knew the extent of his power; but he wanted some entirely new experience, he wanted to be higher than God, and to elevate his power over all kingdoms, and over all of the Godhead." (*Aurora*, xiv. 14.)

God also knew, in His eternal wisdom, that the fall of Lucifer would take place.

> "In eternal wisdom, or, to speak more correctly, in eternal nature, the fall of the devil (and also of man) has been perceived even before the world was created." (*Three Principles*, ix. 22.)

> "The image of the created being has been seen in wisdom according to its aspects in wrath and love. Herein also has the Spirit of God, issuing eternally from the light and the fire of the Father, foreseen the fall— namely, that this image, if shaped into a corporeal being, would be attracted by the wrath, and lose its divine splendour." (*Stief.* iii. 58.)

Although God foresaw that fall, nevertheless it could not be prevented.

> "It may be asked why God did not restrain Lucifer from his evil desire? But how could this have been done? If this being of fire would have been led into still more mildness and love, his glorious light would then have become still more manifest to him, and his fiery self-will would thereby have increased. Should He educate him by punishing him? It was already Lucifer's purpose to excite within himself the magic foundation, and to play with the centre of the qualities." (*Mysterium*, ix. 14.)

Lucifer wanted to know the darkness, and had no desire for the light. Man must know evil for the purpose of becoming able to realise the good, after which he returns to the latter; but as everything seeks for its own corresponding principle, he in whom evil has become paramount will remain in evil.

> "Behold a thistle or a nettle. The more sunshine and power they receive, the more stings will they produce. Thus, if God pours His love

into the devil, the products of the devil are anger and hate." (See *Grace*, iv. 37.)

An end of the hellish torment[19] is inconceivable. Such an end would involve either a change of Lucifer's pride into humility, or a destruction of the whole work of creation.

"If Lucifer were again to become an angel, to become such he would have to draw again from the unity and love of God; his fire-life would have to be consumed by love, and to be changed into humility; but this the hellish foundation (the will) in the devils refuses to permit." (*Theosophical Questions*, vii. 5.)

"The hellish essence, having an eternal foundation, the will cannot perish, unless the whole of creation would cease to exist and eternal nature in her own loveliness be extinguished. But in this case the kingdom of joy would be equally lost." (*Theosophical Questions*, v. 3.)[20]

---

[19] The word "torment" means here not necessarily "pain," but "consciousness." The "devil" does not suffer as long as he is in his own element.

[20] That which has become self-conscious in evil cannot be changed into good without first becoming unconscious of its own evil self; but if the being is wholly evil, such a complete death would also prevent the possibility of its becoming conscious of good.

91

Chapter VI
The Restoration of Nature and the Generation of Man

"IF we speak about heaven and the birth of the elements, we are then not telling of things that are far away or foreign to us, but of that which is taking place within our own self, and there is nothing nearer to us than this birth, for we are therein as in our own mother. If we speak of heaven, we then speak of our home, of our own country, wherein the illumined soul can see, even if that country is hidden before the eyes of the body." (*Principles*, vii. 7.)

The Mosaic account of creation was never intended to be a history of the creation of the world from the beginning, but it is a history of the renewal or the restoration of the natural world that was formerly ruled by Lucifer, and which was thrown into disorder and convulsion by his desertion from God.

"Before the times of the wrath there were in the locality of this world the six sourcive spirits generating the seventh in a sweet and lovely manner, as is even now done in heaven, and there was growing therein not even a spark of wrath. All that was contained therein was light and clear, needing no other light, for the fountain of love within the heart of God was illumining all. Nature was then very ethereal, and everything therein stood in great power. But as soon as in nature the war with the proud devils began, everything took another shape and mode of action. The light became extinguished in the external generation, and therefore the heat became imprisoned in corporeity and could no longer generate its own life. From this cause death then entered into nature, and nature degenerated. Consequently another creation of light had to be inaugurated, and without that the earth would have had to remain in eternal death."[21] (*Aurora*, xvii. 2; iv. 15.)

Everything in nature was to bloom out and become newly-born, as may be seen by beholding minerals and stones, trees, grass, and herbs, and animals of various kinds, and although all these formations were perishable and not pure in the sight of God, nevertheless God intended to extract from them at the end of this time their heart and kernel, and to separate them from the wrath and death, and then that which had thus been regenerated was to bloom eternally, and to bear again celestial fruits outside of and beyond the locality of this world."[22] (*Aurora*, xxiv. 2 5.)

"The same *sal-nitre*" (the material basis or foundation), "which at the time of the ignition of the wrath perished in death, has at the time of regeneration been raised in the flash of fire. It has not become anything

[21]"Lucifer" is to be regarded not as a separate being within this world, but as a power penetrating the whole of the visible universe, in the same sense as that universe may now be regarded as being the body of universal spiritual man.

[22]In other words, the tendency of the spiritual principle is to spiritualise and illumine everything by becoming active therein.

new, but merely another form of corporeity, which is now in a state of death" (existing relatively to us as gross matter).[23] (*Aurora*, xxii. 80.)

The outcast spirits, having produced in nature a state of ignition, God gathered together the essence of that nature, and thereby He withdrew it from the reach of those powers, putting a stop to their insolence by means of water.[24]

"The outcast spirits were still in the quality of the Father, and therefore they ignited the quality of nature by means of their imagination, so that the celestial substance became earth and stones, and the sweet spirit of the water a burning sky. After this the creation of this world took place." (*Menschwerdung*, i. 2–8.)

Creation could not take place as long as all the elements were in a state of revolution; only after the "Spirit of God moved upon the waters of the deep" could the divine Word take form.

"When the eternal Word moved, because of the malice of Lucifer, and for the purpose of expelling this evil guest from his residence into eternal darkness, the essence was rendered compact (coagulated). God was not willing to leave the manifested powers, wherein Lucifer ruled as a prince, any longer in his command, but he caused them to enter into a state of coagulation and spued him out therefrom." (*Mysterium*, x. 13.)

"Therein consists the fall of Lucifer, that he awakened the *mother of fire* and wanted to rule over the benevolence in the heart of God. This fire is now his hell; but this hell God has captured by means of heaven— *i.e.*, the *mother of water*. For while the locality of this world was to burn on his account in the fire, God moved to create, and created the water. From this has resulted the ocean and the unfathomable watery depth. So it was at *Sodom* and *Gomorrha*, for when their sin was great and the devil resided therein, desirous of maintaining his power, God permitted that the prince of this world ignited those five kingdoms with fire and sulphur. But while the devil imagined to be lord in that place, and to have there his dwelling, God thought of breaking his pride; He caused water to come there, and thus He extinguished his glory."[25] (*Threefold Life*, viii. 24.)

By His creative will, full of love, God caused the light to arise, and thus He directed the power of darkness downwards into the depths. Thus, when the soul of man rises up to eternal freedom, the powers of

[23]In the same sense the power of a seed to develop into a tree may remain latent for many years until the conditions present themselves for its manifestation.

[24]Thus the fire of passion is subdued in man by the "water" of eternal life distilled from humility, which baptizes the soul and tranquillises the turbulent elements.

[25]This goes to show the intimate relations existing between the spiritual and the material worlds. There is a "spiritual" and a "material" water, both of which are merely manifestations of the one element.

darkness disappear in the abyss below.

> "The wrath did not touch the heart of God; but His benevolent love issues from His heart, penetrating into the most external generation of wrath, and extinguishing the latter. Therefore He said, Let there be light." (*Aurora*, 85.)

> "When God spoke, Let there be light, the holy power which was conceived together with the wrath, moved, and the power of the devil was entirely withdrawn from him in its essence." (*Mysterium*, xii. 14.)

> "Thus the darkness remained within the quality of the wrath in the substance of the earth, and within the whole depth of this world; and in the substance of light, the light of nature from heaven—*i.e.*, out of the fifth essence, arose that whereof the constellation was created. This essence is everywhere, in the earth and above the earth."[26] (*Aurora*, xii. 15.)

By means of this new creation of the light, the new life had begun to stir everywhere; but this creation, in accordance with the number of the divine spirits which were active thereby, arrived at a state of perfection only on the seventh day.[27]

> "When God spoke the word, Let there be light, the essence, the being within the quality of the light, stirred not only within the earth, but also within the whole depth, in great power; wherefrom on the fourth day the sun was created—that is to say, *ignited*." Mysterium, xii. 13.)

> "When God stirred to create this world, it was not that only one part moved and the other one rested, but there was all in motion at once." (*Aurora*, xxii. 122.)

> "This motion lasted during six lengths of days and nights, when all the seven spirits of God were in complete and moving generation, and also the heart of all spirits, and the sal-nitre of the earth turned around in that time six times within the great wheel." (*Aurora*, xxi. 123.)

> "The day's works refer to the seven qualities, six of them belonging to the actual regiment, but the seventh, or the essentiality, is that wherein the others are resting; for these qualities have been spoken out by God and rendered visible." (*Mysterium*, xii. 2.)[28]

On the second day a separation took place in the power of the light, of the external material from the inner immaterial water, and the

---

[26]The same takes place within the heart of man when his mind becomes illumined by the light of divine wisdom that arises from the divine centre in him.

[27]The seventh "day" for our planet is always and nevertheless it has not yet arrived, because the six days belong to time and the seventh to eternity.

[28]The six "days" are the activities of the seven forms of eternal nature, the seventh is their centre or rest, or the "temperature." In the seventh, "God" appears as the "Christ." (See *Grace*, iii. 39.)

firmament (that which is firm) was put in the middle between these two.

> "The water of life became separated from the water of death; but in such a way that in the time of this world they are linked together like body and soul. But the heaven, having been made from the middle-part of the water, is like an abyss between the two, so that the conceivable water is a death, but the inconceivable one is the life." (*Aurora*, xxi. 7.)

> "The water upon the earth is a degenerated and deadly being, like the earth herself. This material water, contained within the most external generation, has been separated from the inconceivable one." (*Aurora*, xx. 27.)

> "The water above the firmament is in heaven, and the water below the firmament is the material water." (*Mysterium*, xii. 2 4.)

> "The firmament is the connecting link between time and eternity. God calls it 'heaven,' and makes a distinction between the waters; which is to indicate that heaven is in the world, but not the world in heaven." (*Mysterium*, xii. 23.)

Thus the mind of man is the connecting link between the celestial and terrestrial state. Heaven and happiness may be in his mind, but not his mind in an external heaven.

The spiritual and the material water are not separated from each other in an external manner, or according to locality, but wherever there is the material water, there is also the spiritual one, and it comes to aid the former.

> "When I behold the external water, I am forced to say, 'Here in the water below the firmament is also contained water from above the firmament.' But the firmament is the middle, and the link (dividing line) between time and eternity, so that neither one of them is the other. By means of the external eyes, or the eyes of this world, I see only the water below the firmament; but the water above the firmament is that which God in Christ has instituted for the baptism of regeneration." (*Mysterium*, xii. 26.)

> "All the water in this world is degenerated, and therefore the upper water must come to the aid of the earth, and extinguish her fire and pacify her, so that the true water may be born." (*Aurora*, xx. 33.)

Divine inspiration must come to the aid of the material thought, so that heavenly thoughts may be born.

On the third day the fiery and the watery essence, the firmament of heaven and the earth, entered again in Conjunction, and from this there were born grasses and herbs and trees, and at the same time there were also formed gold and silver and ores of various kinds.[29]

> "On the second day God separated the watery and the fiery mercury from each other, and called the fiery one the firmament of heaven. Then in the spirit of external nature there originated a male and a female kind—namely, in the fiery *Mercury* the male, and in the watery the female one." (*Clavis*, 86.)

> "On the third day the fiery and the watery Mercury have again entered in conjunction and mixture, and then the *sal-nitre* gave birth to grasses and herbs and trees." (*Clavis*, 88.)

> "After God had put heaven between the love and the wrath, for the purpose of discernment, there on the third day love penetrated through heaven into the wrath. Then the old and deadened body began to stir and to feel the anguish of generation; for love is ardent, and it ignited the fountain of fire, and the latter caused a friction in the acrid and cold quality of stiffened death, until on the third day the acrid quality became heated, and thus the acrid earth became moveable. (*Aurora*, xxv. 29).

> "When the light contained in the sweet water penetrated through the acrid spirit, the lightning flash, having become ignited in the water, in the acrid, hard, and dead quality, it caused motion in everything, and thus came movability (life) into existence, not only in the heaven above the earth, but also at the same time within the earth. Then there began life to be generated in all things, and from the earth were produced grass, herbs, and trees, and within the earth there were formed silver, gold, and metals of various kinds." (*Aurora*, xxi, 132; xx. 6.)

As the light could be active only in the corrupted essence, there being none other, the products formed thereby were of a mixed kind, half good and half evil.

> "When the light appeared again within the external conceivableness, the Word brought forth life out of death, and the corrupted *sal-nitre* produced fruits again; but this had to take place in a certain relation to the depraved state existing in the wrath, and as the external forthcoming of those fruits took place from the earth, they had to become evil and good." (*Aurora*, xxi. 19.)

Before the ignition of the sun and the stars took place nature was resting as in a state of death, and the formations proceeding from her were devoid of the living, growth-producing power.

---

[29]Three is the number of form, and therefore on the third "day," and by means of the third principle, three dimensional forms (there can be no other) came (and continue to come) into objective existence.

> "Until the third day after the ignition of the wrath of God in this world, nature remained in anxiety, and was a dark valley in death; but on the third day, when the light of the stars became ignited in the water of life, the life broke through death, and the new generation began." (*Aurora*, xxiv. 41.)

> "In the earth there is above all the acrid quality. This contracts the *sal-nitre* and solidifies the earth, causing it to become a corporeal being, forming therein also bodies of various kinds, such as rocks, metals, and manifold roots. When this is formed it has nevertheless no life to enable it to grow and expand. But when the heat of the sun acts upon the soil, various formations prosper and grow in the earth." (*Aurora*, viii. 41.)

Likewise the material and earthly elements in man have no power themselves to rise superior to their own nature. This they can do in no other way than by the power of the Divine Spirit.

Now the eternal light of God shone into the darkness of this world and ignited the heat in the firmament or heaven, and thus out of the fire arose the light—that is to say, the sun and the starry sky.

> "After the heaven had been made, for the sake of distinction between the light of God and the corrupted body of this world, the latter was a dark valley and without light, and all the powers were captured, as if in death, and very uneasy until they became kindled in the midst of the whole body. But when this took place the love in the light of God broke through that heaven of division and ignited the heat." (*Aurora*, xxv. 68.)

> "God, the eternal light and the eternal will, shines within the darkness, and the darkness has captured the will (received its activity). In this will arises now the anxiety, and in this is the fire, and in the fire the light. Thus from the fire the stars have been produced, and from the power of the heavens the sun." (*Three Principles*, viii. 22.)

All this takes place in a corresponding manner during the spiritual regeneration of man.

Thereby divine Wisdom has manifested itself, not in an entirely pure, and therefore not permanent and immutable manner, but nevertheless as in a clear mirror, and it thereby drove the devil backward deep into his darkness.

> "On the fourth day God, out of His eternal wisdom, created the lord of the third principle (the visible world), the sun and the stars. Herein is now truly seen the Godhead and the eternal wisdom of God, as in a clear mirror. This being, visible before our eyes, is not God Himself, but a God in the third principle, which will ultimately return to his

ether and take an end." (*Three Principles*, viii. 13.)

"God has made a solid foundation (firmament) called 'heaven,' between the most external and the most internal generation, between the clear Godhead and corrupted nature, through which one must break if one wants to go to God. Of this foundation it is said (*Hiob.* xiv. 15) that even the heavens are not pure before God, but on the day of judgment the wrath shall be swept therefrom."[30] (*Aurora*, xx. 41.)

"At the time of creation another light, the sun, was awakened in this world, it having been corrupted by Lucifer, and thereby the splendour of the devil was taken away. Thus he has been shut in like a prisoner into the darkness between the realm of God and the realm of this world, so that he has no longer anything to rule over in this world, except in the Turba, wherein is awakened the wrath and anger of God." (*Menschwerdung*, i. 2.)

The sun has been revealed by means of the soul of the world, and is made of the influences of all the stars. He is also the life of all the stars. Thus the sun of divine Wisdom in man is representing the collective knowledge which man has gathered from his experiences, having as a basis his own divine self-consciousness. Without that self-consciousness in God all his intellectual acquisitions are merely vapoury, and will pass away.

"In the soul of the external world, and by means of it, God has awakened a king, or, as I would wish to call it symbolically, a natural deity, together with six councillors, to be his assistants, namely, the sun and the six other planets, which were spoken out of the seven qualities from the *locus* (seat or centre) of the sun. The sun receives his splendour from the tincture of the fire-world and the world of light, and is manifested as a revealed point in relation to the world of fire." (*Mysterium*, xiii. 16.)

"In the death in the centre—that is to say, in the body or the corporeal substance of the earth, God has awakened the *tincture*, its lustre, splendour, and light, wherein is contained the life of the earth; but to the depth above the centre He has given the sun, which is a tincture of the fire, and which, with its power, reaches into the freedom outside and beyond nature, and from which nature receives its splendour. He is the life of the whole circle of stars, and all these stars are His children. Not that he contains their essences, but their life arose from his centre in the beginning." (*Threefold Life*, iv. 27.)

"The sun is the heart of all the powers in this world, and is configurated from the powers of all the stars, while, on the other hand, he illuminates and vivifies all the stars and powers in this world." (*Aurora*,

[30]Man judges himself. According to his conscience will turn the scales of the balance. The judgment-day appears when the judging spirits awaken in him.

99

vii. 42.)

Thus the divine principle in man furnishes the intellect with light and life in the same sense as the sun reflects his light upon the moon. An intellect which has been deserted by God will perish after its accumulated strength is exhausted. Only that which God knows in us remains permanent.

> "The sun is in the midst of the depth, and is, so to say, the light or heart of the stars, extracted from all their powers by the power of God, and brought into form Therefore is he the clearest light of all, and by his lustre and heat he ignites all the stars, each one according to its own special quality and power." (*Threefold Life*, vii. 40.)

> "This is not to be understood as if by calling the sun the centre we meant to say that all the stars were originated from a central point, called the 'sun.' The sun is the centre of the powers of the stars, and the cause why they move in their essence. He unfolds their powers and puts his power into them, and this power constitutes their heart." (*Mysterium*, xi. 32.)

Especially have the seven planets become objective by means of the sun, and in accordance with and corresponding to the seven forms of nature.[31]

> "As the sun is the heart of the life and an origin of all the spirits in the body of this world, likewise is Saturn a beginning of all corporeity and tangibility. Thus he does not derive his beginning and descent from the sun, but his origin is the earnest, acrid, and severe anxiety of the whole body of this world." (*Aurora*, xxvi. 1.)

> "When the light became ignited, the conquered power in the astringency became Mercury." (*Three Principles*, viii. 24.)

> "Mercury is an agitator, sound-maker, ringer; but he leas not yet the true life. The latter originates in the fire. Thus he desires the fierce and storming essence, to cause fire to appear, and this is Mars." (*Threefold Life*, ix. 78.) " When the sun became ignited, the terrible fire-flash went from the locality of the sun in an upward direction like a furious stroke of lightning, and this became Mars. He is now there as a tyrant, a raging element, a mover of the whole body of this world, so that all life takes its origin of him." (*Aurora*, xxv. 72.)

> "As soon as the spirits of motion and life, by means of the ignition of the water, arose from the locality of the sun, mildness, being the basis of the water, penetrated, endowed with the power of light, in a

---

[31]All the illumined philosophers of the past speak of only seven planets, and if we accept the possibility of spiritual perception and agree that this perception was true, then there can be no more than seven original planets in our solar system, and the remaining two may be looked upon as excrescences, or shadows, as would also appear from the maleficent influence of at least one of these, which is known to astrologers.

downward direction, after the manner of meekness, and from this the planet Venus came into existence." (*Aurora*, xxvi. 19–33.)

"When the fiery terror was captured by the light, the light, by its own power, and being a mild, exalting life, penetrated still higher upwards into the depth, until it arrived in the hard and cold seat of nature. There it remained, and from that power the planet Jupiter came into existence." (*Aurora*, xxv. 76–82.)

"The seventh form is Luna, wherein are contained the qualities of all the six forms. She is, so to say, the corporeal being of the other forms, all of which throw into her their desire by means of *Sol*. That which *Sol* (the sun) is spiritually becomes corporeal in *Luna* (the moon)." (*Signature*, ix. 24.)

After the world of stars had begun to exist, the sidereal life appeared by the power of the former—that is to say, that living organisms were produced, representing, so to speak, "stars of the various elements."

"The firmament of heaven, having been made from the medium of the water, this generation penetrates through the external, congealed generation—that is to say, through death, and brings forth the sidereal life, such as animals and men, birds, fishes, and worms." (*Aurora*, xx. 60.)

"After God had unfolded the stars and the four elements, there were produced creatures in all the four elements, such as birds in the constellation of the air, fishes in the constellation of the water, animals and four-legged beings in the constellation of earth, and spirits in that of the fire."[32] (*Mysterium*, xliv. 1.)

These creatures received their spirit from the stars, or rather from the spirit of this world, but their body they received from the earth. According to the predominance of the fiery or the watery form, there resulted also an antithesis of sex.

"By the power of His word, *Fiat*, God caused all beings to come forth from the matrix of nature on the fifth day, all according to their qualities; the fishes in the water, the birds in the air, the other animals upon the earth. They received their corporeity from the fixedness (rigidity) of the earth, and their spirit from the *Spiritus Mundi*." (*Grace*, v. 20.)

"All creatures have been created of the life below and the life above. The matrix of the earth gave the body, and the stars the spirit." (*Threefold Life*, xi. 7.)

[32]For explicit details regarding the inhabitants of the elemental world see Paracelsus. The existence of such beings will become more comprehensible if we remember that the universe is an organised unity, and that each form therein, whether it is visible or invisible to us, is nothing but a relative expanse of manifestation of the consciousness that resides in the All.

"As the spirit of the stars, or the spirit in the fire-form, by the power of its longing, became mixed with the watery one, there resulted two senses from one and the same essence. The one, the male, in a fiery, and the other, the female, in a watery shape (state)."[33] (*Three Principles*, viii. 43.)

Finally, man was created, and out of him there was to come forth a celestial army, and in the midst of the time its king, in the place of the outcast Lucifer.

"God willed to create an angelic army. Thus He created Adam, and he was to generate out of his own body creatures of his own kind; but in the midst of the time there was to be born out of the body of a man the King of all men, and He was to take possession of the new kingdom as a ruler over these created beings, in the place of the degenerated and outcast Lucifer."[34] (*Aurora*, xxiv. 18.)

Man, however, was to surpass the angels (in perfection), for he was to be a complete image of divine glory, while the angels have been created out of only two principles.

"Adam was to be a perfect symbol of God, created out of the eternal *Magia*, the substance of God; he was to be something made out of the nothing, out of the spirit—the ideal—into the body." (*Menschwerdung*, i. 5.)

"The angels are created out of two principles, but the soul, with the body of the outer life, out of three principles. Therefore man is higher than the angels, provided that he remains in God." (*Forty Questions*, i. 263.)

"We human beings are a far greater mystery than the angels, and we shall surpass them in celestial wisdom. They are fire-flames, illumined by the light of God, but we attain the great fountain of meekness and love which is welling up within the holy essentiality of God."[35]

---

[33] All this refers not only to beings such as are visible to us, but likewise to such that exist on other planes of creation, and which can therefore not be seen with our eyes. There are male and female elemental beings, *moll* and *dur* accords in music, positive and negative forces in all departments of nature, from the spiritual down to the most material plane. In all creatures the will is the executing and female, corporifying, and the imagination the superintending, directing, male element.

[34] In regard to the "stuff out of which man is made," *Theophrastus Paracelsus* says: "It is an extract of all beings that exist in heaven and upon the earth, of the souls of all things, all creatures, spirits, elements, and minds, attracted to a focus by means of the spiritual centre residing within each form. It is the quintessence of all things, and man is a microcosm, differing from the macrocosm only in so far as in his constitution the things which constitute the macrocosm appear in another image, order, or shape. In him are all the potencies and qualities that exist in the universe, active or latent. His terrestrial substance is from the earth, his mental faculties from the universal mind, his worldly wisdom is from the light of nature; but the divine wisdom in him belongs to God."

[35] In studying the "anatomy" and "physiology" of the inner man, it will be necessary to remember that, in dealing with anthropology and cosmology from a spiritual point of view, we must be able to discard from our mind all the vulgar conceptions of what is usually called "matter " by that science which deals merely with external appearances, and we must look upon all things as being manifestations of an universal

(Menschwerdung, i. 5.)

Man comprises all three principles: the principle of darkness or fire, from which originates his soul; the principle of light, from which his spirit originates; and the third principle, which is the basic element of his body.

"In the life of man there are three states to be distinguished from each other—first, the *innermost,* that is to say, *God being eternally hidden within the fire;* secondly, the *middle part,* which from eternity has stood as an *image* or *likeness* in the wonders of God, comparable to a person seeing himself in a mirror; thirdly, has this living image received still another mirror in creation wherein to behold itself, namely, the *spirit of the external world,* or the *third principle,* which is also a form (state) of the Eternal." (*Threefold Life,* xviii. 4.)

"The *darkness* in man longing for light is the first principle; the *power of the light* the second; and the *longing power which attracts* and becomes full (substantial), and whereof the material body grows, is the third principle." (*Three Principles,* vii. 26.)

"The *soul,* or the first principle, is founded on the fire of eternal nature; the *spirit,* or the second principle, roots in the light; and the *body* is the third principle, or the substantiality of the visible world."[36] (*Tabulæ Principia,* 65.)

Adam was to rule over all nature, and therefore his body was taken from all the powers of the external world; but the third principle, as well as the first one, appeared in him subject to the second, the light.

"If you will behold your own self and the outer world, and what is taking place therein, you will find that you, with regard to your external being, are that external world. You are a little world formed out of the large one, and your external light is a *chaos* of the sun and the constellation of stars. If this were not so, you would not be able to see by means of the light of the sun."[37] (*Mysterium,* ii. 5.)

"If man, as the image of God, is to rule over the fishes and fowls, the animals, and the whole of the earth, as well as over the essence of all the stars, then must he be out of all three, for each spirit can rule only in his mother, wherein he originated." (*Mysterium,* xiv. 8.)

consciousness, acting upon internal or external planes of existence, while the visible form is nothing but a passing apparition.

[36]Man is made out of will and imagination; in other words, "fire" and "light." The manifestation of fire and light (thought) produces that which appears to us as "substance" or "form."

[37]It is not "man" in the abstract who recognises anything. It is always a certain principle, having become active in him, that recognises its own counterpart in external nature, when it comes in contact with it. Only he in whom is light can see the light; only the element of love can feel love; only the divinity in man can know God in and through man.

103

"Terrestrial man had in. his constitution the kingdom of this world, but there were not ruling in him the four elements (separately); but they were in one, and the terrestrial order of things was hidden in him. He was to live in celestial state, and although everything was stirring (alive) within him, nevertheless he was to rule over the terrestrial anguish (external consciousness) by means of the celestial quality (inner consciousness) of the other (second) principle, and to retain dominion over the kingdom of the stars and elements by means of the Paradisiacal quality." (*Menschwerdung*, i. 2.)

Man must rise, not merely in his imagination, but with his will, above all that which is earthly, sensual, or merely intellectual, if he desires to be a power in the kingdom of the Spirit. Thus will the ideal become real to him.

"Adam's body (the ethereal body of aboriginal man) was created out of the four elements of external nature, and out of the (essences of the) stars, by means of the eternal *Fiat*. Thus he was in possession of divine and terrestrial essentiality; but the terrestrial one was in the divine one like consumed or impotent (latent). The substance or the matter from which the body was made or created contained itself also the first principle within itself, but it was not stirring therein." (*Menschwerdung*, i. 3, 15.)

"As God resides within Himself and penetrates through all His works, incomprehensible to the latter, and without His being affected by anything, likewise His image (man) originated from the pure element. He also was created in this world; but the kingdom of this world was not to comprehend him, but he was to rule powerfully in this world by means of the essences from the pure element." (*Three Principles*, xxii. 15.)

The expression that God created man from a clod of clay is not to be taken in any other sense than that God, by means of desire, drew together all the terrestrial qualities.[38]

"If Moses says that God created man out of a clod of clay, and that he breathed into him the living breath, this is not to be understood as if God had acted in a personal manner—standing there like a man and taking up a lump of earth and making a body out of it; but the *Fiat*, that is to say, the desire of the *Word*, was contained within the eternally-perceived model of man, which stood in the mirror of wisdom, and it drew the *Ens* (the principle) of all the qualities of the earth (matter) into a body, and this was the quintessence made out of the four elements." (*Grace*, v. 27.)

---

[38]Therefore *Theophrastus Paracelsus* says: "Natural man is made out of the world, and not the world out of him. He is a child of nature, and has all of his mother's qualities in himself, neither more nor less. But the true spiritual man is a son of God. Natural wisdom is not divine, but divine wisdom is above all."

But the essence of the soul, being rooted in that whole, did not become manifest in man before God awakened it by the breath of His word.[39]

> "The sourcive spirits within the whole could not become immediately ignited by the soul, for the soul was only as a seed within the whole, hidden away with the heart of God in His heaven, until the Creator expanded the whole by His breath. Then the sourcive spirits ignited the soul, and then body and soul were living at once. The soul truly possessed her life before the body existed; but it was within the heart of God, hidden within the whole in heaven, and was nothing but a holy seed, a centre of power in God." (*Aurora*, xxvi. 126.)

Neither does at this present day the soul of man manifest divine life as long as the Spirit of God is only moving upon the surface and does not stir within the depths.

[39]And thus at this very day each person who has not yet begun to be regenerated in the spirit is in the same condition in which Adam was before the Spirit of God breathed in him. Man's soul resembles a seed containing the potency of conscious immortality in an unconscious state. There is nothing immortal in man except God, and by the awakening of that which is divine in him attains the self-consciousness of his own immortality.

Chapter VII
Man

"God created man in His own image. Male and female (*in one*) created He them."

MAN in his cosmic aspect is a being very superior to that which is commonly looked upon as a "man," and which is described in books on anthropology, anatomy, &c. Such external sciences deal only with the grossly material body of external terrestrial man, while the essential body of macrocosmic and microcosmic man is beyond the reach of external observation. In the study of man as a cosmic being there are three subjects to be considered, although the three are only three aspects of one. These three subjects are God, Nature, and Man, and neither one of them can be understood in its inner essence without an understanding of the other two. External science, "natural philosophy," and theology seek to separate them. They regard man as a being separated, distinct, and independent of nature, and nature as something independent of man; while of God they know nothing, and regard the divine power, which is the cause of all life, as if it were something external to nature and man, and beyond their reach. For this reason the "man" of modern science has become an unnatural being, without any conceivable object for his existence, and nature is to him an organism evolved by accidence and subject to no other than mechanically acting law. The divine, spiritual, creative, and hidden powers in man and in nature are entirely removed from the field of perception of the "rationalist."

Man, as a whole, may be conceived of as a planetary spirit, a self-conscious, luminous sphere of unimaginable extent; as, in fact, at present the mental sphere of man has no defined limits; it reaches as far as his thoughts can go. He was created for the purpose of being the image of God. The glory of God was residing in him, and he was penetrated by the light of divine love.

In man is contained everything, God, and the Christ, and the angels, the celestial and terrestrial kingdoms, and the powers of hell. Outside of him is nothing of which he can conceive; he can know nothing except that which exists in his mind. No god or devil, no spirit or any power whatever, can act within man unless it enters into his constitution. Only that which exists in him has existence for him.

Without a realisation of this fact the mysteries of religion will remain incomprehensible. It may be interesting and amusing to speculate

107

about all the different gods and celestial hosts that go to make up the Pantheons of the various nations, but such a study does not constitute real knowledge. Only when man's spiritual perceptions are unfolded and he attains divine knowledge of self, then will he know the Christ and all the celestial powers whose aggregate goes to make up the kingdom of God existing within himself.

> "The Spirit of God resides from eternity to eternity only in heaven—that is to say, in His own essence, in the power of the majesty. When it became inbreathed into the image of man, then was heaven in man; for God willed to reveal Himself in man, as in an image created after His own likeness, and to manifest the great wonders of His eternal wisdom." (*Stiefel*, i. 36.)

> "Simultaneously with the introduction of His divine image, Adam received also the living word of God (spiritual intelligence) to furnish food for his soul." (*Menschwerdung*, i. 3, 24.)

> "God created Adam to (enjoy) eternal life in Paradise in a state of paradisiacal perfection. Divine love illumined his interior, as the sun is illuminating the world." (*Stiefel*, i. 36.)

> "In Paradise there is perfect life without disturbance, and a perpetual day, and the paradisiacal man is clear like transparent glass, and he is fully penetrated by the light of the divine sun."[40] (*Signature*, xi. 5 1.)

His body likewise appeared luminous, because its terrestrial substance was absorbed in the celestial essence. It radiated a pure, divine light.[41]

> "The inner holy corporeity of the pure element penetrated through the four elements and kept the *Limus* of earth—that is to say, the external *sulphuric* (terrestrial) body within itself as in a state of absorption. Nevertheless, that body was actually present, but in such a way as darkness dwells in light, so that the darkness cannot manifest itself on account of the light." (*Mysterium*, xvi. 6.)

> "All the qualities of the inner and holy body, together with the external ones, were in primordial man attuned in one harmony. Neither of them lived in its own state of desire; but they had their desire in the soul wherein the divine light was manifest. This, the divine light radiated through all the qualities, and produced in them an equal, harmonious temperature." (*Mysterium*, xvi. 5.)

> "The inner man kept the external one imprisoned within itself and penetrated it in a manner comparable to iron, which glows if it is

[40]The term "Paradise" means a state of purity and innocence and happiness, but not necessarily knowledge. Man had to learn to know evil so as to be able to realise good.

[41]His thoughts and will were pure, and therefore his spirit (the union of will and thought) manifested itself in producing a pure and luminous form, not burdened with the gross material elements which form at present the bodies of human beings. Then, as now, his body was the product of his own thoughts.

penetrated by fire, so that it seems as if it were itself fire. But when the fire becomes extinct, then does the black, dark iron become manifest." (*Mysterium*, xvi. 7.)

"The pure element penetrated through the external roan and overpowered the four elements; moreover, the power of the heat and the cold was in the flesh. But as the light of God was shining therein, they were in equal harmony, so that neither one of them became manifest before the other. Thus God the Father is called a wrathful, jealous God and a consuming fire, and He is all that in regard to His qualities; but of these qualities nothing becomes manifest in His light." (*Stiefel*, xi. 75.)

"Primordial man in Paradise, being fixed therein, was in a state such as time is before God and God in time. As time is a spectacle before God, likewise the external life of man was a spectacle before the inner and holy man, who was the true image of God." (*Mysterium*, xvi. 8.)

In the same sense the Bhagavad Gita says that the true self, the God, *Atma*, or " Christ," is not a participator, but merely a spectator in that which concerns the external illusion.

"The inner body was a dwelling-place of the Godhead, an image of divine substantiality. In that body the soul had her meekness, and her fire was rendered mild thereby, for she received there the love and meekness of God." (*Tilk.*, i. 233.)

Owing to this resemblance to God, Adam's will and thoughts were as one. His mind was pure and uncomplicated, childlike, unsophisticated, and devoted to God; he did not need to speculate about the unknown, because he had the power to perceive that which he wanted to know. He enjoyed the perception of divine and terrestrial things.[42]

"The mind of Adam was innocent like that of a child, playing with the wonders of its Father. There was in him no self-knowledge of evil will, no avarice, pride, envy, anger, but a pure enjoyment of love." (*Threefold Life*, xi. 23.)

"When Adam was created in Paradise, there his life was burning like a flame of pure oil. Therefore his perception was celestial, and his intelligence was surpassing and comprehending things beyond nature." (*Signature*, vii. 2.)

"The inner man stood in heaven; his essences were the Paradise; his body was indestructible. He knew the language of God and the angels, and the language of nature, as may be seen by Adam giving names to all creatures, to each according to its own essence and quality." (*Forty*

---

[42]Logical proof is only useful as long as we are blind in regard to the nature of a thing After that thing has become a part of ourselves and we perceive it, no more proof of its existence will be required.

"Adam, after having been created by God, was in Paradise in a state of joy and glorification, beautiful and filled with knowledge. God then brought before him, as the lord of the world, all the animals, so that he might behold them, and give a name to each according to its special essence and power. And Adam knew that he was within every creature, and he gave to each its appropriate name. God can see into the hearts of all things, and the same could be done by Adam."[43] (*Three Principles*, x. 17.)

In this state of godlike being he had power over all things; for all things existed in him and he in all, and there was nothing that could have done him any external injury. To express it in other words, all things existed subjectively in his mind, as they now do in ours, but his mind was his " body," and where the centre of his consciousness was, there was his "form."[44]

"As God is a Lord over all, so man in the power of God was to be a lord over this world." (*Menschwerdung*, i. 4, 7.)

"The soul in the power of God penetrates through all things, and is powerful over all, as God Himself; for she lives in the power of His heart." (*Three Principles*, xxii. 17.)

"As gold is incorruptible in the fire, so man was subject to nothing, only to the One God dwelling in him, and manifested in him by the power of His holy being."

(*Mysterium*, xvi. 12.) "Everything was subject to Adam; his rule extended into heaven and over the earth, and in all elements and stars. This was because divine power was manifested in him."[45] (*Mysterium*, xvi. 2.)

"The will-spirit of man penetrated through all creatures, and was injured by none, because none could grasp it. No creature can apprehend the power and light of the sun in its own will, but must remain passive to become penetrated by it; thus it was then the case with the will-spirit of man." (*Grace*, vii. 2.)

"Before his fall, man could rule over the sun and the stars. Everything was in his power.[46] Fire, air, water, and earth could not tame him; no

---

[43]Adam was in harmony with creation and as one with all nature. Therefore he could experience the feelings of all beings in nature within himself, and express them accordingly.

[44]Even now man is still there where his consciousness exists; but as his physical body is too gross to follow the movements of his thoughts, the body becomes unconscious whenever his consciousness concentrates itself at another place.

[45]This was the divine Man, out of whom the world was created, while the natural man is a product of the world.

[46]Because everything was within his own will, within himself.

fire burned him, no water drowned, no air suffocated him; all that lived stood in awe of him." (*Threefold Life*, xi. 23.)

"No heat, no cold, no sickness, nor accident, nor any fear could touch or terrify him. His body could pass through earth and rocks without breaking anything in them; for a man who could be overpowered by the terrestrial nature, or who could be broken to pieces, would not be eternal."[47] (*Menschwerdung*, i. 2, 13.)

Likewise that nature which surrounded him, and which is called Eden, was illuminated by the celestial light, and it was thereby exalted to paradisiacal magnificence.

"Adam was in Paradise, that is to say, in the temperature. Thereby he was placed in a certain locality, namely, in that where the holy world was blooming out through the earth and bearing the fruits of Paradise." (*Grace*, v. 34.)

"'Eden' means the locality, but 'Paradise' is the out-flowing or the life of God in divine harmony." (*Letters*, xxxi. 28.)

"In Paradise the substance of the divine world penetrated the substance belonging to time, comparable to the power of the sun penetrating a fruit growing on a tree, and endowing it with such qualities as render it lovely to the sight and good to the taste." (*Mysterium*, xvii. 5.)

"Thus the holy divine world was predominant through all the three principles of the human quality, and there was an equal accord, and no enmity or opposite will was manifest betwixt the principles."[48] (*Mysterium*, xvii. 20.)

There were in Paradise all the products which we meet in the terrestrial world, but they were there in a state of ethereality and of supernatural beauty. This paradisiacal beauty was, however, not manifested in all parts of the world.

"In Paradise there are growths, the same as in this world, but not in (terrestrial) tangibility. There *Heaven* is in the place of the earth, the *Light of God* instead of the sun, and the *Eternal Father* in the place of the power of the stars." (*Three Principles*, ix. 20.)

"The Paradise is not anything corporeal or tangible in a terrestrial sense, but its corporeity and tangibility is like that of the angels. It is there a clear, visible, substance, as if it were material, and it is actually "material;" but it is formed only out of the power, without any addition of terrestrial matter, and it is, therefore, perfectly transparent."

[47] This celestial Adam has not died, but still exists in all of us; but on account of our state of degeneration, caused by the attraction of the lower principles, we have forgotten our own divine nature.

[48] It was Adam's own state of feeling and thinking that created an Eden for him, and thus each human being creates his or her own Paradise.

(*Three Principles*, ix. 18.)

"The tangible world, or nature, before the time of the wrath of God, was thin, ethereal, lovely, and clear, so that the sourcive spirits could look through everything and penetrate it. There were therein neither terrestrial rocks nor earth, and there was no created light needed, such as it is now; but the light was generated in all things in the midst of each thing, and everything was in the light." (*Aurora*, xviii. 29.)

"The whole world would have been all Paradise if it had not been corrupted by Lucifer. But as God knew that Adam was going to fall, it bloomed out in only one place, wherein man might find a suitable dwelling-place, and be fortified therein." (*Mysterium*, xvii. 7.)

"God saw and knew that man was going to fall, and therefore the Paradise did not bloom and bear fruits in the whole of the world by means of the earth, although it was manifest everywhere, but only in the Garden of Eden, wherein Adam was tempted, did it become revealed in its full magnificence."[49] (*Letters*, xxxix. 28.)

For all that, man, although having been endowed with great splendour by the Creator, did not yet enjoy true similarity with God.[50]

"In Adam was manifest the kingdom of grace, the divine life, because he lived in the temperature (harmony) of the qualities, but he did not know that God was revealed in him. Likewise his self-will did not know that which is good, because it had as yet experienced no evil. How could there be any joy where no sorrow is known?" (*Grace*, ix. 15.)

"The soul was in her own essence from eternity, but as a created thing she was formed to represent the image of God at the time of the creation of the body. Nevertheless she is *per se* not yet the true image, but only an essential fire for its production." (*Tilk.*, i. 81.)

"The soul of man, which has been breathed into him by God, is from the Eternal Father; but with that she has not yet attained the birth of the Son, wherein is the end of nature, and from which no created being issues." (*Three Principles*, ix. 13.)

Man can attain real similarity to God and perfect beatitude only by decisively willing to put his will into the Son, as the Heart or Light of the Father.

---

[49]This Paradise (*Deva-loca* or *Devachan*) is described in Eastern books as an "illusion;" but it is no more an illusion to its inhabitants than the dream called "terrestrial existence" is an illusion to us. On the contrary, it is far more permanent and beautiful than this terrestrial world.

[50]He could not enjoy similarity with God, because he did not possess divine self-knowledge. To attain this knowledge of self he had to eat from the tree of the self-knowledge of good and evil, and then return to his original divine state.

"God has the eternal and unchangeable will to generate His Heart and his Son, and thus the soul should put her immutable will into the heart of God. Then would she be in heaven and Paradise, and enjoy the inexpressible happiness of God the Father, which He enjoys in the Son, and she would hear the inexpressible words in the heart of God."[51] (*Three Principles*, x. 14.)

"Adam was conceived in the love of God and born into this world. He was in possession of a divine substantiality, and his soul was of the will, the first principle, the quality of the Father. This will should be directed, together with the imagination, into the heart of the Father, that is to say, into the *Word* and the Spirit of love and purity. Then would man's soul retain the substance of God in the Word of Life." (*Menschwerdung*, i. 10, 2.)

"The living soul, from the eternal will of the Father, was breathed into man, and this will has no other purpose than to give birth to His only Son.[52] Of this will God the Father infused into man, and this is the eternal soul of man. The soul ought to put her regenerated will into the eternal will of the Father, in the heart of God. Then will she receive the power of the heart of God and also His holy eternal light, wherein arises the Paradise and the celestial kingdom and eternal joy." (*Three Principles*, xxvi. 16.)

"If the soul sinks her will into the meekness, *i.e.*, the obedience of God, she becomes a fountain of the heart of God, and receives divine power, and all her essences become angelic and joyful. Then her harsh essences will also be useful to her, and appear to her more mild and useful, than if they had already originally been entirely sweet and mild." (*Three Principles*, xiii. 31.)

It was within his power to decide, and he was free to do so, because there was in him not only the principle of light, but also the fire-principle,—not only perception, but will.

"The light and the power of the light is a desire, and wants to come in possession of the noble image made after God's likeness, because it has been created for the world of light. Likewise the dark world or the craving wrath desires the same, for man has all the worlds within himself, and there is a great battle taking place in man. That principle with which he identifies himself with in his desire and his will, will rule in him." (*Tilk.*, i. 381.)

"As the soul is essential and her very substance is a desire, it is clear that

[51]This the soul can surely not do by seeking for the Son or the Heart of God in anything outside of her own sphere, and with which she is in no way related. Therefore the meaning of the words, "Thou shalt worship only one God," is "Thou shalt have faith in no other God except the one who is seeking to reveal Himself within your own conscience, and not worship any strange idols, such as exist in the imagination of men."

[52]God being a unity, has no other will or object in view than to give birth to His Son, *i.e.*, to manifest His outspoken Word as wisdom in man.

113

she is in two kinds of *Fiat*. The first is her own soul-property; the other belongs to the second principle, issuing from the will of God in the soul. The soul desiring for God for the purpose of forming herself in His image and likeness, this desire of God acts as a *Fiat* in her own centre; for the desire of God wants to possess the soul. On the other hand, she herself desires to possess the centre in the power of the fire, wherein the life of the soul originates." (*Eye*, vii.)

"The will of the soul is free, and she can either sink into nothing within herself and conceive of herself as the nothing, when she will sprout like a branch out of the tree of divine life, and eat of the love of God; or she may in her own self-will rise up in the fire and desire to become a separate tree."[53] (*Forty Questions*, ii. 2.)

There existed in man also the third principle, wherein resides sensual desire. He was not endowed with this principle for the purpose of surrendering himself to it, but that he might introduce it into the light of God, and glorify Him by means of that light.[54]

"Man was a mixed individuality, and destined to be an image according to the inner, and also according to the outer world; but as the symbol of God, he was to rule with the inner consciousness over the external one." (*Menschwerdung*, i. 3, 13.)

"When man remains in harmonious order, so as not to let one world into the other, he is then the likeness of God; but the image or the *mirror* of the world of light he should surely introduce into the external world." (*Six Theosophical Points*, vi. 12.)

"The constellation (the astral influences) of the macrocosm should not be permitted to rule over man; but he has his own constellation (the spirit, the idea) within himself, which is capable of becoming attuned to the harmony of the rise and evolution of the divine world within." (*Letters*, i. 8.)

"All of man's desire should have been placed into the light; then would the light have shone within his essence and desire, and filled everything as with one will." (*Tilk.*, i. 542.)

"The soul of Adam could have ruled powerfully over the external principle if she had entered again with her will into the heart of God, into the word of the Lord."[55] (*Forty Questions*, iv. 2.)

[53]The spiritual will of man is free; not so the will of semi-animal man, for freedom depends on the extent of knowledge. When man's knowledge becomes divine, then will his will be free—wholly free.

[54]Man requires the material (animal) element in him to endow him with strength to rise above it by the power of God. Man may be regarded as a god crucified within an animal. The god furnishes him with wisdom, the animal with strength. We are to overcome the animal in us by the power of divine wisdom. He who has nothing to overcome can gain no victory. We cannot rise above a thing as long as we have not attained its highest level.

[55]It would be foolish to worry about what Adam ought or ought not to have done. The meaning is, that we who have "Adam" in us should enter now with our will into the will of God.

Thus it was intended that, by means of the instrumentality of man, the paradisiacal splendour should be continually spread out and increased over terrestrial nature, and that all the hidden treasures of nature should be uncovered.

> "The external world is also of God and belonging to God, and man has been created therein, so that he may bring again the external into the internal one; the end into the beginning." (*Letters*, xi. 18.)

> "Adam was also created in the external quality, so that he may manifest in forms and execute in works that which had been perceived in eternal wisdom." (*Menschwerdung*, i. 4.)

> "Man has been created in Paradise, for it was out-blooming through the earth, and from the earth of Paradise was Adam's body created, because he was a lord of the earth, and it was his destiny to unfold the wonders of the earth. If it had not been for that purpose, God might have endowed him with an angelic body; but in that case the substantiated being with its wonderful qualities would not have been unfolded."[56] (*Menschwerdung*, ii. 12.)

But while in Adam all the three principles were originally in unity and harmony, there was attracting him outwardly in a powerful manner, not only the heart of God, but also the devil and the kingdom of the terrestrial world.[57]

> "Man stood in three principles, and they were in equal concordance in him, but not outside of him; for the dark world had a desire different from that of the world of light, and likewise the external world had a desire differing from that of the dark world and from the world of light. Thus the image of God was betwixt three principles, which all of them in their desire were conducive to that image. Each of them wanted to become manifest in Adam—to have him within its own regiment or as a ruler, and to manifest its wonders through him." (*Mysterium*, xvii. 34.)

> "Everything attracted Adam and wanted to take possession of him. The heart of God wanted to have him in Paradise and to reside in him, for it said, 'He is my image and likeness.' The kingdom of wrath wanted him, for it said, 'He is mine; for he has issued out of my fountain, out of the eternal mind of the darkness. I will be in him, and he shall live in my power; I will manifest through him strong and great power.' Finally, the kingdom of the world likewise said, 'He is mine, for he bears my image; he lives in me and I in him; he must be obedient to

[56]If primordial man had never fallen from his purely spiritual state and "refused to create," he would never have learned to know the wonders of creation, the unfoldment of the third principle. The external world, as we know it, was created by Adam's fall.

[57]The "devil" means spiritual will perverted. If it is perverted in a personal being, then will there be a personal devil.

me, for I have all nay members (organs) in him and he has his members in me, and I am greater than he. He shall be my steward, and manifest my power and wonders.'"[58] (*Three Principles*, xi. 33.)

Adam, making a perverted use of the freedom granted to him, allowed his lower qualities to be awakened to an evil desire—that is to say, to a desire for the terrestrial world, which is divided within itself.

"In primitive man before the fall, the qualities for differentiation and self-enjoyment were in equal will-power, and their desire was introduced into the unity of God. This the devil begrudged to them, and he deluded the seven qualities of life by awakening within them a perverted desire, persuading them that it were good, and that they would become wise, if the qualities, each according to its own kind, would enter into their own accord,[59] and that in this way the spirit would taste and recognise that which was good and evil." (*Tabulæ Principiæ*, 68.)

"The soul of Adam fell in love with the creation of the formed word in its differentiation, and not being conscious of the power of distinguishing, she entered into lust, into differentiation." (*Grace*, vi. 33.)

"The soul wanted to know how it would be if the temperature were to become separated—that is to say, divided, as heat and cold, moisture and dryness, hardness and softness, acridity and sweetness, bitterness and that which is sour; she wanted to taste these and the other qualities all in their separateness, although it had been prohibited to Adam by God."[60] (*Grace*, iii. 34.)

Owing to this perverted desire, there grew in him the tree of temptation, wherein the terrestrial qualities, as such, became manifest.[61]

"Adam's spirit was lusting after terrestrial fruit, such as was of the nature of the corrupted earth, and therefore nature formed for him a tree that was like the corrupted earth; for Adam was the heart in nature, and therefore his spiritual soul aided in the formation of that

[58]God (Christ), nature, and the devil (Antichrist—*i.e.*, Christ perverted) are seeking to attain self-consciousness in man. Man's consciousness is, therefore, continually changing, and in reality not his own. Only when the principle of either good or evil has become self-conscious in man, and he has become identified with it, will he know his true impersonal self. Only then will he be a free and responsible agent.

[59]It was his desire that the lower qualities should become conscious in himself, each according to its own nature.

[60]This is the difference between life in the terrestrial and life in the celestial states of nature, that the former is differentiated into forms, each of which loves to live in the consciousness of its own illusive self—*i.e.*, in a state of isolation and separatedness, and enjoying its own qualities; while in the celestial state the individual powers intermingle, each living, so to say, in the consciousness and enjoying itself in the life of the other. while all strive towards unity and rest in it, like a tree, whose many branches and leaves receive their life all from one common trunk.

[61]This "tree of temptation" is still growing in every human being, as is represented in the allegorical "Adam." The lower qualities in man still strive for outward manifestation, and can be overcome in no other way than by his rising above them into the higher ones.

116

tree, of which he desired to eat." (*Aurora*, xvii. 20.)

"The tree of temptation grew by the power of the hunger after self-knowledge of good and evil. It should not be said that it was any other kind of a product than the rest of such trees; only there was manifest in it the terrestrial desire for conscious evil and good; while the other trees and plants were penetrated by the holy, paradisiacal *Mercury*, so that in them the qualities were in equal accordance, and heat and cold were not separately manifested in them." (*Stiefel*, ii. 80.)

"In the tree of self-knowledge of good and evil there were the qualities in the curse, such as is the case at present—that is to say, each of them was manifest in itself, and seeking to preponderate. They had gone out of their harmony, and thus all the three principles, each separately, were manifest in that tree. Therefore Moses (wisdom) calls it the tree of knowledge of good and evil." (*Mysterium*, xvii. 15.)

The forthcoming of the tree of temptation is not to be wondered at, because Adam was endowed with great powers, and an earthly form as a protection to him against the powers of hell.[62]

"Reason (man's reasoning) says, 'Why did God permit Adam to draw the tree of temptation out of the earth by means of his imagination?' Christ said, 'If you have faith as big as a mustard-seed, and you say to the mountain: throw thyself into the sea; it shall be done as you say.' The soul-spirit (spiritual soul) was produced out of the divine omnipotence, out of the centre of eternal nature, wherefrom all beings have been created. Why should it then not be powerful? It was a fire-spark out of God's power, but after it had been gathered into a created being (individualised as an organism) it gave way to its own selfish desire, and broke away from the whole, and thus it caused corruption unto itself. The soul-power, before vanity entered, was so strong as not to be subject to anything, and would be so now, even this very day, if the understanding had not been taken away." (*Mysterium*, xvii. 41.)

"Divine prevision recognised that the devil was going to winnow mankind, and to introduce them into evil desire; and therefore God put before them the tree of life, and of the knowledge of good and evil, by means of which the breaking up (the death) of the external body was inaugurated. He did this lest man should long after the centre of the dark world."[63] (*Mysterium*, xvii. 38.)

Formerly Adam belonged to the celestial world and to eternity; but

[62]It is self-evident that man can attain knowledge of a thing only by giving attention to it. In doing so, he directs his consciousness to it. Man's consciousness became centred within the lower principles constituting the sensual world, and thereby it lost its seat and centre of gravity in the Supreme. If it had not been for this attraction which the material world exercised upon man, he might have sunk still lower, and approached absolute evil, the kingdom of Lucifer.

[63]"Adam would have fallen into the unfathomable abyss of hell, if, besides the celestial state, which in consequence of his sin became perverted into a hellish one, there had not been still another, namely, the terrestrial region " (*Hamberger*).

117

now, the image of God having begun to pale in him, he sank into the terrestrial state, and thereby into impotency and sleep.

> "A reasonable person will easily perceive that there could be no sleep in Adam as long as he was in the image of God, for at that time he was such an image as we shall be in the resurrection of the dead. We shall then not need the elements, neither the sun nor the moon, and also require no sleep; but our eyes will be open to see always and eternally the glory of God." (*Three Principles*, xii. 17.)

> "The image of God does not sleep. In it there is no time. With sleep, time became manifest in man. He fell asleep in the angelic world, and awoke relatively to the external world."[64] (*Mysterium*, xix. 4.)

> "After Adam had been overcome, the *tincture*, wherein the beautiful virgin had previously dwelt, became terrestrial, faint, and feeble. The powerful source of the *tincture*, wherefrom the virgin had her power, without being subjected to sleep, left Adam and went into its own principle." (*Three Principles*, iii. 8.)

> Thus Adam became a victim of Magic, and now his magnificence was gone. Sleep signifies death and surrender. The terrestrial realm had conquered him and ruled over him." (*Menschwerdung*, i. 5.)

> "After the lust of the spirit of this world had conquered in Adam, he fell asleep. Then his celestial body became flesh and blood, and his strong power became rigid bones. Then the celestial virgin went into the celestial ether, into the principle of power."[65] (*Three Principles*, xiii. 2.)

This impotency was to be a means of salvation for Adam, and moreover there was given to him the terrestrial woman in the place of the celestial virgin, who had passed away from him.[66] This was done to save him from arriving at a still greater depth of degradation.[67]

> "When Adam left God and entered into selfishness, God permitted it to happen that a deep sleep fell upon Adam. If it had not been for that circumstance, he would in his selfishness even have become a devil by the power of the fire."[68] (*Stiefel*, ii. 363.)

[64]God (divine self-consciousness) never sleeps; it is only nature in man that causes him to sleep and wake alternatively. No man is fully awake and self-conscious as long as he has not found his own god.

[65]The "history of Adam" is nothing else but the history of mankind as a whole. Its truth may be recognised by every one capable of self-examination.

[66]Adam having lost the power to recognise the true woman, the eternal virgin within himself, it was necessary that he should have an external objective substitute to whom he might be attracted, so as to stimulate his power to love; which would have entirely died out without such an object, or would have degraded him still lower by turning into desire for still lower beings in the scale of evolution.

[67]From such a degradation may have resulted the tribe of the monkeys descended from aboriginal man. (See *Secret Doctrine*, by H. P. Blavatsky.)

[68]The "*Sal-nitre*" means the fiery material element in man, wherein reside his sensual attractions; in other words, his *Kama-rupa*.

118

"When the devil saw that lust resided in Adam, he acted still more powerfully upon the *Sal-nitre* in Adam, and infected it still stronger. Then it was time that the Creator should build him a wife, who afterwards indeed caused the sin to be acted out, and who ate of the evil fruit. Otherwise, if Adam had eaten of the tree before the woman was made out of him, he would have fared still worse." (*Aurora*, xvii. 21.)

Therefore woman (spirituality) is, and will always be, the saviour of man.

The woman was extracted from all the powers of Adam. Relatively to her substance, she was formed out of a "rib," which at that time had not yet degenerated into stiff bone.[69]

"Eve has been extracted from Adam, not as a mere spirit, but entirely substantial. It should be said that Adam received a cleft, and that the woman is bearing Adam's spirit, flesh and bone." (*Three Principles*, xiii. 14.)

"Reasoning says, 'If Eve has been made out of a rib of Adam, she must be very inferior to man.' This is, however, not so, but the *Fiat*, in its aspect as sharp attraction (the first quality), took her from all essences and qualities of each power of Adam."[70] (*Three Principles*, xiii. 18.)

"Adam's body had not yet received hard bones and osseous substance. This took place only when Eve tasted the apple and gave to Adam to eat thereof." "It is true that the infection and the terrestrial death were already in him as a tendency and deadly disease, but the 'bones' and 'ribs' were nevertheless still power and strength, and thus Eve was created out of that power or strength which (later on) was to become *rib*."[71] (*Three Principles*, xiii. 13.)

Eve was not misshaped. She lived with Adam in Paradise; but the pure likeness of God was then in neither of them.

"Eve was not misshapen, but very lovely; nevertheless she too bore the signs (of corruption), and could not be anything more than a wife of Adam. Both were still in Paradise, and if they had not eaten from the

[69]The woman is made out of the more refined and spiritual essences of man; for this reason woman even to-day is more refined and intuitional than man; while the organisation of the body and also the mind of the male is on the whole more gross and material; and he reasons where woman perceives. There were not all the female elements removed from man in the creation of the woman. If man had no such elements in him he would be a brute. Neither could any woman be visible and tangible and man's associate if she had none of the male and grossly material elements of Adam in her organisation.

[70]It was a part of the higher and more celestial elements which left "Adam" at the time of the creation of "Eve."

[71]It may be well to remember that at the time of Jacob Boehme it was considered a crime to disbelieve even in the literal and external interpretation of the Bible allegories, and that his explanations would have been incomprehensible and unacceptable if his expressions had not been such as to correspond with those of the Bible.

tree, but turned to God by changing their imagination, they would have remained in Paradise." (*Three Principles*, xiii. 36.)

"Adam and Eve had still a paradisiacal consciousness, but it was mixed with terrestrial desire. They were naked, and had animal organs for procreation; but they did not know this, neither were they ashamed of them, for the spirit of the great world had not yet obtained rule over them before they had eaten of the terrestrial fruit." (*Menschwerdung*, i. 6, 15.)

"No one can truly say that Eve, before coming in contact with Adam, had been a pure and chaste virgin, because, as soon as Adam awoke from his sleep, he saw her by his side. He soon imagined into her (fell in love with her). He took her unto himself and said, 'This is flesh of my flesh and bone of my bone. She will be called *woman*, because she has been taken from man.' Eve likewise began to put her imagination into Adam, and each one ignited the desire of the other. Where, then, is the pure chastity and virginity? Is this not animal? Has not the external image become an animal?"[72] (*Forty Questions*, xxxvi. 6.)

God had ordered mankind not to eat from the fruits of the tree of temptation; but the devil thought of inducing them to disobey the command, and they were, moreover, incited to do so by the spirit of the world, and by their own perverted desire.

"The holy-speaking Word of God, after the Trinity of the unfathomable Godhead, gave to the fiery intelligence of the soul the command, 'Eat not of the tree of knowledge of good and evil; or, if you do that, you will die in the image of God on the same day.' That is to say, 'the fiery soul will lose her light, and thereby mortality, the quality of the dark world, from the centre of the first three principles, will creep forth and manifest itself in the tree, and swallow up the Kingdom of God therein.'" (*Grace*, vi. 17.)

"When Adam and Eve were in Paradise as man and woman, being still in possession of a celestial essence, although the latter was mixed (with materiality), the devil would not suffer this to be so, for his envy was great. Then, after Adam had been brought to fall and deprived of his angelic form, and seeing that Eve was his wife, the devil thought that they might generate children in Paradise and remain therein. He then made up his mind to seduce them to eat of the forbidden fruit, so that they might become earthly thereby." (*Menschwerdung*, i. 7.)

"Adam was urged on by the power of the tree, which was also within himself, so that one lust infected another. He was also urged by the spirit of the great world, so that his strength became overpowered."

[72]Woman in all departments of life is a saviour of man. Even the most degraded woman may be a saviour for still more degraded man, by keeping alive in him a feeling for an ideal—a low ideal, it is true, but one that keeps him from sinking into still lower depths, and which may become more refined. The mission of woman to save man ceases only when man has found the celestial virgin within himself.

(*Three Principles*, xi. 40.)

For the purpose of seducing mankind, the devil availed himself especially of the services of the serpent, which, being a living symbol of the tree of temptation, caused them to imagine that, by eating the forbidden fruit, they would become godlike.[73]

"The devil introduced his poisonous imagination into the human quality. Therefrom resulted in man the ardent desire to eat of evil and good, and to live in the self-will; that is to say, his will left the harmony of unity and went into the multiplicity of the qualities. The devil, by means of the serpent, represented to him that he would become like God, and that his eyes would open; which then actually took place in the fall, so that they could now recognise, taste, see, and feel evil and good."[74] (*Mysterium*, xvii. 37.)

"The devil mixed lies and truth together, and said to the first human beings that they would be like God. His meaning was that they would be so, according to the first principle of wrath; but about the Paradise he said nothing." (*Three Principles*, xvii. 96.)

"The substance of the snake, its celestial aspect, was a great power, as there was likewise a great celestial power in the devil, for he was a *prince* of God. Thus he introduced his cunning and lies into a strong state of will, for the purpose of making illusions therewith as his own god." (*Mysterium*, xx. 16.)

"The imagination of the devil poisoned the substance of the serpent, so that the latter, in consequence of the division of its powers that formerly were in paradisiacal unity, formed itself into a serpent. Thus he used the snake as his instrument."[75] (*Letters*, xxxix. 21.)

"The snake was a living symbol of the tree of temptation. The tree of temptation was in mute power, and the serpent was in a living power, and the serpent attached itself to that tree, being of its own nature."[76] (*Mysterium*, xx. 20.)

After Adam had introduced his perverted desire into Eve, the latter was the first to be seduced to fall away from God.[77]

---

[73]The "serpent" is the *astral light*, in whose folds and temptations the will of man is entangled.

[74]Evil desires always enter the heart of man silently and worm-like, until the soul becomes entangled therein as in the folds of a serpent.

[75]The serpent is not himself the devil, but the devil is the evil will that causes the serpent to move.

[76]There is no mortal man to whose tree of life the serpent of desire is not attached during his terrestrial existence.

[77]If woman represents the will and man the intellectual power of mankind as a whole, it naturally follows that the will was seduced by the desire before the intellect followed in its track. If the intellect had become seduced first, it would have become separated from the "woman," and man would have become a clever fool, an intellectual maniac, an unspiritual but cunning scientist, without any soul or faith—a "materialist."

"The lust originated in Adam, but thereupon this perverted desire began to be excited in the woman." (*Stiefel*, ii. 375.)

"Eve was lusting after the fruit of the tree of knowledge of good and evil, but there was the prohibition before her, and she was afraid of God, and did not want to act against the prohibition. Then the devil entered into the substance and cunning of the snake, and turned this power and craftiness around, so that Eve could see and know that the serpent was very artful and cunning. She clung to the forbidden tree, and it did her no harm; but she looked at the serpent and fell in love with his cunning and cleverness, also with his agility and artfulness, and she lusted to eat of the tree. The serpent advised her to do so by the sound and voice of the devil, and pretended that he derived his cunning and artfulness from the tree." (*Mysterium*, xx. 22.)

"The devil told her that the fruit would do her no harm, but that the eyes of her understanding would be opened, and she would be like God. She thought it would be a good thing to be a goddess, and she consented; and in consenting she fell from the divine harmony, from the peace in God, and from divine faith, and entered with her desire into the serpent and into the cunning, the desire, and vanity of the devil."[78] (*Mysterium*, xx. 25.)

While the devil was desirous directly for the fire-life, man at first was only desirous after the terrestrial things, but thereby his lust of pride began to arise.

"The devil went with his imagination into the fiery foundation, but Adam into the watery quality." (*Signature*, vii. 4.)

"Unlike Lucifer, Adam did not actually desire to awaken the first principle; his desire was rather to taste good and evil—that is to say, the vanity of the earth." (*Mysterium*, xviii. 31.)

"In the external part of the soul originated the terrestrial lust to eat of the manifold qualities; but in the interior fiery part of it originated lust for pride, to know evil and good, and to be like God."[79] (*Mysterium*, xviii. 30.)

Thus the first act of the great drama ended, and a god became a man. In the second act He rises again upward toward His former divine state, no more innocent and ignorant of evil, but taught by experience,

---

[78]Actual "sin" begins only where there is a knowledge of evil. A mere evil desire does not constitute "sin" as long as the desire has not the consent of the intellect.

[79]The more man seeks for the object of his existence in external and sensual things, the more will he depart from his spiritual faith or point of gravitation from his own divine centre or God. He becomes experienced in external and superficial things, and loses sight of that which is real and divine. His external knowledge, which after all is only imaginary, as it deals only with passing illusions, awakens his pride and self-conceit; he begins to assert his personality against immortality; he becomes cruel, and selfish, and passionate; and unless he be redeemed by the awakening of spirituality within himself, he will end in awakening in him the "fiery foundation," the principle of evil, the "devil." Instead of the Christ, Lucifer will be revealed in him.

knowing and wise, a conqueror over "matter," and a true Lord over all.

Chapter VIII
Nature, or the Third Principle

"The godless seeks for God outside of his own self, and the Christless sectarians seek for a personal Christ in history; but the man of God and the true Christian know God and Christ within their own soul."

"We surely believe in a personal and historical Christ; but only after Christ has become personal in a man will he realise the true nature and vocation of Jesus the son of Jehovah."—JOHANNES.

THE image of everything that ever existed was in the light at the time when God began to create a new world. The external world, to which Adam had become subjected in consequence of his degradation, has its origin in God's eternal nature and its prototype in His wisdom, wherein it was spiritually contained from the beginning. We may compare the external world to the imagery seen upon a screen, upon which it has been projected by the light of a magic-lantern. The images represent the world, the pictures on the slide the ether, and the light itself is the Spirit of God.

> "The third principle, the spirit and torment of this world, has been hidden from eternity in eternal nature, and was discovered by the light-flaming spirit in God's wisdom and the divine tincture. Then the Godhead moved according to the nature of the producing mother, and the great Mysterium was born, wherein was contained everything that is within the power of eternal nature. This, however, was only a Mysterium, and had no resemblance to any created being. There everything was as if (mixed) together, like a cloud of dust."[80] (*Menschwerdung*, i. 1, 10.)

> "If we rightly consider the creation of this world and the spirit of the third principle, or the spirit of the great world with its stars and elements, we find therein the qualities of the eternal world as if in a state of mixture; wherein Deity willed to manifest the eternal wonders that were hidden, and to bring them into objective existence." (*Six Theosophical Points*, ii. 6.)

> "The external world, in being born (coming into objectivity), makes for itself a new *principium* or beginning. The generatrix of the temporal is a reproduction of the eternal generatrix, time originates in eternity, and even here eternity, with its wonderful production, appears, in its powers and capabilities, in an especially temporal form and shape."[81] (*Mysterium*, vi. 10.)

[80]The external consciousness was hidden within the internal one, in the same sense as the character of a tree is hidden within the seed.

[81]We find the same fundamental law in all departments of nature. A new world is only a "nebular spot," a dust of cosmic matter, as long as it has not formed an organised centre. Likewise man resembles a "*nebula*" of unlimited extent, of which only the organised kernel (the physical body) is visible; and so man begins to exist as a spiritual being only when the universal Spirit takes form within his soul.

In this external world, called the third principle, there are manifest two powers—the holy divine power and the power of the darkness. The latter is even preponderating.

> "The third principle, or the visible elemental world, is an issue of the first and second principles, which is produced by the motion and outbreathing of divine power and divine will. In it is figured the spiritual world according to light and darkness, and brought into a created (objective) condition." (*Tabulæ Principiæ*, 5.)

> "The external world has been outbreathed from the holy and from the dark world. It is, therefore, evil and good, and in love and wrath; but, compared with the spiritual world, it is only like a smoke or a fog." (*Mysterium*, iii. 10.)

> "The word moved the *Fiat* in all forms of eternal nature, in harmony with the world of light and the world of darkness; so that the desire after the quality of both worlds entered into being. This caused good and evil to originate in the essentiality, and thereby was created the external visible world, with stars and elements as a particular life." (*Stiefel*, i. 31.)

> "This terrestrial world is based upon the world of darkness, and if the good had not been also embodied therein, there would be in it no other doing than that of the world of darkness; but this is prevented by the divine power and by the light of the sun."[82] (*Six Theosophical Points*, ix. 17.)

> "This world is rooted in evil and good, and there can be neither one of them without the other. But the great misfortune in it is that evil is preponderating therein over good, and the wrath stronger than love, and this is due to the sin of the devil and of man, who excited nature by their perverted desires, so that the world is now powerfully qualified in wrath, acting like a poison within the body."[83] (*Mysterium*, xi. 15.)

That the darkness has obtained so much power in this world is not the fault of God, but it is due to Lucifer, who corrupted the primordial creation, and who in consequence of Adam's fall is now still more enabled to act within the dark element of nature.[84]

> "Within all nature there is a continual wrestling, battling, and

---

[82]The visible sun in the sky is the exterior manifestation of an invisible spiritual power. As the visible sunlight dries up swamps and destroys impurities, so is the spiritual sunlight opposed to the evil influences that arise from the astral plane.

[83]Nature exists in universal man, and he is existing in her. Nature receives her consciousness from man, and as the will in him has become tinctured with evil desires, so nature—the product of his imagination—became tinctured with evil likewise.

[84]Neither Christ, nor "Lucifer," nor "the Antichrist," is, as the vulgar interpretation has it, outside of the soul of the world, but a power active within the latter, in the same sense as a man's disease does not exist outside of his own body, but within it.

devouring, so that this world may truly be called a valley of sorrow, full of trouble, persecution, suffering, and labour; for when the spirit of creation went into the middle, it had to form the world from the midst of the kingdom of hell." (*Aurora*, xviii. 112.)

"Nature, up to the day of judgment, has two inherent qualities; one is lovely, celestial, and holy, and the other one wrathful and hellish. The good quality works with great diligence for the purpose of producing good fruits under the influence of the Holy Spirit, and likewise the evil quality labours for the purpose of producing evil fruits, receiving power and incitement thereto by the devil." (*Aurora*, Preface, x. 10.)

"The devil resides in this world, and he continually infests external nature; but he has his power only in the wrath, in bitter desire."[85] (*Menschwerdung*, i. 2, 4.)

God acts with the holy power of his inner world against the corrupting power of Lucifer, but the external world is not thereby changed in its own particular essence.[86]

"The inner world, the world of light, dwells in the external world, and the latter receives power from the former. She blooms in the external power, but this power knows nothing of it." (*Six Theosophical Points*, vi. 2.)

"The powers of eternity work through the powers of time, like the sun that shines through water, while the water does not apprehend the sun, but only receives the heat; or, like a fire, which glows in the iron, but the iron remains iron nevertheless." (*Mysterium*, xii. 20.)

"The spiritual world is hidden within the visible elementary world, and acts through the latter, and by means of the *separator*, or the soul of the outer world, it shapes itself in all things according to the character and quality of each thing; but the visible being receives the invisible one not in its own power, neither does the external thing become changed into the inner one, but the inner power merely takes shape therein, as we may see if we observe the growth of herbs, trees, and metals." (*Contemplations*, iii. 19.)

"We see that the earth has a great hunger and desire after the power and the light of the sun, and likewise the external being craves for the interior one. Thereby it receives the form of the latter as a light and power, without, however, being able to grasp the interior spirit itself;

[85]If it had not been for Lucifer's seduction and Adam's fall, primordial man would have remained for ever in blissful ignorance of the lower qualities, in a spiritual state, which he could not have fully enjoyed, because he did not know its opposite, namely, suffering. Thus the devil brought suffering into the world, and is therefore man's benefactor; provided that man learns by the experience afforded to him in this way, and does not become absorbed by evil, but conquers it.

[86]If it were not for the omnipresent and superior power of good, there would be no possibility for man to conquer his evil desires. This absolute good is the One, without which the Two (relative good and evil) could not exist.

for the spirit does not dwell in the exterior, but has possession of its own self in its own interior state."[87] (*Six Theosophical Points*, vi. 9.)

God exercises this blissful power especially by means of the sun, who, being a true image of the divine heart of love, illuminates all the visible world, and restrains the wrath of the dark world.

> "The Godhead, the divine light, is the centre of all life, and likewise in the manifestation of God the sun is the centre of life." (*Signature*, iv. 17.)

> "God the Father generates love by means of His heart, and the sun symbolises His heart. He is in the external world a symbol of the eternal heart of God, which gives to all beings and existences their power." (*Signature*, iv. 39.)

> "God gave to the external world the light, by the out-breathing of His power through the rays of His light, and with the sun and the moon He rules within the things of this world. The stars take their light from the outpoured radiance . of His light, and by means of this very light God ornaments the earth with beautiful plants and flowers, and makes glad everything that lives and grows. (*Prayer*, xlvii.)

> "This world has a natural God of its own, namely, the sun; but he takes his being from the fire of God, and this again from the light of God. Thus, the sun gives his power to the elements, and they give theirs to the creatures and herbs of the earth." (*Six Theosophical Points*, v. 13.)

> "The abyss of hell is in this world, and the sun is the only cause of the existence of water, and of the fact that the depth above the earth is lovely, pleasing, mild, and delightful." (*Threefold Life*, vi. 3 6.)

> "All that is powerful in the essence of the holy world is hidden in the wrath and curse of God in the quality of the dark world; but it blooms by means of the power of the sun and the light of external nature through the curse and the wrath."[88] (*Mysterium*, xxi. 8.)

As the sun rules over all the terrestrial world, he must be present in his essence and power everywhere in that world.

> "The sun is not very different from water, for water has the quality and essence of the sun. Without that the water would not receive the light

---

[87]The earth, like every other cosmic body, is a form of manifestation of will, and has a sensation of its own. Every part of the earth strives for the full enjoyment of the beneficent sun-rays, and when arriving at the meridian it would fain stand still, as if in mute adoration and worship of the glory of the celestial orb, but is pushed on by those parts that follow. Thus every part alternately embraces the sunlight and sinks again into darkness once during the daily revolution of our planet.

[88]The world is the body of universal man; the spiritual sun is his heart, and the moon is the symbol of his imagination (or fancy). The true meaning of Boehme's writings, like those of the Bible, will only be understood if we cease to look upon the cosmos from our limited personal point of view, and, by becoming identified in our consciousness with the All, realise that the All is our Self.

of the sun. Although the sun is a body having a form, nevertheless the essence of the sun is also in water, but not manifest. In fact, we recognise that the whole world is all *sun*, and the locality of the sun would be everywhere if God would want to ignite it and cause it to become manifest, for all existence begins in the light of the sun."[89] (*Six Theosophical Points*, vi. 10.)

"If God would ignite the light by means of the heat, the whole world would be sun (manifest), for the power of the sun is everywhere, and before the body of the sun existed the whole locality of the world was as shining as the sun is at present, but not so insupportable, but mild and delightful."[90] (*Aurora*, xxv. 63.)

The planets are also ruled by the sun, from which they receive their powers, and they communicate these powers in their turn to terrestrial objects.

"The sun is the centre of the constellation (solar system), and the earth is the centre of the elements. Both, if compared with each other, are like spirit and body, or like man and woman. But the constellation has still another woman, wherein it breeds out its substance, namely, the moon, she being the wife of all the planets, but especially of the sun."[91] (*Mysterium*, xi. 31.)

"As the stars, full of desire, draw unto themselves the power of the sun, likewise the sun penetrates also powerfully into the stars, so that they receive their light from the power of the sun. The stars then send again their ignited power as their product into the elements." (*Grace*, ii. 26.)

But as the stars have their origin from the world of light and from the world of darkness, not only the good, but also the evil, existing in the terrestrial world comes from them.

"With the creation of the constellation good and evil became manifest, for in them is manifest the wrathful fiery power of eternal nature, as well as the power of the holy spiritual world, as an outbreathed essence. Thus there are many dark stars which we cannot see, and there are

[89]It may be remarked that at the time of Jacob Boehme it was not generally known that the sun has a hydrogen atmosphere, nor that water was composed of oxygen and hydrogen, the most combustible gas.

[90]The same doctrine applies to the light of the spirit. The Christ-spirit is everywhere; but it is not manifest in every person. Little would it benefit the blind to know of the light merely from hearsay. Little would it profit the "Christian" if he knew of a historical Christ, and could not perceive the glory and majesty of the *Atma Buddhi* within his own soul. Boehme says—

"The light and the power of Christ arises within His children in the interior foundation and illumines the whole course of their life. Within this fountain of light is the kingdom of God in man. He who is not in possession of it cannot bring it into himself by means of any creed, opinions, or theories; but if he possesses it, then from that fountain will arise many streams of pure love." (*Communion* v. 18.)

[91]So with the mind of man, it being the "constellation of stars, thoughts, and mental powers wherein he lives," he receives its light from the divine sun that shines in the centre of his own being. There are thoughts of which we are conscious, and others which remain hidden until they are called forth by that power which rests in the spirit of man.

many shining ones which we see."[92] (*Mysterium*, x. 36.)

"The evil, like the good, in all things comes from the stars; and as the creatures upon the earth are in their qualities, likewise are also the stars." (*Aurora*, ii. 2.)

"All that lives and exists is awakened and brought to life by the stars, for they are not only fire and water, but they also possess hardness and softness, sourness and sweetness, bitterness and darkness, even all the powers of nature, and everything that is contained in the earth." (*Threefold Life*, vii. 46.)

"The constellation is the cause of all arts and science, also of all order and harmony in this world, because it awakens the trees and metals, enabling them to grow. In the earth is everything that is contained within the stars; the constellation ignites the earth, and all this taken together is only one spirit."[93] (*Threefold Life*, vii. 48.)

In their relations to the earth and the elements, the stars act the part of a higher, living, and, so to say, male power.

"The stars are a quintessence, a fifth form of the elements, and, so to say, the life of the four." (*Threefold Life*, vii. 45.)

"The starry sky rules in all creatures as it were in its own property. This sky is the man, and 'matter,' or the watery form, is his wife, who gives birth to what heaven creates."[94] (*Three Principles*, vii. 33.)

"The upper desires the lower and the lower the higher. The hunger of that which is above is directed powerfully to the earth, and the hunger of the earth strives for that which is above. Thus, compared with each other, they are like body and soul, or like man and woman, generating children with each other." (*Grace*, v. 19.)

But it must be understood that there is a distinct life in the earth. This is proved by her products, and also by her desire for the sun, in consequence of which she is continually turning around.[95]

"If you behold the earth and the rocks you will acknowledge that there

[92]This is also asserted in Sinnett's *Esoteric Buddhism*. Ideas have their regular revolutions in the mental world, comparable to the planets in the sky. They arise and disappear from the mental horizon of the individual, and also from that of humanity as a whole, according to cosmic laws.

[93]To realise the nature of the relation existing between the macrocosm and the microcosm, it is necessary that man should learn to realise his own existence as a macrocosmic being. Without such a practical realisation, a merely theoretical study of such mysteries is difficult, and of little use.

[94]All material forms are nothing but ultimate expressions of ideas, shaped into forms by thought and caused to grow and become objective by the power of will which is inherent in everything.

[95]There is only one universal life; but its action becomes differentiated and modified in each individual form by the qualities of the latter. It then becomes therein, as it were, a distinct and separate life, differing not in essence but in quality from that of other forms. This individual life constitutes the individuality of the form. The external expression which results from the action of this individual life constitutes the personality.

is a life in them; for if this were not so, there would be in them neither gold nor silver, and neither herbs nor grasses." (*Aurora*, xix. 57.)

"Each being desires the other. That which is above desires that which is below, and the lower desires the higher. Thus the earth is filled with hunger after the stars and after the *spiritus mundi*, so that they have no peace." (*Clavis*, 110.)

"The earth is turning around because she has both fires, the hot and the cold fire, and that which is below always desires to rise upwards towards the sun, because she receives spirit and power only from the sun. Therefore she is turning. The fire, her desire for light, is turning her, for it wishes to be ignited, and to have a life of its own. Having nevertheless to remain in death, still it desires after the life above and attracts the latter, and opens its centre for ever to receive the *tincture* and fire of the sun."[96] (*Threefold Life*, xi. 5.)

The four elements are actually only qualities of the true one element, which is hidden behind the external four elements.

> "That which we call at present four elements are in fact not elements, but merely qualities of the one true element." (*Three Principles*, xiv. 54.)

> "The quintessence is a paradisiacal substance in the celestial world, but enclosed in the external world; that is to say, not imprisoned therein, but only rendered invisible." (*Clavis Specialis*.)

> "Fire, air, water, and earth have issued from the centre of nature, and consisted in the ignition of one substance. Since that ignition took place they appear in four forms, which are called 'elements;' but they are still interiorly, and in reality there exists, only one. There are not four elements in heaven, but only one; but all four states are contained therein." (*Threefold Life*, v. 105.)

From this superterrestrial basis have proceeded the external terrestrial elements. There was first separated from it the fire, next the air, then the water, and finally the element of earth.[97]

> "The four forms which are hidden within the one true element have become active by means of the ignition or excitation of the lower principles, and they now appear in their external substance comprehensible to the creatures." (*Threefold Life*, v. 105.)

---

[96]If the whole world is a manifestation of consciousness, there can be nothing absolutely unconscious in it. Each thing has its own state of consciousness, but is not necessarily therefore self-conscious or aware of its own qualities. If it were so, the world would be a hell.

[97]The same order may be observed in the microcosm of man. First comes the desire, which is of a fiery nature; then the idea, which is still airy and indefinite, but which becomes concrete as a thought by the aid of the "watery element," and ultimately there results the act or the material corporification.

"From the fire originates the air, and from the air the water, and from the water earth; *i.e.*, a substance which is of an earthly nature, and thus the elements are merely an external manifestation of the inner eternal element and an ignited smoke of the latter." (*Mysterium*, vii. 19.)

The elements having issued from their original unity, strongly desire each other, but at the same time there are dissensions and strifes among them.

"The four elements are only qualities of the one in-differentiated element. Therefore there is a great anxiety and desire among them. They constitute interiorly only one sole principle, and therefore they instinctively long one after the other and each seeks for the inner principle within each other." (*Clavis*, 106.)

"After from the one element, which has only one single will, the four elements had originated, which are now existing in one single body, there is among them much strife and dissension. Heat is against cold, and fire against water; the air is against earth, and each causes the death and breaking-up of the other." (*Signature*, xv. 4.)

In many of the products of the earth—for instance, in many of the minerals—the true essence seems to be entirely hidden in death; but in others, especially in the noble metals and precious stones, it still manifests its brightness.[98]

"It seems strange to the reasoning mind, if we observe the earth with its solid rocks and its rough and harsh appearance, that big rocks and stones have been created, whereof a part is useless, and which are only an obstacle for the creatures of this world." (*Mysterium*, x. 1.)

"The terrestrial consciousness corrupted the celestial one, and the former became the *Turba* of the latter. Likewise, the *Fiat* made the earth and stones out of the eternal essentiality." (*Menschwerdung*, i. 9.)

"But in the earth we find still another *tincture* hidden away which is like the celestial one, especially in the precious metals."[99] (*Six Theosophical Points*, vi. 2.)

"Gold is nearly related to the divine substantiality or celestial corporeity. This would be seen if we could dissolve the dead body of the gold and cause it to become a volatile, active spirit, but this is only possible by means of the power of God."[100] (*Signature*, iii. 39.)

[98]In the mineral kingdom precious stones may be compared to the eye in the animal realm, in so far as the same is said to be the mirror of the soul; *i.e.*, of the interior quality.

[99]All forms are expressions of originally spiritual powers, and the qualities of such powers are more manifest in precious stones than in any other material substance.

[100]For this reason it requires the possession of divine power to practise alchemy. It is a divine and not merely a "natural" science.

"As far as precious stones are concerned, carbuncles, rubies, delphines, onyx, &c., they have their origin there where the flash of light arose within love. This flash is born in meekness, and is the heart in the centre of the sourcive spirits. Therefore are such stones so mild, lovely, and at the same time so powerful."[101] (*Aurora*, xviii. 17.)

As it is in regard to the mineral kingdom, so it is in regard to the vegetable and animal kingdoms. There the power of death has also penetrated into everything; but there also are formations existing which show a relationship with the paradise.

"Before the fall the paradise was efflorescing through all trees and through all the fruits which God created for man. But when the earth was cursed, the curse penetrated into all fruits, and now everything became good and bad. In all things was death and rottenness, which formerly was only in the one tree, called the tree of knowledge of good and evil." (*Threefold Life*, ix. 15.)

"The fruits of the earth are not entirely in the wrath of God, for the incorporated word, being immortal and imperishable, was blossoming out again in the body of death, and produced fruits from the mortified body of the earth." (*Aurora*, xxi. 24.)

"Some animals, especially the tame ones, are closely related to the one element; others, especially the ferocious ones, have more relationship with the four elements." (*Three Principles*, xviii. 10.)

"There are poisonous animals and worms grown out of the wrathful quality, and formed after the centre of the dark world. They love to dwell only in the dark, and hide themselves away from the sunlight. Furthermore, there are many creatures which the *spiritus mundi* has formed out of the realm of phantasy, such as monkeys and certain animals and birds, who like to play pranks and torment and disturb other creatures, so that one is the enemy of the other, and they are all fighting against each other. On the other hand, there are also good and kind creatures, made after the type of the angelic world, such as the tame animals and birds: among them, however, there are also bad qualities to be found." (*Grace*, v. 20.)[102]

In each external thing there is hidden an eternal and imperishable something, which issues again in an ethereal form out of the degraded body of the terrestrial substance.[103]

"In each external thing there are two qualities, one originating from

---

[101]For the true signification and magic powers of precious stones see "*In the Promos of the Temple of Wisdom.*"

[102]For description of the elementals inhabiting the astral plane see *Paracelsus.*

[103]The spiritual being is the one that is not subject to the dissolution of the physical form, but "reincarnates" periodically; that is to say, it creates for itself again other forms in which it may find to a certain extent an outward expression. (Compare *Myster. Magn.*, 29, 45.).

time and the other one from eternity. The first or temporal quality is manifest, the other one hidden." (*Signature*, iv. 17.)

"In the beings of this world we find everywhere two beings in one— first, an eternal, divine and spiritual being, and then one that has a beginning, and is natural, temporal, and corruptible. The outbreathed desire—that is to say, the love of the divine power for nature, wherefrom nature and self-will have originated—is longing to get rid of the natural perverted self-will, and is destined, at the end of time, to be free of the illusion thus acquired, and to be brought into a clear, crystalline nature." (*Contemplations*, i. 30.)

"Behold a tree. Outwardly it has a hard and rough shell, appearing dead and encrusted; but the body of the tree has a living power, which breaks through the hard and dry bark and generates many young bodies, branches, and leaves, which, however, all are rooted in the body of the tree. Thus it is with the whole house of this world, wherein also the holy light of God appears to have died out, because it has withdrawn into its principle, and therefore it seems dead, although it still exists in God. But love ever again and again breaks through this very house of death and generates holy and celestial branches in this great tree, and which root in the light." (*Aurora*, xxiv. 7.)

All these external formations proceed from the fire-life by means of the *tincture* and the oily, spiritual quality, which manifests its power and activity in contrast with the elements.[104]

"Each thing is like a fire. However, the torture of the fire is not a true life, but the tincture that originates from the fire." (*Threefold Life*, viii. 18.)

"As the spirit is in a thing, so is the *tincture*, for the tincture issues from the spirit and is its delight." (*Three Principles*, xiii. 45.)

"Where a desire exists there is a fire, for the fire desires substantiality, so that it may have something to consume. It cannot make for itself any substantiality, but it makes a *tincture*, and that tincture produces the substantiality." (*Threefold Life*, viii. 33.)

"The *tincture* produces all colours, because it introduces the quality of fire and light into the water. Thus it also transforms water into blood." (*Six Mystical Points*, i. 5.)

"The oily quality is in stones, metals, herbs, trees, animals, and men. The deadly quality is in the earth, in water, fire, and air. Those four qualities are, in fact, like a dead body; but the oil therein is a light or a life, wherefrom results the desire or the growth, the outblooming from this deadly quality. The oily quality could not, however, be a life if it

[104]In other words, each thing is an expression of will-power. The will alone, however, does not constitute its true consciousness; the latter results from the action of the will upon the imagination.

134

were not in the anxiety of death. The latter arouses the former, and renders it movable, because the oily quality desires to fly from the anxiety, and to issue from thence, and thereby the growth is caused. Thus death itself has to be a cause of life and motion." (*Signature*, viii. 5.)

The external appearance or *signature* of things is a symbol of what they actually are in their inner essence, or of what principle is preponderating in their character, and therein is the basis of the language of nature.

"All the external visible world, in all its states, is a symbol or figure of the internal spiritual world. That which a thing actually is in its interior is reflected in its external character." (*Signature*, ix. 1.)

"That principle which in the spirit of its action is superior to the rest, engraves its character principally upon the corporeal being, and the other qualities are only secondary additions to it, as may be seen in all living creatures." (*Signature*, ix. 4.)

"The inner form characterises man, also in his face. The same may be said of animals, herbs, and trees. Each thing is marked externally with that which it is internally and essentially. For the internal being is continually labouring to manifest itself outwardly. Thus everything has its own mouth for the purpose of revealing itself, and therein is based the language of nature, by means of which each thing speaks out of its own quality, and represents that for which it may be useful and good."[105] (*Signature*, i. 11–17.)

[105]See *Magic, White and Black.*

135

Chapter IX
Generation

"Let every Brahman, with fixed attention, consider all nature, both visible and invisible, as existing in the Divine Spirit. For when he contemplates the boundless universe in the Divine Spirit, he cannot give his heart to iniquity."—MANU.

GOD evolves the centre of light from eternity to eternity within Himself, and likewise there is in the soul of man a desire to penetrate into the second principle and to live in the light of God.[106]

"The soul in its substance is a magical gush of fire from the nature of God the Father. She is an ardent desire for the light. Thus, God the Father very strongly, and from all eternity, desires his heart, the centre of the light, and He generates it in His desiring will out of the quality of the fire." (*Four Complexions*, ii.)

"God makes also the second principle in His love, wherefrom He generates from eternity to eternity His eternal word and heart, and the spirit ignites the bond of nature, and renders it luminous in the love and the life of His heart by the power of the light. Likewise the soul of man desires to penetrate into the second principle, and to still its hunger with the power of God." (*Threefold Life*, i. 11–13.)

But if the soul, as has been the case with Adam, does not surrender her will to God, then will the divine idea not become annihilated, but is rendered inactive in man.

"The soul has the seven qualities of the inner spiritual world (modified) according to nature; but the spirit is without any qualities; it is outside of nature and in the unity of God. By means of its fiery nature the spirit becomes manifest in the soul, because it is the true likeness of God, an idea wherein God Himself acts and resides, provided that the soul enters with her desire into God and surrenders her will to Him. If this does not take place, then will that idea, namely, the spirit, be mute and inactive, like a picture in a mirror that has faded and is without substance, as was the case with Adam in his fall." (*Tabulæ Principæ*, 66.)

"It should not be supposed that the celestial *Ego* of man had become a nothing. It has remained in him, but in his (personal) life it was then like a nothing. It was then hidden in God and inconceivable to man, and without (manifested) life." (*Mysterium*, xx. 28.)

---

[106]It is the principle of light in man that causes him to seek for the light, and to desire that it should become manifest. If man were something entirely different from God, and had consequently nothing divine in him, he would be an atheist, incapable of conceiving of justice or truth, and have neither any desire nor understanding for that which is divine.

"The essence of the soul, that issued from the unfathomable will, has not died. Nothing can destroy it. It remains for ever a free will. But it lost the divine state, wherein was burning the light of God and the fire of His love. Not that the latter has become a nothing, although within the created soul it became like nothing (unmanifested), and unconscious; but the holy power, that is to say, the spirit of God, which was the active life therein, became hidden." (*Grace*, vi. 2.)

If the soul thus permits her true light and life to be extinguished, then it naturally follows that her opposite power, the principle of wrath, becomes perceptible (conscious) in her.[107]

"As the word or heart of God takes its origin in the light of the majesty, in the eternal fire-tincture of the Father, likewise is this the case with the image of the soul. The true image of God resides in the light of the soul-fire, and the fiery soul must draw that light from the love-fountain in God, in His majesty, by means of her imagination in God, and surrender of her self-will to God. If the soul does not do this, but imagines within herself, in her own fierce forms or states conducive to the fire-torture (passion), and not in the fountain of love, then will her self-torture arise from her harshness, acridity, and bitterness, and the image of God will be swallowed up in the wrath (the dark fire)." (*Eye*, xiii. 15.)

"The soul is *per se* a fire-torture, and contains within herself the first principle, the harsh acridity, which has for its object the fire. If from this birth (evolution) of the soul is withdrawn the mildness and love of God, or if she becomes infected with very strong matter (gross material desire), she will then remain a severe harshness, consuming itself, and nevertheless continually generating new hunger within her own will." (*Menschwerdung*, i. 2.)

Thus has man, by his withdrawal from God, attracted unto himself the wrath of God and opened for himself the kingdom of hell, and he now forms in himself hellish figures.[108]

"After Adam had lost the pure and beautiful image, his soul stood then only in the quality of the Father; that is to say, in eternal nature, which, apart from the light of God, is a wrath and a consuming fire." (*Tilk*. i. 285.)

"By means of the fall there was in man a door opened in the wrath of God, namely, hell. The jaws of the devil were opened, and thereby was inaugurated the realm of illusion." (*Grace*, vii. 7.)

[107]In proportion as the will of man is not controlled by reason, that will becomes unreasonable and follows its lower impulses.

[108]To express this in other words, we may say that the will of man ceased to act within his own higher nature, *i.e.*, the celestial virgin of divine wisdom, wherein his power was united to sweetness, and became active within the lower and animal elements of his constitution, so that brute passion took the place of divine self-conscious will. This animal will produces corresponding animal images in his soul.

"If we investigate the substance of the soul and its essences, we find that it is the most harsh thing in man; it is fiery, acrid, and bitter. If it entirely loses the virgin of divine power who accompanies it, and from which the light of God (in the soul) is born, it then becomes and is a devil." (*Three Principles*, xiii. 30.)

"After man had entered the realm of his selfish enjoyment and turned his will away from God, he then began to produce hellish figures, such as cursing, blaspheming, and lying." (*Prayer*, 53.)

"We, the poor children of Eve, have to feel within ourselves, in great suffering, sorrow, and misery, how the wrath moves, guides, and torments us, so that we now no longer walk together in the love of God, but, full of poison, envy, murder, and animosity, we persecute each other, we denounce, dishonour, and vilify, wishing to one another death and all kinds of evil, and enjoying each other's misery." (*Tilk.* i. 4.)

"That which malicious persons of this world do in their malignity and falsehood is also done by the devils in the world of darkness." (*Six Theosophical Points*, ix. 18.)

"Each person causes suffering to another, and is therefore the other's devil." (*Threefold Life*, xvii. 10.)

God has, however, given to man protection, so that he may not so easily become a devil, and He did this by causing him to enter into external terrestrial life.[109]

"God caused the soul to enter into flesh and blood, so that she may not so very easily become capable to receive the wrath. Thus (during her terrestrial existence) she enjoys herself in the mirror of the sun, and is glad in her sidereal essence." (*Six Theosophical Points*, vii. 19.)

"Not without cause has God breathed into the nostrils of Adam the external spirit, the external life. Adam might have become a devil, like Lucifer, but the external mirror prevented it." (*Forty Questions*, xvi. 2.)

"Many a soul in her malignity would become a devil within one hour if the external life did not prevent it, so that her complete ignition cannot take place." (*Forty Questions*, xvi. 12.)

"In examining our own selves we find that, on the whole, the external spirit (our human nature) is very useful to us. Many souls would become corrupted if the animal spirit did not hold captive the fire and present to the fire-spirit terrestrial, animal occupation and joy, wherein

---

[109]If man's imagination were not excited by the pictorial representations which the objects of the surrounding world call forth in his mind by means of his external senses, but if his mental activity were restricted to forming images by its own power, his fiery will, from which the recognition of his divine bride has departed, would cause him to become self-conscious in evil. For this reason asceticism without divine wisdom leads to the acquisition of the powers of black magic.

it may amuse itself until it obtains again a glimpse of its nobler image, and begins to seek for it again." (*Forty Questions*, xvi. 10.)

"If the matter of this world (the imagery of external nature) were broken, as it will be broken one day in the future, the soul would have stood in eternal death, in the darkness. The beautiful creature (the living image) would then have been captured by the realm of hell, and the devil would have been triumphing over it." (*Threefold Life*, viii. 38.)

As the soul of man became captured by the spirit of this world, and as she allowed its *tincture* to enter within herself, the terrestrial qualities necessarily arose (became pre-eminently active) in him.[110]

"The poor soul of Adam was made captive by the spirit and principle of this world, and allowed the tincture of this world to enter within her." (*Threefold Life*, viii. 63.)

"That in which the imagination of the spirit enters becomes expressed in the corporeal form by means of the impression of the spiritual desire. Therefore God commanded Adam, when he still was in Paradise, not to eat with his imagination from the tree of self-knowledge of good and evil, so that he should not sink into suffering and death and die to the kingdom of heaven, as has actually occurred."[111] (Baptism, i. 22.)

"The terrestrial quality, which formerly was in Paradise in an unmanifested condition, manifested itself by means of the desire of the soul. From this resulted heat and cold, the poison-life of all adversities, and the supremacy of the body, so that the beautiful image of Heaven and Paradise faded out of sight." (*Stiefel*, ii. 83.)

The bodies of the first human beings were of a spiritual, celestial nature; but, in consequence of eating of the forbidden fruit, they became terrestrial and material.

"God had given to man a body constituted of pure, essential power, after the nature of the soul, and which, if compared with the grossly terrestrial substance, may be looked upon as being a spiritual body." (*Mysterium*, xvi. 3.)

"The body of the first human beings was of a celestial kind; but when they ate of the terrestrial fruit and absorbed it into the bodies the temperature separated, and the terrestrial body became manifest according to all its qualities." (*Grace*, vii. 5.)

"When Eve reached out for the tree and broke the fruit, she did it

[110]Man became an organism wherein the powers of nature are acting, and in identifying himself with nature he began to enjoy and to suffer with her.

[111]Man's constitution resembles a garden, wherein all kinds of seeds, good and evil, are sown. Those which he cultivates or permits to glow will become predominant in him.

through the earthly *limus* and through the will of the soul, which desired knowledge from the centre of nature. In eating actually of the fruit, her body's essence, *i.e.*, the human essence, took in the essence in the tree."[112] (*Mysterium*, xx. 29.)

Man hereby lost the life in eternity, and became subject to death.[113]

"We cannot say of man that in the beginning he was enclosed in time. In Paradise he was embraced in eternity. God created him in His image; but when he fell he became subject to the limitation of time." (*Grace*, vii. 51.)

"Time has a beginning and an end, and as the will with its desire has surrendered itself to the temporal guide, the body dies and perishes therefore likewise." (*Signature*, v. 9.)

"After the fall man with his interior body lived only in time; the precious gold of heavenly corporeity, which should tincture, penetrate and bless the external body, had lost its colour."[114] (*Signature*, v. 8.)

Moreover, the powers of animal life have gained so much room in man, and become preponderating in him to such an extent, that in his external essence he has become an animal himself.[115]

"Man was not, like the animals, created from evil and good (out of the merely terrestrial substance). If he had not eaten of evil and good there would not be in him the fire of the wrath; but now he has also an animal body." (*Aurora*, xviii. 109.)

"Before the sin the celestial image penetrated wholly the external man, clothing him with divine power. The animal element was then not manifested in him; but when that image, formed of the celestial essence, paled and disappeared, then the poor soul, formed out of the first principle, found herself surrounded by the animal body, naked and bare." (*Mysterium*, xxi. 15.)

"After Adam and Eve had eaten from the tree of self-knowledge of

[112]If "Eve" had not plucked the fruit from the tree of knowledge for "Adam," that is to say, if he had not desired it merely in his imagination, but plucked the fruit himself by entering therein with his own fiery will, the consequences would have been still more disastrous to him. The universal man (Adam) would then have become a devil, instead of a semi-animal human being.

[113]This does not mean to say that the true divine and immortal man did lose his immortality; but man in his aspect as a human being became unconscious of his immortality, and is now seeking for external proof for the purpose of becoming convinced that there may be something immortal in him.

[114]The more of man identifies itself with the body and its lower principles, the more of him will die. That part of man which identifies itself with the immortal part within becomes immortal with the latter. Man should, therefore, not identify himself in thought and will with the lower elements in his constitution, but employ the powers of the latter for the unfoldment of his spirituality.

[115]As the whole of the animal kingdom exists in macrocosmic man, likewise the representative forms or germs of all animals exist in the animal soul of microcosmic man, and they grow and become predominant in him according to his predominant animal tendencies or desires. They are the elementals which take possession of godless man and render him subservient to their will.

good and evil, they soon became ashamed, because in their ethereal form there had grown up such a gross animal, made of common flesh and hard bones and animal bowels. The animal being had swallowed up the celestial state, and arisen in them as a creature foreign to their true nature, such as they had not known heretofore." (*Mysterium*, xxiii. 1.)

"Let no one imagine that man before the fall had animal organs of reproduction, neither did he have bowels such as he has now. Such uncleanliness does not exist within the Holy Trinity, nor within Paradise; it belongs to the earth. Originally man was created an immortal being and holy, like the angels." (*Three Principles*, x. 7.)

"By means of the fall man, in regard to his external body, became the animal of all animals; that is to say, he became the animal image of God, wherein the word of God became manifested in an earthly manner. Thus he became a master and king of all animals; but nevertheless only an animal; endowed, however, with a higher intellect than the merely animal forms." (*Grace*, vii. 6.)

The senses of man also became of an earthly and animal nature, so that he is no longer able to perceive God and that which is divine.[116]

"When man left the Paradise and entered into another generation, namely, into the spirit of this world, into the quality of the sun, the planets and elements, then his paradisiacal perception became extinct." (*Three Principles*, xiv. 2.)

"After the fall man became degraded to an animal state of being, so that Heaven, Paradise, and divinity became a mystery to him." (*Menschwerdung*, i. 2, 14.)

"The serpent (of desire) said to Eve, 'You will not die; but your eyes will be opened, and you will be like God.' It is true that her earthly eyes became opened, but her celestial eyes became closed."[117] (*Stiefel*, i. 44.)

Man's will and mind were captured by the spirit of this world, and are now held by one or another element, as is shown by the power of the temperaments.

"The soul entered with Adam into a strange habitation, namely, within the spirit of this world. There are actually four dwellings in which that precious jewel is imprisoned. Of these four there is always one

---

[116]If man were truly to realise his own divine state, there is no power that would retain him against his will in his semi-animal body. He would then be the god which in the course of ages he aspires to become.

[117]In the same sense, the more we cling to merely external pursuits, the more are we liable to lose the power of the true recognition of internal truth, and for this reason we usually find the least amount of spirituality and intuition among those that are very learned. The more we close our eyes and speculate, the less shall we become capable to see.

especially manifest in a person, and not all four, according to the four elements which are within each man, and of which always one predominates in the life of a person. These four states, forms, or temperaments are called the choleric, the sanguine, phlegmatic, and melancholy temperament. In the choleric one is the nature and quality of the fire manifested, in the sanguine that of the air, in the phlegmatic the nature of water, and in the melancholic the quality of the element of the earth." (*Four Complexions*, i. 6.)

Man's enjoyment and desire is now turned away from the divine, and directed towards that which is earthly and animal.

"The angelic image in man became entirely destroyed both as to mind and senses, as we may plainly see at present, both thoughts and senses are shaped by an animal will, and it is very difficult for them to arrive at a state in which they love God and justice." (*Grace*, vii. 36.)[118]

"After the fall the creatures (elementals) obtained -power in man and arose in him. There are persons who live in the quality of a snake, and are full of cunning and poisonous malice; others live in the quality of a toad or a dog, a bear or a wolf; or one may have in him the quality of some good and tame animal. All men are outwardly formed in the human image, but within the quality is seated an animal."[119] (*Grace*, vii. 3, 4.)

Man's present animal method of reproducing himself originated in his fall, as is proved by Eve having been projected from Adam at a later period of time, and also by the inherited sense of shame in regard to the organs of generation.

"If God had created man for this earthly, corruptible, poverty-stricken, sickly, and animal life, He would not have put him into Paradise. If He had originally intended that mankind should procreate themselves like the brutes, He would have made them into men and women already at the start." (*Mysterium*, xviii. 5.)

"The poor degraded soul is ashamed of the possession of animal organs of generation, and of the way in which impregnation takes place. Does not every one feel this? If we had been created beastlike in Adam, why should we be ashamed of our beastliness? Why is it that the soul is ashamed of the monstrosity of her outward body, and of its animal

---

[118]If the senses of man were educated to love that which is true and divine, then would the inner realm become opened to their perception, and man would know "supersensual things."

[119]Every character, when it is to be expressed, finds its expression in a certain form. All the animals in this world are incarnations of certain characters, and likewise the qualities of animal man are expressed in his animal soul (on the astral plane) in corresponding animal forms. The above assertion of Jacob Boehme is, therefore, not a mere figure of speech; but the animal soul of every human being resembles a menagerie composed of different animals, which may be seen by those that are sifted with the astral perception, and according to the quality of the will of man, whereon these animals live, some become sick and die, while others are born and grow. The conditions of these animal elementals in the constitution of man are some of those causes of his bodily ills of which modern medical science is entirely ignorant.

143

method of procreation?" (*Tilk.* i. 608.)

If there had occurred no sin, man, being the living image of God, and therefore possessing the power to create, could have produced his equals out of his own self without the existence of severed sexes.

"The sum of all mankind constitutes the one original Adam. God created him alone, and left it to him to produce other beings. He should have surrendered his self-will entirely to God, and with God generated other men out of himself, and in conformity with himself." (*Mysterium*, lxxi. 31.)

"Adam was a complete image of God, male and female, and nevertheless neither of them separately, but pure like a chaste virgin. He had in himself the desire (power) of the fire and the light, the mother of love and wrath, and the fire in him loved the light, receiving from it calmness and beneficence; while the light in him loved the fire as being its life, in the same sense as God, in His quality as Father, loves the Son and the Son loves the Father." (*Stiefel*, ii. 351.)

"Adam was man and wife in one individuality. However, he must not be considered as having been a woman in the usual sense of this word, but as a pure, chaste, virginal power. That is to say, he had within himself the *tincture* or spirit of fire, and also that of water, and he loved himself and God. He could generate in a virginal state, and procreate by means of his will and out of his own substance, without any pain or laceration." (*Threefold Life*, ii. 24.)

"If man had withstood the temptation one human being would have been born from another, in the same way as Adam in his virginal state was projected into objectivity as a human being and image of God, because that which is of the Eternal can also procreate (multiply) itself according to the law of eternity." (*Threefold Life*, xviii. 7.)

These descendants of man would have issued one from the other, and one would have surpassed the other in his qualities and dignity before God.[120]

"It is unnecessary to know whether, if man had remained in his original state, all (future) individuals would have been the products of one individual, or whether they would have been produced one from another; but in seeking within the depth, in the centre, I find that one would have come from the other. In the course of time they would have differed in their qualities; some would have grown to be superior to others, as is the case at present where not all men are equals, but some have more genius and intelligence than others." (*Menschwerdung*, 1. 5, 4.)

---

[120]This is the way in which the "personalities" mentioned in the Book Genesis were "begotten."

But now, after the generative powers, which were formerly united in man, appear in a state of separation in males and females, each sex seeks within the other the child that is to be generated, and strongly desires to unite with the other.[121]

> "In the beginning of creation all was born from one being, and a separation of sex took place later on. Therefore each sex strongly desires the other, as is seen in the process of procreation." (*Three Principles*, viii. 40.)

> "There is now a strong sexual desire in all creatures. The male spirit seeks for the beloved child in the female, and the female seeks for it in the male." (*Three Principles*, viii. 44.)

> "The water-mother strongly desires for the fire-mother, and seeks for the child of love. Likewise the fire-mother seeks for it in the water-mother, and therefore both sexes have a strong desire to mingle with each other." (*Three Principles*, viii. 42.)

This desire, wherein the two sexes are burning in regard to each other, is an abomination before God; but if it is governed by faithfulness and orderly conjugal love, it is patiently tolerated by the Lord.[122]

> "Conjugal sexual cohabitation is not sinful, because it is in accordance with man's human nature. It is incited by the power of nature, and tolerated in divine patience by the spiritual soul." (*Stiefel*, ii. 409.)

> "Lust, however, without being ennobled by faithful conjugal love, is merely an animal and sinful desire; and if you seek in marriage only the gratification of sexual lust, you are then not superior to an animal." (*Three Principles*, xx. 64.)

> "Beware, O man, as to how you use the sexual animal desire! It is an abomination before the Lord (the divine Being in man), whether it be within or outside of legalised wedlock; but true lawful love and faithfulness hides the desire before the sight of God." (*Three Principles*, xx. 65.)

> "If a couple generate children, their imagination or desire (during the sexual act) is not holy, but the noble part of the soul is ashamed of it. There are even animals that are ashamed of that act. Even in its best aspect the performance is disgusting before the sanctity of that which is divine, it having been caused by sin in consequence of primordial man's degradation, but being patiently submitted to by that which is

---

[121]Since the "woman" has issued from man, his manner of reproduction has necessarily become an external and animal one, and will continue to be so until the true divine marriage has taken place, by which the Will of man becomes again one with the goddess of wisdom.

[122]Each sex seeks within the other that of which it is itself deficient, and therefore, seen from the spiritual point of view, all sexual "love" may be regarded as a manifestation of selfishness.

divine in man, because it is a necessity of his present animal state."[123] (*Stiefel*, ii. 396.)

It is an error to suppose that one person is a descendant from others merely as far as his corporeal form is concerned. The human soul is likewise generated in that manner. If the heart were absent even the body could not come into existence.[124]

> "The soul is not every time created anew and breathed into the body, but she is reproduced according to human natural law, like a branch growing out of the trunk of a tree, or as a kernel or seed that is sown. Thus the soul is sown that it may grow to be a spirit and body."[125] (*Forty Questions*, x. 4.)

> "The souls of men, all taken together, are as only one soul, for they have all been generated out of one soul."

> "The soul is a cause of the existence of all the members necessary for the life of man, for without the soul no organ would come into existence to live in the life of man." (*Three Principles*, xiv. 14.)

> "The heart is the true origin of the soul, and in the interior blood of the heart (the will) is the soul, the fire, while in the *tincture* the soul is its spirit (its light); the spirit floats above the heart, and communicates itself to the body and to all of its organs." (*Forty Questions*, xi. 3.)

In so far as by the connubial act a soul is generated, there is in it even something of a paradisiacal nature.[126]

> "While Adam remained in the love of God, and the woman (the female principle) in him was a chaste virgin, the *tincture* of the fire (in him) could have experienced much joy in the embrace of the *tincture* of the light contained (in him); but the present external body is not worthy of enjoying such an intercourse with the kingdom of delight, wherein the life of the soul is sown. Only the inner essences, which originate (directly) from the Eternal, are capable of participating in

[123]"Sin" is that which constitutes a disobedience against the will of God, which is also the law of nature. He who resists the law of nature without being able to rise above his own animal nature commits a crime against nature, and therefore against God. But if we rise above our animal plane into the higher regions of feeling and thought, then shall we be no longer affected by the laws that govern that animal nature, and no resistance will be needed, as the desires of the flesh do not affect the spirit that is not identified with the flesh.

[124]Here Jacob Boehme evidently refers to the human soul, the *Manas*, and not to the *Buddhi*, or spiritual soul, which overshadows each new incarnation.

[125]The spiritual soul in man has its origin in God, and its individual qualities are gathered from the efflorescence of its experiences in previous incarnations; but the human and animal soul are the products of the mental and astral influences acting through the bodies of the parents; while the visible material form is made of the elements of the earth.

[126]The highest sensual pleasure which human beings can possibly enjoy is experienced by them during the connubial act; but as this act constitutes the exercise of the highest power which is still within man's dominion, namely, the power to create a being like unto himself, therefore this power should not be prostituted for baser motives, such as the gratification of sensual desire.

such happiness; external animal man merely gratifies an animal desire, and knows nothing of the delight of the (spiritual) essences. If, however, the (external and internal) tinctures intermingle, then there is therein something (a sensation) belonging to Paradise; but the earthly essence (lust) soon becomes mixed therewith." (*Menschwerdung*, i. 7, 6.)

"The desire for conjunction in men and women results from the separation of the fire and light-tincture in Adam. These principles in their own essence are still much more noble and pure than the flesh. It is true that they are now separated, and do not contain the true life; but they are full of desire for that true life, and when they again meet with each other in the unity of all being, they then awaken the true life to which their desire is directed. They want to be again that which they were in the image of God when Adam was man *and* woman."[127] (*Stiefel*, ii. 388.)

"When the two tinctures are brought together into one, then the quality of the eternal kingdom of joy, the highest desire and its fulfilment, becomes manifested. If this could be done in purity, and without the admixture of that which causes disgust, then would it all be holy; but even the *sulphur* (the terrestrial element) of the seed is a cause of disgust in the sight of true holiness." (*Stiefel*, ii. 402.)

During the connubial act a divine interaction takes place; but there are also influences coming from the terrestrial and the satanic worlds. More especially is the nature of the child dependent on the quality of its parents.[128]

"The will called into action during the connubial act is threefold. Firstly, there arises between the parents of the child the animal desire to commingle, and during the commingling the centre of love becomes opened, even if they were otherwise dissatisfied with each other. That love then participates in the qualities of the one element, and this element with paradise; but the paradise is before God." (*Three Principles*, xv. 30.)

"On the other hand, the external seed has also its own essences, and they participate in the qualities of the external elements. These external elements participate in the qualities of the external planets, and they

[127]In the male is represented especially the fiery essence (the will or obstinacy), in the female the essence of light (spirituality or gentleness). The sexual distinctions, however, do not belong to the external body exclusively, but to the inner man, of whom the outer man is not always a correct image, because there are other factors besides the true soul entering in his formation. Therefore it sometimes happens that the sex of the external body does not seem to correspond to that of the inner man. We meet with male persons apparently inhabited by a female soul with female tastes and tendencies, and vice versa; and in such persons there are sometimes manifest apparently inexplicable sexual perversities.

[128]It should always be remembered that man's constitution is not the result of the action of only one principle, but of three, manifesting themselves in the seven qualities of eternal nature, in seven different forms, and that, therefore, his external body is not the expression of only one principle, but of three. His spirit is from the innermost fountain, his soul from the internal world, his body from external nature.

are connected with external wrath and malice; while the latter are connected with the abyss of hell, and that abyss belongs to the devils." (*Three Principles*, xv. 31.)

"If a branch grows out of a tree, its form approximates that of the tree. Thus, if a mother produces a child, the child is formed in her own image." (*Forty Questions*, v. 1.)

"An evil tree cannot produce good fruits. If both parents are bad and in the power of the devil, a soul inclined to evil will be sown. It would be well for parents to remember this fact. You are saving up money for your children, but if you would furnish them with a good soul, that would be more useful to them."[129] (*Forty Questions*, x. 7–9.)

"To the extent in which the parents have the essentiality of God connected with their own souls will the seed not be introduced into the Turba; for Christ says, 'A good tree cannot bring forth evil fruit.'" (*Forty Questions*, x. 5.)

Each soul, however, is an individual being, and therefore a child born from bad parents can again turn to God, or the reverse of this may take place.[130]

"Although the soul is a branch from the tree, she is, nevertheless, an individual being. Therefore a child, after being born, has a life of its own, and the centre of nature is within its own power." (*Forty Questions*, vi. 2.)

"Even if a child has good parents, it may afterwards enter into the *Turba*. Likewise a child born of evil parents may become converted by means of its imagination, and enter into the *Word* of the Lord. This rarely takes place, but it is nevertheless possible. God throws no soul away, unless the soul throws herself away. Each soul judges herself."[131] (*Forty Questions*, x. 6–8.)

---

[129]The absence of words in modern languages for expressing internal facts in a comprehensible manner leads to a continual confusion of terms. Thus the term "soul" refers here not to the divine soul that originates directly from God, nor to that part of man which becomes reincarnated (the *Karana Sarira*), but to the "inner man" (the *Manas* and lower lsencippri). Unless this distinction of the various aspects of man is kept in mind, we are always exposed to mistaking the leaves of the tree of life for the branches, and the branches for the trunk, and the trunk for the roots.

[130]Each soul constitutes an individual, but for all that not an independent, part of the tree of life. The trunk (Christ) remains, but the leaves (the personalities of men and women) drop off. The branches (the individual human spirits) grow from year to year, and by the power of the sap which the branches receive through the trunk they produce new leaves (personalities) every spring. Thus it is not the Christ, *i.e.*, the divine, man, who becomes reincarnated; neither do the same identical leaves reappear upon the same tree, but the spirit of man (his higher *Manas*) through the power of Christ (the *Atma-Buddhi*) produces new personalities in whom is expressed the power which the spirit receives from God.

[131]Each soul is receptive of good and evil influences, but especially to such as are predominant in her own nature. Whether or not a soul will inherit the desire or power to overcome the evil in her own constitution, or whether she will be more inclined to evil, will depend on the *Karma* acquired by her in previous incarnations.

Chapter X
The Christ

"The inner element which holds the whole body of this world has become the eternal body of Christ; for the whole of Divinity in the word and heart of God has entered therein in eternity; and the same Divinity has become a created being; but such a creature, as can be everywhere, like Divinity itself." (*Princ.* xxiii. 20.)

"WITHOUT special divine aid, humanity would have gone to eternal perdition on account of the sin."[132] (*Hamberger.*)

"Adam would have been lost eternally if the heart of God with the word of promise had not entered his soul, awakening the spiritual hope which maintained him." (*Forty Questions*, viii. 5.)

"If the divine principle of love were not still pervading all nature in this terrestrial world, and if we poor created beings had not with us the warrior in the battle, we would all be sure to perish in the horror of hell."[133] (*Aurora*, xiv. 104.)

God, on account of His infinite mercy, desired to aid mankind.[134]

"God desires that all mankind shall be saved. He does not desire the death of the sinner, but that he become changed, and turning again to God, find life in Him." (*Three Principles*, Preface, i. 6.)

"(Superficial) reasoning represents God as an unmerciful being, and teaches that He has thrown His wrath upon man, and cursed him to death, because He found disobedience in him. But you should not

---

[132]This does not mean to say that any extracosmic God worried or "studied" about finding a method by which he might save mankind; but the "Heart" of God moved, because its own love caused it to move.

"God is threefold in His personal aspect, and willed to move three times, according to each of these aspects, but not in eternity. At first there moved the centre of nature in the Father, for the purpose of creating the angels, and through them the world. The second time the quality of the Son moved, whereby the Heart of God became Man, and this will never take place again in eternity; but whenever it now takes place, it will occur merely through this only (universal) Man (Divinity in Humanity), who is God, manifesting Himself through and in many. For the third time, and at the end of the world, God will move in the name (quality) of the Holy Spirit, when the world will return into the Ether (*Akasa*), and then its dead will be resurrected." (*Threefold Life*, vii. 22.)

This may perhaps be expressed in other words by saying: At the first impulse the latent will became active, at the second move the latent wisdom or light, and at the third move or impulse the third principle will enter from the latent state into activity.

[133]Whether such an event took place some 1900 years ago or at any other date may be left to the historian to find out. At all events, the Bible account is a description of the redemption of the world from spiritual ignorance by the entering of a ray of the light of God, and likewise of the spiritual regeneration of man. The external "Christian" Church, with its ritualism, is based upon a belief in a person of Jewish history, who died and left his powers in the hands of the clergy. The religion of the living Christ is based upon the recognition of an eternal process going on in the macrocosm of nature and in the microcosm of man. To the externally-reasoning "liberal" Christian, Jesus of Nazareth, whether He ever existed or not, represents the type of an ideal man, a teacher who, by example and words, taught men virtue. To the internal perception of the seer He is the type of the personification of the divine *Logos* in man.

[134]The expression "God" is here not to be taken as the primordial absolute Will, but as God in His aspect as the Father.

believe this. God is love and goodness, and in Him there is no angry thought. Man would be all right if he had not punished himself." (*Three Principles*, x. 24.)

There was no other way to save mankind, except that the Son or the Light of God should enter into them.[135]

"When the soul went out of the light of God and entered into the spirit of this world, then began the torment of the first principle. She saw and felt herself no longer in the kingdom of God, until the heart of God came and appeared between her and that kingdom, so that she could enter therein and become regenerated." (*Three Principles*, ix. 6.)

"There was no other salvation for the divine image in man unless divinity had moved according to the second principle, *i.e.*, according to the light of eternal life, and by the power of love rekindled the substantiality (of the soul) that was imprisoned in death." (*Menschwerdung*, i., 11, 22.)

"The soul has separated her will from the will of the Father and entered into the lust of this life. There could have been no other way of redemption, except that the pure will of the Father should again enter into her substance and bring her again into the state which she formerly occupied, so that her will would be directed again into the heart and light of God." (*Three Principles*, xxii. 67.)

"If the soul was to be aided, the heart of God with its light, and not the Father Himself, had to enter her, for in the Father she was anyhow; but she was turned away from the entrance to the generation of the heart (the beginning of the divine self-consciousness) of God, and her desires were directed towards this external world."[136] (*Three Principles*, xxii. 68.)

The preparations for that redemption were already made before the creation of this world, as the name of *Jesus* was embodied in man.[137]

"The name of *Jesus* embodied itself into the *tincture* of the soul in Paradise when Adam fell, and even before Adam was created; as *Peter* mentions in his first letter (i. 20), where he says that we have been

---

[135]God never went outside of universal man, neither did His light become extinguished in him. In its macrocosmic aspect the "re-entering" of that light may be compared to a ray of light in the centre of a body penetrating to the periphery. In its microcosmic aspect it is comparable to the life giving power of the sun, awakening the life in an individual organism.

[136]The true Christ is, therefore, neither an "Adept" nor a "*Mahatma*," nor a Reformer, a mortal person, nor anything whatsoever that differs from God, but he is Divinity itself manifesting itself in Humanity, and thereby saving mankind as a whole, and each individual person separately considered, from ignorance and suffering, to the extent as mankind or such an individual person receives Him (the light) in him or her. The redemption from spiritual darkness depends on the presence of the redeeming power of the spiritual light within the darkness itself.

[137]As the future regenerated Man, the second Adam was contained hidden within the first Adam; likewise the name of *Jesus* was hidden in the name of *Jehovah*, the latter being Himself Universal Man.

150

provided for in Christ, even before the foundation of the world was laid." (*Menschwerdung*, i. 8. 1.)

"The name *Jesus* was incorporated into the image of eternity as a future Christ, that it may become a redeemer of men, and out of the dying in the wrath regenerate them again into the pure being of divine and paradisiacal power." (*Stiefel*, ii. 74.)

"The word which God spoke in regard to the power that was to bruise the head of the serpent, was a spark of love from the divine heart of God, and therein has the Father from eternity seen and elected humanity. In this spark of divine love-light the whole world was to live, and Adam was already therein while his creation took place, as is also expressed by *Paul* (Eph. i. 13), where he says that man was elected in Christ before the foundation of the world was made."[138] (*Three Principles*, xvi. 107.)

As long as Adam had not ceased to resemble God, the Redeemer within him did not render Himself perceptible. This, however, took place immediately after the fall.[139]

"From all eternity stood the name *Jesus* in immovable love in man as the image of God. But when the soul lost the light, then the Word spoke the name of *Jesus* into what was movable; into the faded *ens* of the heavenly world's substance."[140] (*Grace*, vii. 34.)

"Before the fall Adam received the divine light out of *Jehovah;* that is to say, out of the one only God, wherein was hidden the name of *Jesus*. But during the time of suffering when the soul fell, God manifested the treasure of His glory and holiness, and by means of the living voice of the Word He incorporated Himself with the divine fire of love into the eternal image, representing the banner of the soul, which she was to follow as a guide. But if she was not able to penetrate therein, being as one dead relatively to God, nevertheless the divine breath penetrated into her, and warned her to stop her evil activity, so that its voice might again begin to become active within the soul." (*Grace*, vii. 32.)

"As Adam manifested in himself the centre of wrath, God instituted opposition to evil, and manifested in him the power that bruises the heel of the serpent, which heretofore, at the time when sin had not yet

---

[138]Christ (*Atma-Buddhi*) being Divinity in Humanity, there can be no other Redeemer than He, because man cannot be saved from mortality in any other way than by becoming immortal; nor can he become immortal unless he does become divine. ("That which is unclean cannot enter the kingdom of cleanliness.") The reason why the divine *Logos*, in its aspect as the "Christ" or Redeemer, is not spoken of as an "it," but as "He," is evidently because the Word, by becoming human in man, naturally assumed the qualities of man.

[139]There was no occasion for the voice of conscience to speak in "Adam" as long as he had not acted against the Law.

[140]From all eternity there was in man latent the power of becoming divine; but that power did not act as long as there was no cause to incite it to do so. This cause was created by the second moving of the fundamental will (of God).

appeared, had been hidden (latent) in the power of God, and in Jesus as the love of God, in divine unity."[141] (*Stiefel*, ii. 161.)

The power of the future Redeemer became first of all active in Eve.[142]

"The in-speaking of the devil, wherefrom evil will originated, took place in Adam while he was still man and woman, and yet neither the one nor the other, but an image of God. From Adam it penetrated into Eve, who began to sin. Then occurred the in-speaking of God, and this took place at first in Eve as the mother of all mankind, and opposed itself through her to the consciousness of sin that had begun to be manifested in Adam." (*Grace*, vii. 47.)

"Not in the *tincture* of man, which represents the fiery essence, did the word of promise desire to become incorporated, but in the *tincture* of the light, in the virginal centre, which was to generate magically in Adam, in the celestial substance of the holy generatrix, because in that tincture of light the fiery soul-essence was weaker than in the fiery nature of man." (*Mysterium*, xxiii. 43.)

"Not through Adam's fire-tincture was this event to take place, but in and through Adam's light-tincture, wherein the love was burning that had become separated from him to constitute woman, the mother of all mankind. It was she in whom the voice of God promised again to introduce the living, holy substance from heaven, and to generate anew and in divine power the faded image of God that was contained therein."[143] (*Grace*, vii. 18.)

This, however, did not take place in her terrestrial body, but in her celestial essence, which on account of the sin had weakened.

"When God said, 'I will put enmity, and the seed of the woman shall bruise the head of the serpent,' then the holy voice went from Jehovah into the weakened celestial substance of the woman for the purpose of introducing therein a new living and celestial state, and to conquer the kindled wrath of God by means of the most exalted divine love, whereby the monstrosity and its desire should be entirely killed and exterminated." (*Mysterium*, xxiii. 29, 37.)

"The voice of God, speaking to Eve, entered into the seed of the woman; but the true woman was the eternal virgin, and this virgin became revealed by the power of the voice speaking into her in the name of Jesus, which (name) had evolved from Jehovah, and promised that in the fulness of time the holy, celestial love-essence would again

141"Jesus" means "Wisdom." Divine wisdom is love.

142Woman, being on the whole more refined, more submissive and intuitional than man, is also more receptive for the germ of true spirituality.

143Whether a person is of the male or the female gender, it is always in his or her female elements (in the intuitive faculties, and not in the fiery will), that the divine and redeeming power of the love-light becomes first manifest.

be introduced into the weakened image."[144] (*Grace*, vii. 33.)

From Eve, out of whom the Saviour as an incarnation was to issue in the fulness of time, the blissful power radiated and expanded over the whole of humanity.[145]

> "God spoke into the image of Adam, that had become weakened relatively to its divine life, His holy word, 'The seed of the woman shall bruise the head of the serpent.' By the action of this voice the destitute soul regained a divine life, and this very voice (inner consciousness) was perpetuated from man to man as the covenant of mercy." (*Grace*, vii. 16.)

> "Christ was perpetuated in all men as a glowing spark of divine light, according to the quality of the true image, and as a potentiality (or seed of immortal being), but, as a matter of course, not in the external flesh of the terrestrial world, but within the second principle." (*Stiefel*, ii. 318.)

> "The word that had been incorporated in the seed of Eve became perpetuated from man to man in his celestial part as a sound (conscience) or spark of the divine and holy fiery light, until the time when Mary was awakened, when the time for the fulfilment of the covenant had arrived and the doors of the closed chamber were opened."[146] (*Mysterium*, xxiii. 31.)

This event could not take place earlier on account of the great depth of human corruption, but in the minds of those that were willing to submit to divine mercy this power resisted Satan, and even awakened prophets among them.[147]

> "Christ remained in Adam and Eve as a divine mystery, and did not take human substance in them. He remained motionless until the time (for His manifestation) arrived; only then He moved within the seed of

[144]The "seed of woman" is the universal female principle, the celestial image which finds its reflection and representation in terrestrial woman, upon the earth. For this reason woman is more beautiful than man. Beauty in a male results from the presence of the female principle of beauty in him, combined with his strength. Strength (rigidity) without mildness (harmony) cannot be beautiful.

[145]"Eve " means the celestial woman, the vehicle of the divine spirit, wherein the divine will moves, in a terrestrial aspect.

[146]Jesus of Nazareth represents the incarnation, personification, and fruition of the divine Logos in man. Likewise Mary represents the personification of the celestial virgin-mother, the universal celestial kingdom which furnishes the conditions necessary for the unfoldment of divinity in humanity.

[147]It is obvious that, as Universal Man became more and more differentiated in His external forms as individual powers or human beings, the original power contained in Him must also have remained in all His successors; but as there may be millions of seeds of a plant while only one of them finds the conditions necessary to grow into perfection, likewise the Atma was in all human beings, but not active in their material nature, while in Mary it is represented as having begun to stir and to become incorporated in visible form, manifesting itself outwardly and externally as an incarnation of divine power. If we apply the rules laid down in the *Secret Doctrine*, the appearance of the Christ—*i.e.*, the incarnation of the divine Word, or the awakening of the Divinity in. Humanity—would have had to take place during the middle of the fourth race in the fourth "round."

the woman." (*Stiefel*, 448.)

"The seed of the woman received its anointment by means of the motion of the name of Jesus only in Mary, but not in Adam, Abel, Enoch, Noah, Isaac, Jacob, and David. The ancient prophets did not know Christ in their seed, and that He had moved within their carnal seed, but only within their spirit and soul, within their desire for faith (spiritual knowledge)."[148] (*Stiefel*, ii, 453.)

"The (astral) soul of Adam and Eve and of all human beings was still too rough, unmanageable, and impregnated by the first principle. Therefore the Word and the bruiser of the head of the serpent did not enter into form within their souls; but it stood within the mind to oppose the devils and the kingdom of hell with those that were willing to surrender themselves to it." (*Three Principles*, xviii. 26.)

"The saints of God being prophets, and prophesying in the spirit of Jesus, all spoke aiming at the covenant, *i.e.*, out of the promised *Word*, which was again to move within the flesh; that is to say, that the *Word* was contained within the weakened interior image, and unfolded itself, and indicated to the external man what was to happen to him in the future, when it would manifest itself, and destroy therein death and the loathsomeness resulting from the battle taking place within the forms of life."[149] (*Stiefel*, 385.)

As our progenitors (in their terrestrial aspect) were governed by external reasoning, Eve believed that in giving birth to Cain the bruiser of the head of the serpent had already come into the world.[150]

"Hear and see what was Adam and Eve's desire before and after the fall. They desired the terrestrial kingdom, and Eve's mind was directed to terrestrial things. When she gave birth to Cain she said, 'I have the Man, the Lord.' She thought that he was the one whose heel was to bruise the head of the serpent, and that he was to drive the devil away.

[148]"*Adam*" is the trunk of the tree representing humanity. He is the primordial man, or the collectivity of the first "anthropoid beings" (spirits;—not apes), which were of an ethereal kind.

"*Abel*" and "*Cain*" are the two branches of that tree.

"*Cain*" represents the external, sensual realm; "*Abel*" the supernatural—*i.e.*, transcendental kingdom.

"*Enoch*" means the outbreathing of life and reconceiving of it within itself, such as constitutes contemplativeness.

"*Noah*," the end in the beginning; the "*Word*" that enters from the end into the beginning.

"*Isaac*" is the prototype of the kingdom of grace.

"*Jacob*," the uprising and consolidation of the spiritual will coming from the fiery will.

"*David*," the power of grace arising from the submission of one's personal will to one's divine will. (Compare *Mysterium Magnum*.)

[149]The "*Christ*," the light, existed therein essentially, but not substantially. It was a state of feeling, but not of understanding. It may be compared to the heat in a body, which renders the body hot; but not luminous, until the ignition takes place.

[150]"*Eve*," the soul of the world, had not yet become spiritually enlightened enough to produce a divine being.

She did not think that it was for her to die to her own false, earthly, and fleshly will, and to be reborn in a divine will. Such a (selfish) will she carried within her seed, and Adam likewise, and from that resulted the will in the soul-essence.[151] The tree produced a branch of its own nature, for Cain's thoughts were bent upon becoming a lord of this earth. As Cain saw that Abel was higher in the love of God than he, his free animal will arose for the purpose of killing Abel, for he cared only for the possession of the external world, and to be lord therein, while Abel was seeking only for the love of God." (*Mysterium*, xxvi. 23.)

As an antithesis to Cain, there was born to Adam another son, namely, Abel, who was not so much an image of his earthly as rather of his celestial essentiality, that had been restored to a certain extent by divine mercy.[152]

"After the fall Jehovah spoke the name of Jesus in Adam into an actual life; that is to say, he manifested it in the celestial being that had been weakened on account of the sin. In consequence of this in-speaking, there was awakened out of the spiritual death or state of dying, into which Adam had sunk, a divine desire once more, and this awakened desire was the beginning of faith. This very desire separated itself from the quality of the false desire, and formed an image, and thus Abel came into existence; but Cain was the product of Adam's soul-quality, according to his earthly lust." (*Grace*, ix. 101.)

Thus Abel on the whole, and especially on account of his forcible death which he suffered, represented an anti-type of the Redeemer.

"Relatively to his external human state, Abel was also sinful; but in his interior the angelic world and image of Paradise began to bud. Then the interior man put his heel upon the monster-serpent of false desire, and on the other hand the monster-serpent stung the heel of his angelic will." (*Mysterium*, xxviii. 2.)

"The killing of Abel's external body by Cain symbolises that the external man must be mortified in the wrath of God. The wrath must kill and consume the external image that has grown in the wrath, but from its death springs forth the eternal life." (*Mysterium*, xxviii. 14.)

"Abel, representing an antitype of Christ, who was to suffer death for humanity, had to pass through death without having produced fruits or branches; for the fruit which Christ was to generate was the tree of humanity, that was to be reborn in the spirit, but not new branches of the old one. Thus Abel, as the anti-type of Christ, was to produce no new branch from his loins." (*Mysterium*, xxix. 22.)

[151]"Eve imagined that in Cain she had produced *Jehovah*, the future King of the external world; and likewise the apostles supposed that Christ Was going to establish au external kingdom." (*Three Principles*, xx. 50.)

[152]It should be remembered that these allegorical names do not refer to individual men, but to states of the universal mind.

In the place of Abel, Adam was to produce a third son, namely, Seth, in whom was to be perpetuated the line of generation from which the Saviour was to be born in the flesh.[153]

> "Adam, by means of his Eve, was to produce still another branch from the tree of life, a son, who would be in his image similar to Adam and like himself, namely, Seth; (a race) wherein a ray of the love-will is perceived within the fiery will; being, however, still imprisoned by the essence of the external world, the corrupted house of (matter which afterwards became) flesh." (*Mysterium*, xxix. 24.)

> "In Seth the line of the covenant was perpetuated, wherein Christ was to manifest Himself relatively to the tree of humanity." (*Mysterium*, xxix. 26.)

To Cain also was shown the mercy of the Lord, who protected him against his hellish enemies, so that he might repent.[154]

> Cain was afraid that the spirits (elementals) that had influenced him to commit murder would kill him. To prevent this God decreed that whoever should take away Cain's life should be punished eternally through the seven qualities of the world of darkness." (*Mysterium*, xxix. 55, 58.)

> "By the command, 'Upon him who kills Cain vengeance shall be sevenfold,' the terrible avenger, the abyss of hell, was driven away from Cain, so that he did not fall a victim to despair. Cain had departed from God, but nevertheless the kingdom of heaven was before him, so as to enable him to turn and enter into repentance. God did not want to reject Cain, but merely his wicked murder and his false belief." (*Three Principles*, xx. i.)

Cain and his descendants, however, preferred to give themselves up to mundane desires and occupations, while the generation of Seth entered into divine contemplation.

> "Cain was made of flesh and blood, and understood not these words about eternal death; but being assured that no one would kill him, he became again glad, and began to turn to terrestrial arts; not only to agricultural pursuits, but also to working the metals." (*Three Principles*, xxi. 5.)

> "From the descendants of Cain resulted the arts as a wonder of divine wisdom acting in and through nature, but in Seth the Word entered into spiritual contemplation." (*Mysterium*, xxx. 2.)

---

[153] "*Seth*" is a ray of love-light escaping from the fiery will. (*Mysterium Magnum*, xxix. 24.)

[154] If "*Cain*"—*i.e.*, the external "church,"—had been annihilated, there could have been no further progress therein. The destruction of the intellect would make an end to all prospects of its becoming spiritual.

In the descendants of Noah—Sem, Ham, and Japhet—are represented the mental tendencies of the three principal races of mankind before the flood.[155]

"After the first terrestrial world of human quality had been drowned in the flood, its form became reconstituted again in Noah and his three sons." (*Mysterium*, xxiv. 30.)

"Sem represents the world of light; Japhet the world of fire, wherein, however, the light is visible. Japhet also represents an image of the Father, and Sem that of the Son; but Ham is an image of the external world."[156] (*Mysterium*, xxxi. 10.)

From these fundamental directions result the different fates of these races, such as they were already predicted by Noah.

"The configuration of Sem descended upon Abraham and Isaac, for there the Word of the covenant was manifested and contained within the sound; but Japhet's configuration went through the wisdom of nature in the realm of nature, and from that originated the heathen (intellectual but unspiritual people) who were giving (preeminently) attention to the light of nature (natural things). Thus Japhet—that is to say; the destitute, imprisoned soul, belonging to eternal nature—lived within the "huts" of Sem—*i.e.*, within the covenant—for the light of nature lives in the light of grace, constituting a form or a conceived state of the unformed light of God. Ham's descending line overshadowed animal man, formed from the *Limus* of the earth, wherein is the curse, and from that resulted the sodomitic semi-animal race, that pays attention neither to the light of nature nor to that of grace in the covenant." (*Mysterium*, xxxiv. 14.)

"Noah said, 'Praised be the God of Sem, and Japhet shall live in the huts of Sem.' Here by the expression 'God of Sem,' is meant the holy Word in the covenant, and how it would manifest itself, that the Japhites or heathen—that is to say, those who lived only by the light of

---

[155]"*Sem*," the outbreathing of divine power.

"*Ham*," a breath from the centre of nature, conceived within the "flesh."

"*Japhet*," the will penetrated by light.

[156]In regard to the Bible allegories Boehme says:—

"The written Word is only an instrument wherewith the Spirit leads. The Spirit must be alive in the literal form. Without this there can be no divine teacher, but only teachers of letters; only reciters of stories." (*Regeneration*, viii. 6.)

"Christ alone is the Word of God, teaching by means of His children and members the way of truth. The literal Word is merely a guidance and symbol, a testimony to illustrate and represent objectively to man what Christ has done (and is doing) for us; so that we may draw and conceive our faith therein; but then we should enter with our desire into the living Word, into Christ Himself, and become ourselves born to life therein." (*Mysterium*, xxviii. 53).

"Babel does not like to hear it if it is taught that Christ Himself has to be the teacher within the human spirit. They call upon the written Word, and say that if they teach that, then would the Spirit be poured out. Oh yes! All right! I claim the same thing. If the Word is taught in the spirit and power of Christ, then is this so." (*Mysterium* xxviii. 51).

nature—would come to the light of grace that was manifested in Sem, and thus enter into the 'huts of Sem' and live therein. But Ham, the spirit of fleshly lust, was to become a servant of the children of light, according to his quality and selfhood, because the children of God were to force him to become submissive to Him and take away his scoffing self-will."[157] (*Mysterium*, xxxiv. 31.)

The name of Abraham had not a terrestrial meaning, and in this, as in many other respects, he was an anti-type of Christ.[158]

"The great name which God was to give to Abraham in his seed was not to be taken in an especially terrestrial sense; for Abraham was upon this earth like a stranger, owning no principality or kingdom. He was to be in the promised seed and blessing a stranger upon the earth, and therein resembled Christ, whose kingdom was likewise not of this world."[159] (*Mysterium*, xxxvii. 23.)

Nevertheless the sons of Abraham represent the same antithesis as those of Noah and Adam.

"Isaac was not made entirely of celestial essence, but of both—namely, of Abraham's Adamic essence and of the word conceived of faith, or the substance of Christ; but Ishmael was only of Adam's own nature according to the corrupted quality, and not from the conceived word of faith, which was acting with superior strength upon Isaac."[160] (*Mysterium*, xl. 13.)

---

[157]Those are the favoured people of God in whom lives the light of Christ, and not those who exclaim, "Lord! Lord! " using the name of Christ in vain, while the devil is occupying their souls. Boehme says:—

"All beings are created out of the Father. The Father is in all and maintains everything. He gives to all life and substance, and the Son is in the Father and gives to all things power and light. He is our light, and without Him we cannot know God. How can we, then, say anything about Him? If we wish to speak of Him truthfully, we must speak out of His Spirit, because He testifies of God." (*Threefold Life*, xi. 90.)

[158]"Abraham," a collection of people—*i.e.*, of minds—in whom spirituality has become manifest. (See *Mysterium Magnum*, xli. 1.)

[159]This again goes to show that Boehme's conception of these intracosmic powers and processes had nothing in common with the narrow views of orthodox "Christianity," which sees in those Biblical personifications nothing but terrestrial men and women.

[160]These representations of intracosmic powers, personified in the Bible, are all to be found in the theogonies of the "heathen," although under different names.

"The saints in their teachings and writings did not all use the same words, but what they taught and wrote was all out of one spirit." (*Three Principles*, xxvi. 19).

"The Spirit of Christ in His children is not bound to a certain form, so that He could say nothing but what is found in the writings of the apostles; but as the Spirit was free in the apostles, and as they did not all use the same expressions, but were all teaching in one spirit and foundation, each one as he was influenced by the Spirit to speak, likewise the Spirit of Christ still speaks out of His children, and needs no previously prepared formula of the literal Word, but itself reminds the spirit of man of that which is contained within the letter." (*Mysterium*, xxviii. 52).

"You need not be surprised that reason is manifesting itself in many different forms, in one in a way different from that of the other, and that the children of God do not all speak the same language and words. Each one speaks out of the wisdom of the mother, whose number is without beginning and without end. Their aim is the heart of God, wherein they all meet. This, then, is the test by which you must know whether the spirit speaks out of God or out of the devil." (*Threefold Life*, v. 73.)

The same may be said about the sons of Isaac, in whom there is plainly represented an image of the first and the second Adam, and of the final conquest of the first by the second.[161]

"Esau and Jacob both, and also the races descending from them, have originated out of one seed. The former, coming solely out of the Adamic nature, was the greater one, and comparable to the first man whom God created in His own image, which image, however, became corrupted and died relatively to God. The other one (Jacob) came also from the same Adamic nature; but in that nature was the realm of grace in the essence of faith, constituting a conqueror. Even if the latter was inferior according to the Adamic nature, nevertheless God was (more) revealed in him, and therefore the greater one was to serve and be subject to the smaller one. It is not shown that Esau became subject to Jacob, but the story represents to us a spiritual symbol, showing how the kingdom of nature in man was to become subjected and to be made to submit in humility to the kingdom of grace; how it should become entirely submerged in divine humility, and out of that humility become regenerated." (*Mysterium*, lii. 29.)

"Upon Esau followed Jacob as the image of Christ, conceived in the essence of faith and clinging to Esau's heel. The Adamic image created by God had to be born first of all and to live eternally, but not in its gross and animal state of existence. With the expression of 'Jacob holding on to Esau's heel' is symbolised that the other Adam, namely, Christ, should be born after the first Adam, and grasping him from behind, draw him back from the direction of his own self-will into the first matrix, wherein nature originated, so that he might be newly born." (*Mysterium*, lii. 37.)

"Esau was born of holy parents, and represented an image of corrupted nature only in regard to his state of separation. God separated also the image of Christ from the same seed of Esau's parents (as Jacob), and put it before him as a contrast to his brother (Esau). Moreover, Jacob by his gift and humility excited the greatest compassion in Esau, and therefore we should not condemn Esau."[162] (*Grace*, ix. 121.)

More important than these opposites are those of the descendants of Japhet, because they selected for themselves false gods from the powers of nature, and were now led by them by means of oracles.

"The idolatry of the heathen consisted in their departing from the one only God and turning to the magic generation of nature, selecting false gods from the powers of nature."[163] (*Mysterium*, xi. 6.)

[161]"*Esau*," gross, sensual nature. (*Mysterium Magnum*, iv.)

[162]Evidently all these Bible allegories represent cosmic processes which have actually taken place in the history of the world. They are, so to say, the genealogy of Humanity, in which at the fulness of the times the Divinity became manifest.

[163]The "heathen," then, seem to be those prehistoric races that were cultivating magic arts.

"The heathen worshipped the planetary system and the four elements, because they knew that these ruled the external life of all things. Thus by means of their intellectually conceived word they entered into the likewise conceived and formed (manifested) word of nature. On the other hand, the spirit of the formed word of nature became a part of themselves, and thus one intellect moved the other. The human intellect moved the intelligence within the soul of the external world as far as the desire of the latter is concerned, and by means of this intelligence (residing within the *astral light* or the mind of the external world) the prophetic spirit out of the Spirit of God indicated to them how in future times the formed word of external nature would manifest itself in the up-building and in the destruction of kingdoms, &c. Out of this soul of the world the heathen received answers by means of their images and idols, because their faith which they very powerfully introduced into them moved them; and this has therefore not all been accomplished by the devil, as it is supposed by those who, knowing nothing about the mystery, make the devil responsible for everything, while they are ignorant of what either God or the devil is." (*Mysterium*, xxxvii. 10–13.)

Those heathen who led a pure and blameless life arrived at a knowledge of the symbols of celestial things by means of their ability to see within the mirror of external nature.[164]

"The heathen remained within their own magic, but those who went out from the desire of corruption and entered into the light of nature, because they did not know God, but who, nevertheless, lived in purity, these heathen were the children of the free will, and in them has the spirit of freedom unfolded great wonders, as may be seen in the works of wisdom which they left behind them." (*Terrestrial and Celestial Mysterium*, viii. 9.)

"In those heathen that were highly intellectual in the light of nature the interior holy realm was mirrored, and although the true divine intelligence was closed to them, and although they beheld merely an external reflection, nevertheless at the restoration of all beings, when the veil will be removed, they shall live in the huts of Sem." (*Mysterium*, xxv. 24.)

Not only in the "Israelites" (in spiritually awakened races), but also in the "heathen" (in those races that lived on a more material plane) was active the power of the Redeemer (the Word), that had been spoken into Eve, and thereby into all mankind.

[164]"The mysteries of nature were not so deeply hidden to those (prehistorical) peoples as they are to us, because they were not so deeply hidden (immersed) in materiality and sin. Therefore they knew the relationship between the paradisiacal (ethereal) forms of nature and their corporeal visible embodiments. They knew the qualities and the true nature, not only of animals, but likewise of plants and minerals. Man himself was the heart of all beings, and he created them. He could therefore give to each its appropriate name, as if he were in these things himself, and (felt and) experienced their conditions himself." (*Three Principles*, xxi. 8.)

"Adam issued from the one only God, and entered into a selfhood, into ignorance, and he led us all with him into that ignorance (or misunderstanding); but then came the grace out of the same one and only God, and is offering itself to all those that are ignorant, to the heathen as well as the Jews." (*Mysterium*, lxx. 78.)

"The heathen were not out of that seed of Abraham with which God made a covenant; but the first covenant, the word that had been in-spoken in mercy, was as a foundation in them. Therefore, says Paul (Rom. ix. 24), that God had not called and elected merely the Jews in their covenant, but also the Gentiles in the covenant of Christ, and that He called 'My people' and My 'beloved' those that did not know Him, and who, not knowing Him, were not His people in an external sense. The proposition of grace, which had incorporated itself by means of the in-speaking in Paradise after the fall, was contained in them, and according to that God called them His beloved ones. Only the children of wrath must be excepted, because in them the incorporation of the name of *Jesus* does not take place, but only the incorporation of wrath. The latter, however, never extends over whole races, but merely over such individuals among them as are like thistles among the wheat."[165] (*Grace*, x. 24.)

Before the Redeemer appeared in the flesh His reconciling and blissful power was participated by man by means of sacrifices.

"Before the incarnation of Christ mankind became redeemed by means of the incorporated word and name of Jesus. Those who directed their will in (and to) God have received the word of promise, because the soul was accepted therein. Thus the whole law in regard to sacrifice is nothing else but an antitype of the manhood of Christ. That which Christ did as man, when by means of His love He reconciled the divine wrath, the same was (symbolically) done by means of the blood of the

[165]Thus it appears that a person's true Christianity does not depend on his or her being learned in regard to theology, nor in subscribing to a certain creed or belief, nor in going through certain ceremonies, but in their being penetrated by that principle of love and wisdom which constitutes the Christ.
"It is very deplorable to see the world revile and storm, blaspheme and denounce, whenever the gifts of God manifest themselves in mankind in different ways, and if they have not all the same quality of knowledge. What can a man take if it is not generated within him? This (the quality of his understanding) is not a matter of his choice, but as his heaven (his mental constitution) is, so will God become revealed to him." (*Letters*, i. 14.)
"We ought not to persecute each other on account of the difference of the gifts given to us, but rather rejoice in love towards each other, seeing that the wisdom of God is so inexhaustible, and we should think thereby of the future, and what would become of us if all knowledge were to become manifest only from one and within one single soul." (*Grace*, xiii. 21.)
"If there were even a thousand persons well taught by God and regenerated in the Spirit of Christ assembled together, and if each of them had his own particular gift and self-knowledge in God, nevertheless they would all be one in the root of Christ, and each of them would be desirous only for the love of God in Christ; for which one of the disciples would exalt himself above his own Master? If, then, we are one body in Christ, why should one member dispute with another about the food? If the mouth that desires eats, all the members receive strength, and each member has its own office to unfold the wonders of God. We do not all use one and the same expression, but we all have only one spirit in Christ. To each one is given that which he ought to unfold in God, so that the great mysteries of God may become manifest, and the wonders that are in His wisdom from eternity be revealed." (*Threefold Life*, xvi. 24.)

161

animals. The word of promise was within the covenant, and in the meantime God conceived of a figure (symbol), and by the power of the covenant He caused Himself to be reconciled symbolically, for the name of Jesus was within the covenant, and by means of the imagination it reconciled the fury and wrath within the nature of the Father." (*Menschwerdung*, i. 7, 12.)

"The sacrifices were symbols of the object which God had proposed unto Himself. The divine imagination saw through the object of the covenant the animal blood wherein Israel performed the sacrifice. Man had become earthly, and therefore God put before Himself the object to a covenant of mercy, so that His imagination might not enter into the terrestrial consciousness of man, and that His wrath-fire might not be ignited with the earthliness and the sins of mankind."[166] (*Tilk.* i. 289.)

This reconciliation (or atonement) could surely not result from the merely external act of sacrificing animals, but by means of the faith that accompanied it. This faith required an external action or form wherein to become conceived.

"All sacrificing without faith and divine desire is an abomination before God, and does not reach the gate of divine glory; but if man enters therein with the power of faith, he surrenders to it his free will, and desires by that means, and through its instrumentality, to enter into the eternal free will of God." (*Mysterium*, xxvii. 13.)

"Why did the two brothers (Cain and Abel) wish to sacrifice to God, while atonement is only to be found within the earnest desire for the mercy of God, in prayer and in man's persuading himself to depart from his own evil will, to change and to repent, and by bringing his faith and hope into the mercy of God? The free will of the soul is as thin as a nothing, and although within its (material) body it is surrounded by something (substantial), nevertheless its own conceived essence is in a state of false desire on account of the sin. If, then, this free will, with its (accompanying) desire, is to proceed towards God, it will have first to issue from its own illusive something, and whenever it issues from thence it is then naked and impotent, and again within the original nothing. If the will desires to go with or to enter into God, it must die to its own selfhood and leave that (illusive) self; and whenever the will leaves that self it is then like a nothing, and can therefore not act, strive for, or accomplish anything. If it wants to show its power, it must be within something wherein it may conceive and form itself, as is the case with Faith; for if there is to be an active faith, then that faith must conceive of something (have some object) wherein it may act.

---

[166]Surely an internal and spiritual God could want no other sacrifices than internal and spiritual ones. The animals in man, the snake of envy, the peacock of vanity, the ox of self-will, &c., had to be killed, so that God could manifest Himself in the purified soul. Any external sacrifice could at best be a symbol of the internal one.

Even the free will of God conceived itself within (has for its object) the internal spiritual world, and acts through the latter. Thus the free will of the soul of man, having its origin from the abyss (the primordial, unfathomable will), must conceive itself into something, so as to become manifest and to move before God." (*Mysterium*, xxvii. 1, 4–6.)

The earthly and impure substance of the victim was to be destroyed by the fire, but this fire was not of a terrestrial but of a celestial kind.[167]

> "The spirit of man has issued from God, and has gone from God (the Eternal) into time, and within the temporal it has become impure. Now it will have to leave its impurity, and by means of the sacrifice enter again into God." (*Mysterium*, xxvii. 34.)

> "Adam's body has been created out of the *Limus* of the earth, and also out of the *Limus* of the heaven of holiness; but the *Limus* of heaven, wherein the free will could conceive itself into a celestial form and move, act, think, and pray before God, was weakened in Adam, and therefore the two brothers ignited (sacrificed) the fruits of the earth. Cain brought of the fruits of the earth (matter), but Abel of the first-born of his flocks (of the spirit), and these they ignited by means of *fire*." (*Mysterium*, xxvii. 7.)

> "An animal medium, namely, the flesh of animals, was to come within the holy (will-)fire of Moses, because man had become of an animal nature, so that the animal nature, by means of the wrath-fire of the Father, may become consumed, and that the love-fire might ignite the fire of the human soul by means of the desire introduced within the victim. Thus the desire of God in the Word perceived the desire of man through the fire; for in the (divine) fire was consumed the animal vanity in the will of man, by means of the wrath, and then the purified human will, with the incorporated paradisiacal grace, entered as a sweet odour into the love-fire of God." (*Communion*, i. 31.)

> "Although wood and animals have been used at the sacrifices, nevertheless the fire used thereby was not produced by external means, but originated from the highest *tincture* of the paradisiacal foundation. This holy fire consumed the victims by means of the imagination and ignition of God, and thus the human will, that had been introduced therein, and which was still clinging to the earthly condition, was (and still is) purified in the fire and redeemed from sin. The grossness of the elements was to be consumed, and out of the consummation by fire was to issue the true, pure, beautiful, and spiritual image that had been created in Adam, and which, while it was contained within the fire of divine wrath, could now be made to appear in its clearness by means of this holy fire." (*Baptism*, ii. 2, 16.)

---

[167]Such animal sacrifices are still taking place, whenever man kills his sensual desires and sacrifices them upon the altar of his soul. Then the animal symbols in his astral light are destroyed by the magic fire of his spiritual will.

Within this holy fire, wherein was represented the light of the Christ and also the reconstitution of man to his true state of being, man was to enter with his mind, and thereby become reunited with God.

"At the times of the Old Testament the at-one-ment by sacrifice took place by means of the holy fire, which was a symbol of the wrath of God that was to consume the sin together with the soul. The Father's quality in wrath was manifest in that fire, and the Son's quality in love and meekness introduced itself into the wrath. They sacrificed the flesh of animals, but they introduced their imagination and prayer to the grace of God." (Baptism, i. 2, 23.)

"There was an animal quality, the animal soul, that originated from the planets, attached to the mind of man, in consequence of which their prayer and will was not pure before God, and therefore the wrath-fire of God consumed this animal vanity of men by means of the sacrifice; but the conceived image of grace went with the prayer into the holy fire. Thus the children of Israel were reconciled with God and relieved of their sins in a spiritual manner, and with respect to a future fulfilment, because Christ was to come and to take up the human state, and to enter into God as a sacrifice to His wrath-fire, and thus to change the wrath into love."[168] (*Baptism*, ii. 2 5.)

"The victim, the wood, the smoke, were all terrestrial, and likewise was man earthly, as far as his external body is concerned; but after the sacrificial object was ignited (by the magic fire) it became of a spiritual nature, for from the wood issued the fire, which accepted and consumed the object. From this consummation resulted the smoke of the fire, and was followed by the light, and this light was the symbol wherein entered the imagination of man and that of God, which produced a conjunction of both." (*Mysterium*, xxvii. 29, 30.)

"God desired to smell (during the sacrifice) nothing except the *will* of man, that is to say, the human life, which before the time of this world was within the word of God—not yet as a created being, but as a power—and which was breathed into the created image. This it was that was "smelled" by God by means of the sacrifice, and within the essence of Christ or the grace, that had been spoken into man, and it readjusted the will by means of grace in the fire, so that the will became again divine. At the same time it made one fire out of the combination of the human life-fire and the divine love-fire, and therewith was constituted a true sacrifice of sin and restitution, because the sin was sacrificed to the fire of divine wrath, to be consumed therein." (*Communion*, i. 32.)

"The sacrifices of the children of God, especially the first fathers after Adam, were nothing but symbols, wherein was represented how the

---

[168] If the light of wisdom, the Son, enters the fiery will, the Father, then does the Son become one with the Father, and the wrath of the Father becomes reconciled and changed into that light which is love.

(animal) soul was sacrificed within the wrath-fire of God and transformed therein into a love-fire; that is to say, that she was to enter into a state of death and dying in regard to self-will, and that thus her false willing would be consumed, and that she would issue into a clear light, through the fire and by means of the in-spoken grace, and enter into a new birth; not dark, but clear and radiant. Furthermore was it to signify how the poison introduced within the soul by the serpent would have to be eliminated, like the separation of smoke from the fire, so that the latter appears as a clear shining splendour, and no longer imprisoned (latent), as is the case in wood (before it is ignited). Thus the children of God represented to themselves the process of regeneration by means of the sacrifice through fire, and imagined the bruiser of the serpent's head within the fire; how in the fire of the soul He would transform the wrath-fire of God into a fire of light and love, and how the enmity would become separated from the soul, and the soul be transformed into an angel by means of the death of Christ and the entering of the love of God into that fire." (*Baptism*, i. 2, 10.)

Thus the faithful "Israelites" (the children of light) received, within the blissful covenant and in the flesh of the sacrifice symbolically, the flesh and blood of the Christ.

"The soul, that is to say, the mouth of faith within the soul, took in the sweet divine grace at the time of the sacrifice, not as a substance, but in power (spiritually) and in the foreknowledge of future fulfilment, when those powers were to become manifest in the flesh. Thus the body ate of the blessed bread and flesh, wherein was the power of grace, *i.e.*, the imagination of the covenant. Thus the 'Jews' ate of the flesh of Christ and drank His blood symbolically, for the power had then not yet become flesh and blood; but they enjoyed therein the word of grace that afterwards became human." (*Communion*, i. 34.)

"The animal flesh which was sacrificed to the Lord and afterwards eaten was sanctified for man, because the imagination of God entered therein, and therefore Moses called it a holy flesh, and there was also a holy bread." (*Communion*, i. 33.)

Chapter XI
Incarnation–The Celestial Virgin

The doctrine of the incarnation of Christ, or, to express it in other words, of the awakening of the germ of divine self-knowledge in man, is so grand, that it is impossible to form a conception of it as long as we occupy a narrow-minded, personal, or sectarian point of view. If we desire to feel the power of the universal Redeemer within our heart, we must allow our mind to expand and embrace in our love all that is divine, noble, and ideal in humanity.

IN considering the contents of the following chapter it will be especially recommendable to keep in mind the great occult maxim, that it is below as it is above, and that everything above has its corresponding part below; so that the great processes taking place in the macrocosm produce corresponding processes on the microcosmic plane, and that which exists eternally in heaven (the spiritual plane) seeks to be embodied and represented in terrestrial forms upon the earth. It is also well to remember that completion is attained only by the reappearance of the third principle in the seventh; that is to say, by the spiritualisation of matter and the acquisition of form. A being or power belonging to an entirely ideal plane cannot produce any direct reaction in the grossly material state of existence, no more than a tree can grow out of the idea of a tree existing within the mind, but it needs a material seed or kernel to serve as a material focus for the attraction and distribution of material principles. For similar reasons it was necessary that the *Logos*[169] should actually become flesh and enter the human state so as to produce a fundamental and radical change in the will of humanity by starting a new activity of light and love in its very centre or heart.

This process is beautifully and allegorically described in the New Testament.

In the configuration of the person of our Redeemer there are to be distinguished three factors: the eternal generation of the Son of God, His birth as a celestial Man, and, finally, His being incarnated as a terrestrial person.[170]

---

[169] The *Logos* is everywhere, and did not enter from any external locality. Likewise the body of the sun is everywhere, although it manifests its light only in one locality in the sky.

[170] All disputes about the nature of Christ only prove that the disputants are not Christians, because if they were true followers of the Christ they would have the living Christ within themselves, and know His true nature. The misunderstandings of the "Christians" regarding the Christ arise from the fact that they regard Him as something external and incompatible with human nature; neither will any merely theoretical research regarding this mystery lead to any satisfactory result. The only way in which this matter can be settled for once and for ever is that those who have doubts about the divinity of Christ succeed in raising Him from His tomb within their own souls, when He will become revealed to them.

"Christ is greater than any angel in heaven, because He has a celestial human body; He also has the eternal celestial bride, the virgin of divine wisdom, and, finally, the Holy Trinity in His possession. We can truly say of Him that He is an individuality in the Holy Trinity in heaven, a true man in heaven, and an eternal king in this world, a lord of heaven and of the earth." (*Three Principles*, xxii. 8 6.)

"The Word, or the second person in the Godhead, has been from eternity in the Father, and by becoming incarnated in humanity it did not change its nature and become something else, but remained in. the Father, in its centre and seat, as it had been from eternity. The other (second) formation took place in a natural manner at the time of the annunciation by the angel Gabriel,[171] when the virgin said to the angel, 'Let it be done as you say.' The fulfilling of this Word was effected in the celestial element, as was the creation of the first Adam before the fall. The third formation took place simultaneously with the second, and at once, as when a terrestrial seed is sown whereof a child grows." (*Three Principles*, xviii. 45.)

"The holy Spirit of God formed the celestial, angelic substantiality within the one element by means of the virgin; but the planets and elements of this world formed the external man, providing him with a natural body and soul exactly like that of other human beings, and both in one person. Thereby each form had its own particular state of perception and sensation, and the divine state did not mingle in such a manner (with the terrestrial form) as to cause the former to be diminished, but remained what it was (before the incarnation took place), and that which it was not it became (by means of the incarnation), but without any separation, differentiation, or division of the divine being. Thus the Word remains in the Father, the created being of the holy element remained before the Father, and the natural human state was attained in this world in the womb of the virgin Mary."[172] (*Three Principles*, xx. 86).

Those who regard Christ as being not a person, and who claim that Mary was an eternal virgin and not born from terrestrial parents, are in

---

"Each one desires to be a child of God in his knowledge, and nevertheless disobedience and unfaithfulness are as great in one people as they are in another. A belief that Christ has once been born and died for me and arisen from death does not make me a child of God. The devil knows that also; but it is of no use to him. I must clothe myself in Christ by means of the desire of faith; I must enter myself into His obedience, His incarnation, His suffering and death; I must myself arise in Him and adopt the obedience of Christ. Only in this way can I be a Christian, and not in any other way." (*Mysterium*, li. 43).

[171]"'Gabriel,' an angel or god of sound, an internal, sourcive spirit." (*Aurora*, xii. 86.)

[172]There is no doubt that, as some will have it, the legend of the descent of the Redeemer is the description of an astrological process; but this theory, far from disproving the incarnation of divine wisdom into a human form, confirms it; because that which takes place in the macrocosm produces corresponding effects in the microcosm. In man is the sun, the moon, the stars, and the whole of the zodiac. In the microcosm is represented every part of the macrocosm in its material and spiritual aspect. When man sees the external sun rise in the outer world, the sun in him arises and gives joy to his heart. Any individual person, or also humanity as a whole, may become either a god or a devil incarnate.

error.[173]

"Those err who say that Christ is not a created being. As far as His divinity is concerned, He is certainly not a created being; but relatively to His celestial state, regarding which He says that He had come from heaven and was still in heaven, He is there both a creature in human nature, and without humanity an untreated being." (*Letters*, ii. 54.)

"There are some who have said that the virgin Mary was not a terrestrial being, and not the daughter of Joachim and Anna, because Christ is called the seed of the woman, and would therefore have to be born from an entirely celestial virgin. If this were so, it would serve very little to us poor children of Eve, as we have become earthly and are carrying our souls in earthly tabernacles."[174] (*Menschwerdung*, i. 8. 1.)

"It has been said that Mary was an eternal virgin of the Holy Trinity, and that from her Christ had been born; because, according to His own testimony, He did not come front human flesh and blood, but from heaven. It is true that our Lord said that He had come from God and was to return to God, and that no one would go to heaven except the Son of Man, coming from heaven and being in heaven; but in thus saying He spoke evidently of His human aspect, and not merely of His divinity; for the eternal God could not have been the Son of Man, neither could a son of man come out of the Trinity; but if it had been possible to redeem man by means of a foreign soul brought down from heaven, where would then have been the necessity for God to enter into our (human) shape and to be crucified therein."[175] (*Three Principles*, xxii. 61.)

If Christ had brought a foreign soul with Him from heaven, and not taken a human soul from His mother Mary, He would have been foreign to us, and could not have become our Redeemer.

"It is not true, as some say, that Christ has taken a soul unto Himself from the Word in the eternal virgin Mary, so that Christ was coming from God and the soul in His human nature had a beginning." (*Mysterium*, lvi. 19).

"Christ is not only a seed that came from heaven, so as to have no other quality received from man except a human covering (body). If He had not a human nature He would not be the Son of Man, neither

[173]Christ, or the Universal *Logos*, is not a personality in the usual acceptation of that term, but becomes personal if personified in man. Likewise the celestial virgin is personified in woman, in the same sense as the light of the sun becomes individualised in a flower, a diamond, or precious stone.

[174]"Outside of a body the spirit cannot remain in its perfection, for as soon as it is separated from the form it loses its rule. The body is the mother of the spirit. In the body the spirit is born, and receives therein its power and strength. If it is separated from the body it still remains a spirit, but loses its ruling power." (*Aurora*, xxvi. 50.)

[175]And the divinity in man continues to be crucified in him until the self-will is dead and the Christ arisen in His own light.

169

would He be my brother." (*Tilk.* i. 245.)

"The soul of Christ is a creature like our own soul, and He has received it from humanity and in the body of Mary. Therefore we rejoice eternally that the soul of Christ is our brother and the body of Christ is our body in regenerated man." (*Three Principles*, xxiii. 30.)

"What would it benefit me if Christ had brought with Him a strange soul? Nothing! But I rejoice that He has introduced my soul into the holy *Ternary*. Now can I truly say, 'The soul of Christ is my brother, and the body of Christ is the nutriment of my soul.'" (*Three Principles*, xxii. 78.)

But if Christ had come only from a terrestrial virgin He would not have come from above, and would not have been pure.

"Christ said to the Jews, 'I am from above, but you are from below; I am not of this world, but you are of this world.' If He had become human in an earthly tabernacle, and not in a pure, celestial, and chaste virgin, such as Mary had become in consequence of her having been blessed, He would have been of this world." (*Menschwerdung*, i. 9, 20.)

"All that is born from the flesh and blood of this world is impure, and a pure virgin cannot be born in this corrupted flesh and blood; but Christ has been received and born without sin from a pure virgin."[176] (*Three Principles*, xxii. 36.)

According to the external flesh, Mary descended from Joachim and Anna; but she was also the daughter of the covenant, and as such she was blessed (penetrated) by the virgin of wisdom.[177]

"Mary was generated from the seed of Joachim and Anna in the same manner as other human beings are generated; but she was blessed among women, so that in her the eternal virgin became revealed." (*Threefold Life*, vi. 72.)

"Mary, in whom Christ became man, was truly the daughter of Joachim and Anna, according to the external flesh, and generated out

[176]The Christ can never be born or revealed in any impure soul. A soul wherein regeneration is to take place must be an immaculate virgin, having no intercourse with any external god; but executing the will of God dwelling within herself.

[177]"Ana" is the Chaldean name for the astral light (see *Secret Doctrine*). "In the language of nature the name 'Mary' means 'salvation from this valley of sorrow.'" (*Principles*, xviii. 37.)

No man can be saved without the grace of Mary, *i.e.*, without the presence of that which is noble, exalted, saving, and sanctifying in him.

"Human reason can understand nothing about the kingdom of Christ, nor about His person or office, because the testament of Christ is celestial, and human reasoning is terrestrial; the latter seeks Christ in time, while He can only be found in eternity."

"All misunderstanding is caused by the circumstance that the heaven wherein Christ is seated to the right of God is not understood, and because it is not known that this heaven is in this world, and this world rooted in heaven. They are both one in the other, like day and night." (*Baptism*, i.)

of their seed; but in regard to the will she was the daughter of the covenant of promise, the object of the covenant, wherein the same became accomplished." (*Menschwerdung*, i. 8. 2.)

"The pure and immaculate virgin in whom God was born is before God, and an eternal virgin. She was pure and without blemish even before heaven and earth were created; and this pure virgin became incorporated in Mary, so that it rendered her a new being within the holy element of God. Therefore she was blessed among women, and the Lord was with her, as was said by the angel." (*Three Principles*, xxii. 38.)

The celestial virgin did not become terrestrial in Mary (or enter into her mechanically from the outside); but the omnipresent celestial virgin became revealed (unfolded) within Mary's innermost being.[178]

"We cannot say that the celestial virgin, when she entered into Mary, became terrestrial by the order of God, but we say that the soul of Mary took hold of the celestial virgin, and the latter adorned the soul of Mary with the pure garment of the holy element, a pure, regenerated human being, and therein has Mary received the Saviour of the world, and given birth to Him in this world." (*Three Principles*, xxii. 44.)

"No other woman, ever since the time of Adam, became clothed with the celestial virgin except Mary; but this took place in the soul-principle, and not in the terrestrial flesh." (*Forty Questions*, xxxvi. 12.)

"Mary received the celestial token which was unknown to nature, and which was also unknown to her in her external womanhood, namely, the celestial virgin, and in that virgin she received the Word of the Eternal Father." (Three Principles, xxii. 43.)

By means of this unfolding or state of bliss the Word was enabled to take up the human state in Mary, and thus the celestial virgin that had become weakened in Adam became again strong and substantial in her.

"The Word of promise, which was before the Jews as an antitype, or as an image in a mirror, wherein the wrathful Father imagined and wherewith He extinguished His wrath, began to move essentially, as it had not moved from eternity; for when the angel Gabriel brought to Mary the message saying that she should become pregnant, and when she expressed her willingness, saying, "Let it be done to me as you said," then the centre of the Holy Trinity moved itself; that is to say, the eternal virginity which was lost by Adam, became opened in her in the Word of life. The fire of divine love in Mary's being, in the virginal essence that had been corrupted in Adam, was again restored."

[178]The spiritual soul does not become an animal soul in man; neither is the former a separate entity to be put into the latter; but as the vibrations of light awaken corresponding vibrations within the ether that is in darkness, so the divine harmony existing in the spiritual soul of the universe awakens corresponding harmonies in the soul of man.

(*Menschwerdung*, i. 8, 3. 4.)

"The Word, that stood in the virgin of wisdom and surrounded by eternal wonders, entered again, out of great love to our image, which had been destroyed in Adam, and it became human in Mary in consequence of the benediction." (*Forty Questions*, xxxvi. 10.)

"The eternal virgin, being without substance, entered also into the incarnation, and thus the tine soul was received out of the essences of Mary. In this way the eternal virgin came into substantiality, for she received the human soul within herself." (*Threefold Life*, vi. 75.)

Mary could not by her own power put herself in possession of that celestial blessing, but it came to her by divine grace and in the power of the Holy Spirit.

"The true being of humanity, that had died and disappeared (become latent) in Adam, awoke again to life in Mary, and thus she became highly exalted and like man before the fall. This, however, did not take place by her own power, but by the power of God. If the centre of God had not moved within her, she would not have been different from all other daughters of Eve." (*Menschwerdung*, i. 8. 5.)

"Mary is called a holy and pure virgin merely with reference to the celestial virgin that had taken possession of her, and clothed her with the pure element of Paradise. Mary did not obtain possession of this state by her own power, as is shown by the angel saying to her, 'The Spirit of God will come over you, and you will be overshadowed by the power of the Supreme; therefore the Holy One that shall be born of thee shall be called the Son of God.'" (*Three Principles*, xx. 41.)

"The words of the angel, 'The Spirit of God will come over you, and you will be overshadowed by the power of the Supreme,' means: The Holy Spirit shall open the closed centre within, in the moribund seed, and the Word of God will enter with living and celestial substantiality within that which had been closed in death, and become one flesh with it."[179] (*Three Principles*, xxii. 41.)

It is certain that the soul of the Redeemer could issue from Mary only on account of her being of a character full of humility and in accordance with the will of God; and it is furthermore certain that she spiritually enjoys a high state of glorification for having had the qualifications necessary for becoming the mother of the Redeemer.

"The first thing that a child (in the womb) receives is the *tincture* of its mother. Thus it was in the case of Christ. When the angel announced

[179]Perhaps the same idea might be approached by saying: The divine harmony underlying the original order of nature, which was thrown into confusion by the action of an evil will within the seven qualities of eternal nature, created a centre of harmony within the soul of Mary, which, expanding from within outwardly, rendered her whole nature harmonious and spiritual.

to Mary the coming incarnation of Christ, it was the mother's will, and the *tincture* which received the *Limbus* of God and impregnated her, belonged to her. If, then, the soul of the child is in the Holy Trinity, do you then not think that its glorious light beautifully illuminates the mother, and does not that mother rightfully put her feet upon the Moon,[180] as being exalted above all that is of an earthly nature? She gave birth to the Redeemer of the world without any carnal commingling, and from her issued the body which attracts all members, namely, the children of God in Christ, *i.e.*, the children of Light." (*Three Principles*, xviii. 93–98.)

Mary, however, was not deified. In spite of all her greatness she could only through her Son become perfect and inherit heaven.[181]

"The Word which was promised by God in the garden of Eden came to bloom in the life-light of the virgin; and when the angel Gabriel, by order of the Father, came to give to it an impulse by means of the message, it then entered into the one element of the chaste virgin, but not so entirely within her soul and body so as to deify her person." (*Three Principles*, xviii. 89.)

"The virgin Mary entered into great perfection, like the star of the morning, which is more glorious than the rest of the stars. She attained perfection and beatitude through her Son, Jesus Christ." (*Three Principles*, xviii. 88.)

"The virgin Mary did not become deified. Christ Himself says, 'No one goes to heaven except the Son of Man, who came from heaven and is in heaven.' All others have to attain heaven through Him. Christ is their heaven, and the Father is the heaven of Christ." (*Three Principles*, xviii. 89.)

The external kingdom of this world did not become separated from the virgin; but it lost its power over her. The quality of her inner life communicated itself to her physical body.

"When God moved in Mary as His object, then was she highly blessed, and in that benediction of the Redeemer she became impregnated. Now, it is known that the seed of man communicates its qualities to the body. When the divine life entered into the essence of the seed (power) of Mary, her whole body, which was then surrounding the body of the (divine) image, became highly blessed, and quickened by this wonderful moving of God. The external kingdom of this world was

---

[180]The sunlight of wisdom (self- knowledge and self-perception) is superior to all that is merely imaginary, fanciful, and illusive. Wisdom sees the illusion, but is not captivated by it.

[181]No soul can become divine or deified by merely contemplating God as if He were something foreign to herself. God must become substantial and corporified in her. The mere idealist is satisfied with enjoying in his imagination the beauty of the ideal, but does not embody it within himself. The so-called "realist" is satisfied with what he believes to be real, and acquires nothing better than what he already has. The true Christian, *i.e.*, the "ideo-realist," seeks to realise the ideal, so that it becomes a part of himself.

then not separated from Mary, she was still imprisoned therein; but the tincture of her blood became kindled with the divine tincture; *i.e.*, with the tincture of the *seed;* communicating its qualities to the corporeal form." (*Tilk.* i. 331.)

"The soul of Mary became surrounded by the divine living substantiality, not relatively to her terrestrial but to her celestial nature, so that the terrestrial state was merely supplementing her being. Her soul, with the Word of life that became human in her, was to pass with it through the death and wrath of the Father into the celestial consciousness, and thus her external human nature had to (he in regard to earthly life, so that she could live in God. But because she has been blessed, and has carried in her womb the object of the covenant, that which was celestial in her consumed her terrestrial part." (*Menschwerdung*, i. 9, 18.)[182]

The Saviour had to receive earthly essences from Mary, and He became in her, in the normal way, a terrestrial man.[183]

"The virgin comprised Christ as a mother her child. She gave to him natural essences, such as she had inherited from her parents, and these essences from her flesh and blood he received to the element, and became therein a living soul." (*Three Principles*, xviii. 90.)

"The living Word that dwelt within the eternal virgin attracted to itself the flesh of Mary—that is to say, the essences from the corporeal body of Mary—and thus there grew in nine months a complete human being with soul, spirit, and flesh." (*Threefold Life*, vi. 79.)

"The life of Christ did not begin to stir immediately at the time of conception, or in any supernatural manner, but this took place at the proper natural time, as is the case with all the children of Adam. Thus in nine months he grew to be a complete human being, and was born like all other children of Adam. He might have caused himself to be born magically, but if this had been done he would not have been in this world in a natural manner." (*Menschwerdung*, i. 10.)

In Christ, as the son of Mary, there were united all the three principles, but without commingling with each other, so that, in spite of His terrestrial body, He remained nevertheless free from sin.

"Christ in Mary accepted all the three principles, but in divine order, and not intermingled, such as they became in Adam, who, by means of his imagination, introduced the external realm into the internal realm,

---

[182]The *Manas* became absorbed in the *Buddhi.*

[183]"God lives also in man." (*Threefold Life*, xi. 106.) Each human being (if he is not godless) carries God and the Christ, the Holy Spirit, the virgin Mary, together with the angel Gabriel and all the rest of the angels and spirits within himself. It is, therefore, of little use to seek for all that in history. We can find it nowhere except within ourselves.

174

into the soul-fire, in consequence of which the light became extinguished. He (Christ) had on Himself the soul-essence, or the first principle, the substance of the image of the second principle, and finally the external form, *i.e.*, the third principle." (*Tilk.* i. 336.)

"Christ took from Mary the interior seed that had been weakened in Adam, and to this was attached the external seed of the flesh, but so that they did not mix with each other, neither were they separated; but they were relatively to each other like God, who dwells in the world, while the world nevertheless is not God." (*Stiefel*, ii. 204.)

"Christ did not by means of His external body produce sin and dishonour. No, this cannot be; but He has taken upon Himself as a burden the sin which we have inherited from Adam, and which He was to carry as if He were Adam, while He still was not Adam." (*Stiefel*, ii. 499.)

"Christ did not take upon Himself the awakened and conceived vanity (selfishness) which the devil introduced into the flesh by means of his imagination, and which caused the flesh to sin; but He took the awakened forms of life (principles) which from a state of harmony had issued, each one in its own desire. Therein He took upon Himself our sin and disease, and death and hell; but only for the purpose of tincturing them by His love, by means of. His celestial blood which He had poured into our external human nature, and this was to change hell into heaven, and to introduce the human qualities again into divine harmony." (*Regeneration*, iii. 11.)

Still less has the innermost essence of the Lord, the eternal Word, ever mingled with His terrestrial body; it did not even mingle with His human soul.[184]

"God has become revealed within the external seed (principle) of Mary, for Christ did not differ while upon the earth from other human beings in form, substance, or external appearance. In that external seed He did not take up divinity; His external form was mortal, and He annihilated death therein." (*Stiefel*, ii. 203.)

"Christ truly attracted to Himself our human essences while in the body of the virgin Mary, and He has become our brother (thereby). But the human essences cannot apprehend His eternal divinity; only the new man, born in God, conceives of it as the body apprehends of the soul." (*Three Principles*, xxii. 48.)

"The soul and the Word are not one or one being. The soul is born

[184]The divine spirit, *i.e.*, the spiritual consciousness of each or any individual person upon this earth, never was, is, or will be imprisoned, incarnated or reincarnated, or absorbed in any material mind or person. It for ever remains in heaven, *i.e.*, in its own celestial state. The mind and the body are merely reflections of the light of the spirit as it shines into "matter." The true Man is in heaven; his shadow walks upon the earth.

175

from the centre of nature, from the essences, and belongs to the body, for she issues from the essences of the body, and attracts to herself the body; but the Word is from the centre of the majesty, and draws the majesty unto itself." (*Threefold Life*, vi. 83.)

The Word and the soul are not standing separately side by side, but the latter is penetrated and illumined by the former.[185]

"The soul and the Word are not standing side by side like two persons, but the Word penetrates the soul, and out of the Word shines the life-light; whereby, however, the soul remains free to herself. A red-hot iron is in itself dark and black, but the fire penetrates it, so that it becomes luminous. There has no change happened to the iron itself; it remains iron and the heat remains heat; one is as free as the other, and neither one is the other. Thus has the soul been put into the fire of divinity, so that divinity may penetrate and illuminate the soul, and dwell therein and conceive of her, although the soul cannot conceive of divinity; nevertheless she does not become transformed. Divinity conceives the soul and endows her with the power of majesty." (*Threefold Life*, vi. 83.)

Christ did not become human merely within the virgin Mary, but also in an unlimited celestial manner.

"While Christ lived upon the earth His external form was limited like our own bodies, but the internal man was immeasurable." (*Three Principles*, xxiv. 88.)

"The Word has become humanity everywhere; that is to say, everywhere became unfolded the divine substantiality wherein our eternal humanity exists. We ought to exist in the same corporeal substantiality in eternity, wherein exists the virgin of God, and we must clothe ourselves with the virgin, for Christ has clothed Himself with her." (*Menschwerdung*, i. 8, 12.)

"The whole angelic world is the substantiality of Christ according to His celestial essentiality, 'created' in regard to the personality of humanity, but outside of it is untreated and eternal." (*Letters*, xii. 56.)

The celestial and unlimited corporeity of our Redeemer is incomprehensible to the reasoning intellect; but it is nevertheless logical to accept it, because in Christ the infinite God became man.[186]

[185]Whenever I speak of the man Christ, and of what a triune God and man He is, I make a distinction between the human creature, that came from us human beings, and the triune Divinity, the revealed word of the power and omnipotence. Not that they are separated from each other, but the Spirit of God is higher than the being to which that Spirit gives birth in its outbreathed word. I do not say that the sweet and beloved Christ is the man, but it is the holy sunshine in the flame of love in the man; for whenever I see a holy Christian man stand or walk I do not say, "Here stands or walks Christ;" but I say, "Here stands and walks a Christian man in whom shines the sun of Christ." (*Stief.* 421.)

[186]It is universal and nevertheless individual, like that of a god.

"Reason says: 'The body of Christ is in one place; how then can it be everywhere? It is a creature, and one creature cannot be in every place at once.' But listen, dear Reason. 'When the Word of God became a human being in the body of Mary, was it then not also (at the same time) high above the stars? While it was at Nazareth was it then not also at Jerusalem and everywhere? Or do you think that God, while He became a man, had been confined to His human form?' This is an impossibility, and thus, while God became man, His humanity was everywhere where His divinity existed."[187] (*Three Principles*, xxiii. 8.)

"Christ has not become man solely in the body of the (terrestrial) virgin Mary (in that sense), as if His divinity or divine essentiality had been captured, imprisoned, or seated therein. As little as God, who is the fulness of all things, resides in one place alone, so little has God moved in only one small portion (of the Word); for He is not differentiated, but everywhere one and a whole, and wherever He becomes manifest there He is manifest as a whole. Neither is God measurable, and there has no place of residence been discovered in Him, unless He should establish for Himself such a dwelling in one of His creatures; but even then He remains a whole apart from and beyond such a created being." (*Menschwerdung*, i. 8.)

In this respect Christ may be likened to the sun, who is also immeasurable in his aspect as a power, but which is nevertheless existing as a separate body in space.

"We may compare the sun to Christ in His aspect as a created being, and the whole depth of space may be compared to the Father. If we then see that the sun shines within the whole depth of space, and sends his heat and power everywhere, we cannot then say that within the depth the power and light of the sun is nowhere outside of the body of the sun; for if the light and substance of the sun were not everywhere, space could not receive the power and light of the sun. It requires two powers or principles of a similar nature to be receptive of each other. The depth (of space) contains its light, but hidden (latent). If it were the will of God, the whole depth would all be sun." (*Menschwerdung*, i. 8.)

"As the sun shines through all the external world, causing everything to become more powerful and fertile, and as nevertheless the world and the sun are (in their corporeal centres) to be distinguished from each other, so Christ, as a manifested Sun, shines out of (the depth of) Jehovah or Jesus, in the created humanity of Christ. Jehovah is the eternal divine Sun, and within that Sun has been hidden to all creatures the great Love-Sun of Christ, as a heart in the centre of the Holy Trinity; but by the moving of the Godhead He has become

[187]This would be like imagining that the trunk of a tree was dwelling within the leaves.

revealed as a holy Sun of divine love." (*Stiefel*, ii. 422.)

"The sun illumines the world; but this would not be possible if there were not within the depth a similar state of being as that which constitutes the sun. Likewise the corporeity of Christ is all the fulness of the heavens, as a created being in the person and without the person; but (both) exist in one spirit and one power as one, and not in a state of duality or as two things separated from each other." (*Tilk.* ii. 251,)[188]

This unlimited, celestial (state of) being of the Redeemer is nevertheless lower than the Godhead.

"When the Word enters into the one pure element, the virginal matrix, it does not become separated from the Father, but remains eternally, and is everywhere present in the heaven of the element wherein it entered, and wherein it has become a new creature, called a 'god.' This very new creature is naturally not born from the flesh and blood of the (physical) virgin, but of God, out of His element (the celestial virgin), and in the power of the Holy Trinity, which remains therein eternally in its fulness. But the corporeity of the element of that created being is lower than the Godhead, for the Godhead is spirit, and the holy element is born out of the Word from eternity. Thus the Lord has entered into the servant, whereof all the angels in heaven are filled with surprise. It is the greatest miracle that has occurred from all eternity, because it is against (human) nature, and could only have been accomplished by divine love." (*Three Principles*, xviii. 42.)[189]

---

[188]The universal life and the individual life are only one principle.

[189]"You must not seek for any historical knowledge in our writings. It is not possible to see God with earthly eyes, and therefore it is impossible for an unillumined mind to comprehend heavenly thoughts and perceptions in its terrestrial vehicle. Like can be grasped only by like." (*Princ. Appendix*, 30.)

Chapter XII
Redemption

"God lives also in man. Therefore if we are but seeking and loving our own (true) self, we then love God. That which we do to each other we are doing to God. He who seeks and finds his brother and sister has sought and found God. We are in Him all one body with many members, each of which has its own functions." (*Threefold Life*, xi. 106.)

IT was the will of God, by means of becoming Himself human, to reinstate man, who in consequence of his sin had become degenerated into an earthly being, into the glorious state in which he had been created originally.

As this statement, on account of the old theological ideas which it is liable to awaken in the mind, will probably be misunderstood, we will attempt to express its meaning in different terms. God, the will of eternal wisdom, willed that His wisdom should become manifest in a human form, because the universal man, having become absorbed by the attractions of the sensual plane, had lost that divine state of consciousness which renders possible the perception of divine truth. As it is only the truth in man that can know universal truth, and as this principle of truth had become inactive in him, it was necessary that the Christ (the Truth, the Life, and the Light) should become active in him, and by rendering man truthful, self-conscious, and living within the light, reinstate him in his former position which he occupied in the macrocosmos before he sank into materiality and degradation.[190]

"The spirit of this world has captured the body[191] and rendered it earthly, so as to cause body and soul to be corrupted. Thus we are no longer in possession of the pure element necessary for the formation of a (pure) body, but an outgrowth of the four elements in combination with the influence of the stars. This body does not belong unto the Godhead. God does not unfold Himself within an unclean body, but only in holy (regenerated, interior) man, in the pure image which He created in the beginning. There was then nothing else to be done than to regenerate that image by means of the heart and light of God." (*Three Principles*, xxiii. 21.)

[190]If we take of the history of redemption the ordinary theological view, and regard it as the work of an extracosmic God, getting offended and angry, and becoming reconciled by having his son killed by man, it becomes at once absurd and incredible; but if we look at it in its true light, namely, as an allegory describing an intracosmic process going on in the body of macrocosmic and microcosmic man, it then becomes intelligible. It was not an outside deity, but the divine will, active within the heart of humanity, that willed that humanity should be saved by the awakening of the divine will in man, and the same process takes place even now in the organism of every individual on entering from spiritual darkness into light.

[191]The term "body," as a matter of course, does not refer to the visible form of earth, which is merely an instrument for its inner inhabitant, but to that principle of which that form is an external expression.

"Man must again go out of the spirit of the planets and elements and enter into a new birth, into the life of God. This the soul cannot accomplish by her own power, and therefore the life of God out of love and mercy came to us into the flesh and took our human soul again unto itself, into the divine life, into the power of the light; so that in this life we may enter into a new birth and penetrate unto God." (*Threefold Life*, i, 17.)

"To the human spirit (as such) it was impossible to issue from the torment of anguish and enter into the region of heaven, and therefore God had to come again into humanity and aid the human spirit in bursting the doors of the darkness, so that it may enter within them (clothed) in divine power."[192] (*Threefold Life*, xxi. 21.)

"Christ came for the purpose of healing the injury which Adam had suffered when he died relatively to the celestial kingdom. He came to awaken the inner man who had disappeared in Adam, and to regenerate him in His power, and to bruise for ever the serpent's head of wrath and falsehood, (that is to say) to kill the (selfish) terrestrial will." (*Stiefel*, ii. 168.)

To effect this reconstitution the direct action of God upon humanity would not have been sufficient. Without the incarnation a real union of God and man, and a resurrection of the latter from death, would not have been possible.[193]

"It was the will of God to transmute humanity, after it had become earthly, again into the celestial quality, to turn the human earth (material element) into heaven, to make out of the four elements only one, and to transform the wrath of God in human quality into love. But the wrath of God, having become ignited in man, was a power of fire and fury, to resist which, and to transform it into love, it was necessary that love itself should enter into the wrath and surrender itself wholly to it. It was not enough for that purpose that God should remain in heaven (in His own divine self-consciousness), and look lovingly down upon humanity. This would not have subdued the power of the fury and wrath, neither would they have entered into a state of love." (*Signature*, xi. 7.)

"In the holiness of God the human essence could not have been conceived without the presence of an appropriate medium; the will was separated from it. Therefore God became man, so that He might endow or bless humanity with His divinity, and that He may become conceivable to us." (*Baptism*, ii. 36.)

"Before the incarnation took place, the Word could redeem the soul, so

[192]In other words, there is no other way of restoring the order except by means of its restoration.
[193]If the light shines merely upon the surface, it then does not penetrate into the depths. The will had to become active within the flesh. This divine will is love, which is substantial and not a mere dream.

that she could stand the test before the Father in the fire; but not (the test) in the love and delight before the light of the Holy Trinity. A rising from the tomb was not thus to be accomplished. If man was to be raised from the tomb, the Word had first to become man."[194] (*Three Principles*, xvi. 35.)

"The pious have clothed themselves in Christ before His incarnation in the covenant of promise, not in substance, but merely in power; not in the flesh, but merely in the spirit." (*Stiefel*, ii. 442.)

In consequence of sin the power of death had become a ruler, and therefore the Redeemer entered Himself into death for the purpose of conquering it, and to obtain for us again the fulness of divine life.[195]

"In consequence of the sin there was no salvation for man; if the eternal Word and heart of God had not become human and entered into the third principle, into the human flesh and blood, taking upon itself (the state of) a human soul, and entering into the death of the destitute soul, whereby it could take away from death its power and from hell its terrible sting, and thus conduct the soul out of death and redeem her from hell." (*Threefold Life*, viii. 39.)

"Adam's soul had turned from God and died relatively to the essentiality of tile light. Thus the second Adam brought the soul again into the fire, *i.e.*, into the fountain of wrath, and ignited again the light in death. Then shone the light again into the darkness, and death died itself, and for the wrath or hell there was created a plague." (*Tilk.* i. 513.)

"As we had gone out from the freedom of the angelic world and entered into the dark torture, therefore the power and the word of the light became man, and led us out of the darkness and through death in the fire into the freedom of divine life, into the divine essentiality. Therefore Christ had to die and to enter into the divine essentiality through hell and through the wrath of eternal nature, and to open a road for our soul through death and through the wrath, on which we may enter with Him by means of death into divine life." (*Menschwerdung*, i. 3, 7.)

"When the two kingdoms, the wrath of God and the love of God, were battling with each other, then appeared Christ as the hero. He willingly surrendered Himself to the wrath (to the suffering caused by the lower principles that had been awakened to consciousness in consequence of the sin), and He extinguished it by His love. He came from God into this world and took our soul into Himself, so that He might take us out of the earthly state into Himself and lead us thus into God. He

[194]The tombs from which man must arise are error, passions, and temptations.

[195]The light could not have redeemed the darkness in any other way than by entering therein; neither could anything entirely spiritual and unsubstantial have acted upon matter.

regenerated us within Himself, so that we would become capable of living again in God, and that we should put our will into Him. In Him He led us to the Father, into our first home; that is to say, into the Paradise which Adam had left." (*Menschwerdung*, i. 11. 6.)

"The Word took our own flesh and blood into the divine essentiality, and broke the power which held us imprisoned in the wrath of death and fury. It broke that power on the *Cross;* that is to say, in the centre of nature (the fourth natural form, whose symbol is the Cross), and ignited again in our soul (that had become dark) the burning white light-fire." (*Menschwerdung*, ii. 6, 9.)

"Christ sacrificed our human image to the wrath of His Father, to be swallowed up in death, and introduced His life into death; but He manifested His love in that life which death had devoured, and thus He brought that life out of death by means of His love (with which it had become one and immortal). As a seed sown into the earth must die (as such and relatively to its form) within the earth, and as by means of this dying a new body grows, so the corrupted body of Adam had to be sacrificed to death and to the wrath, and out of the death and wrath issued the *body of the love of God.*" (*Mysterium*, xxviii. 17.)

The conquest of the power of death took place, in a certain sense, already at the time of the overcoming of the temptation of the Redeemer, which, like that of Adam, was caused by the envy of the devil, but in which the devil was conquered by the Lord.[196]

"Adam was to take possession of the kingly throne of Lucifer, because the latter had turned away from God. From this results the great envy and the spite of the devil against mankind. From this also originates the temptation of Christ in the wilderness, because Christ was to take possession of the throne which the devil claimed, to break his power, and to become his judge who was to reject him eternally." (*Grace*, vi. 13.)

"All that which had seduced Adam; and wherein he became imprisoned as in the death of darkness, was offered to the Saviour at the time of temptation." (*Signature*, vii. 46.)

"The temptation is the hard fight in the garden of Eden, in which Adam fell; but the new warrior came out of it victorious, and remained conqueror." (*Three Principles*, xii. 91.)

"When Christ withstood the temptation in the place of Adam, then the newly introduced celestial *Ens* broke the sword in the death of the external body of Christ, and by means of the holy substance it brought the external body, which He had taken up in Mary and out of her seed, through that sword of the wrath and into the holy state. In this very

[196]Little would it benefit man to believe that another person overcame his temptations, while he himself would succumb to his own. He who conquers that which is mortal in him conquers death.

power the external body became raised from the dead, and conquered both, death and the fiery sword." (*Mysterium*, xxiv. 24.)

The first factor in the temptation was that Christ was requested to take earthly food instead of celestial nutriment, and that He should thereby gratify the desire of His body.[197]

> "After the Spirit of God had led Christ into the wilderness, then was the devil permitted to approach Him in the kingdom of wrath and to tempt the second Adam as he had tempted the first one. There was then no earthly food or drink, and the soul of Christ knew very well that she was in God, and that she could make terrestrial bread out of stones, as there was no other bread there. But she did not desire to eat with her celestial body terrestrial but celestial bread, and to leave the terrestrial body to its hunger, because the divinity in Christ said, 'Eat of the word of the Lord and you will issue from the earthly man and rest in the kingdom of heaven; live in the new man, and then the old one will be dead for the sake of the new.' However, the devil spoke to the soul: 'Thy earthly body is hungry, and as there is no bread, therefore make thou bread out of stones.' Then the strong soul in Christ stood there as a warrior and said, 'Man lives not alone of bread, but of each word that passes through the mouth of God. Thus he rejected the terrestrial bread and life, and put his imagination into the word of God and ate of it. Then was the soul alive in the kingdom of heaven, but the body like one dead; that is to say, it became the servant of heaven and lost its powerful rule (over the soul)." (*Three Principles*, xxii. 100–105.)

Furthermore, the devil thought of turning the Redeemer away from the divine will by exciting the spirit of vanity.[198]

> "After the soul of Christ had received the heavenly bread, it was to be

---

[197]The first temptation which meets every one on the road to regeneration is the hunger of the lower qualities in him.

"The first cause of real temptation is the transcendent abundant love of God. The human will refuses to submit itself entirely to the exquisite grace which offers itself out of divine love, and seeks for its own self and for the love of that self which belongs to that which is impermanent. It loves itself and the state of this world better than God. Here man is tempted by his own nature, which in her centre stands outside of the love of God, in anguish, combativeness, and dissension, and in which the devil puts his perverted desires for the purpose of leading man away from the sublime grace and love of God. Here the dragon within the soul turns its eyes in vanity towards the world, and shows to her the glory and beauty of this world, and derides her because she desires to become another creature. He puts before her the kingdom wherein she exists and wherein she has her foundation." (*Letters*, xliii. 3.)

[198]The second temptation for the regenerated is spiritual pride.

"The second temptation is, that the soul, after having tasted of divine love, and having once been illumined, desires to have that light in her possession, and to act therein in her own power. The fiery nature of the soul ought to be transformed into a love-fire, and she ought to give up her natural right. This she does not like to do, but looks about, prefers to see herself in her own power, which she, however, does not find. Then the soul begins to doubt the power of grace, for she sees that she has to desert therein her natural desire and will. She then trembles, and will not sacrifice to the divine will the rights conferred upon her by nature and die in the divine will; and she imagines the light of grace, which acts without such a fierce power, to be a false light." (*Letters*, xliii.)

seen whether she would now arise in the power of the fire of vanity, or, full of humility, behold only the heart and the will of God, and surrendering herself to it, become an angel of meekness. Herein is seen the cunning of the devil, because he quotes the Scripture and says, 'The angels will carry him upon their hands.' This passage has been misapplied, because it did not refer to the physical body, but to the soul. This he wanted to introduce into pride, so that it should rely upon being carried by the angels; but the Redeemer said, 'It is also written, Thou shalt not tempt the Lord thy God.' Thus he overcame the pride of the devil and entered into the humility and love of His celestial Father." (*Three Principles*, xxii. 108.)

Finally, he offered to the Saviour the rule over the external world; but the Lord did not accept it from the hands of the devil, but from His celestial Father.[199]

"After the devil had thus failed twice, he came forward with the last powerful temptation (saying) that he would give to Him the whole world if He would fall down and worship him. Adam already had been anxious to come into possession of this world, and he wanted to make it his own; but in doing so he departed from God, and became himself captured by the spirit of this world. Now the second Adam had to submit to this temptation of the first Adam. It was to be tried whether the soul would remain within the new, holy, and celestial man, and live in the grace of God or in the spirit of this world. But the soul of Christ said to the devil, 'Depart from me, Satan! for it is written, Thou shalt worship the Lord thy God, and serve Him alone!' Thus the valiant warrior conquered, and the devil had to depart; and thus all that is earthly has been overcome by the Christ. Now the Lord is higher than the moon,[200] and takes all the power in heaven and hell, and is Master over death and life. He now began His sacerdotal kingdom with signs and miracles. He changed water into wine, made whole the sick, the blind seeing, and enabled the lame to walk, and even awakened the dead to life. He now sat in the chair of David, and was the true priest in the order of Melchisedec." (*Three Principles*, xxii. 3.)

But the victory which the Redeemer had gained over Satan at the time of the temptation could not be sufficient for the purpose of the redemption of mankind. To that end the complete transmutation, consequently the (bodily) death of the Lord, had to take place.[201]

"When Christ was born the heaven existed within the earth—*of man;*

[199]In the regenerating man the third temptation is, that the soul thinks of employing the spiritual powers which she has acquired for purposes which are not divine, namely, for awakening the sourcive spirits of the lower qualities, and thus of raising her head higher than God, as was the case with Lucifer.

[200]The sun of wisdom is higher than the moon of imagination.

[201]Thus in each individual man the overcoming of the temptations on this or that occasion is not sufficient for permanent salvation; for as long as the germ of evil exists, it may sprout again. Final safety is attained only after the battle, when the root of the evil is torn out of the heart.

but this was not sufficient. The two worlds were to wrestle with each other. Therefore came the temptation, and as the divine world conquered, the great wonders (of the spiritual world) became revealed in the external human world. All this, however, could still not be sufficient, because the human quality was still active in her selfhood (self-consciousness) within the movable wrath. It was necessary that the human state should be transmuted into the celestial one, and for that there was no other way than that the name of Jesus in divine love and celestial essentiality would give itself wholly to be devoured by the wrath. Thus the Son was obedient to the wrathful Father, even unto the death on the Cross." (*Signature*, ii. 12–17.)

The physical death as well as the temptation of the Redeemer was caused by Satan, who for that purpose excited the animosity of the mundane and clerical authorities against the Lord.[202]

"Christ said that He was a king of love and Son of God, having come to save His people from sin. The devil then thought that he would lose his kingdom, and the authorities thought, 'If this is a king and Son of God, our supremacy will be at an end;' while the clergy said to themselves, 'He is much too insignificant for us; we want a Messiah who will give us temporal power and glory; one who will make us rich in the world and give us high places in society, so that we shall have all the honour of this world. This man we will not have; He is far too poor for us, and if we were to follow Him we might lose the favour of the mundane authorities. We will remain in our glory and power, and do away with this king of beggars and with His kingdom of love.'" (*Signature*, x. 78.)

By means of His corporeal death, the wrath, or that which was in antagonism to celestial magnificence, was to be taken away from the external being of the Redeemer.[203]

"The human fire-life exists in the blood, and therein rules the wrath of God. Therefore another kind of blood, one that was born from the love-essence of God, had to be brought within the wrathful human blood. Both, however, had to enter together into the wrath of death, and thus the wrath of God had to be extinguished in the divine blood. Therefore external human nature had to die in Christ, so as to exist no longer in the quality of the wrath; so that the power of the celestial blood, namely, the speaking Word, may alone live in external human nature, and rule in its own divine power in external and internal man; that is to say, that the sense of the *I* (the selfishness or illusion of isolation and separateness) cease to exist in humanity; that the Spirit of God should be all in all, and the personality only His instrument living

[202]A more modern way of expressing it would be: When the disciple becomes an accepted "*Chela*," his evil *Karma* begins to assert itself. In other words, the awakening of a new life in an organism stimulates also the lower qualities therein, whether it be a man, a people, or a whole world.
[203]When that which is mortal in man dies, that which is immortal in him returns to freedom.

185

in humility." (*Signature*, ii. 10.)

"In the external flesh of the Redeemer was contained the evil part which came to the surface in Adam when he died relatively to God. Now this evil product was to be received again within the love of God, as Isaiah said of Christ, 'He took all our sins upon Him.' Now the cursed Adam was hanging at the Cross as a curse, but Christ redeemed him by His innocently suffering pain and shedding of blood. Adam's body died on the Cross, and Christ, born of Jesus and the sanctified seed of the woman, tinctured (blessed) him with His dear blood of love." (*Stiefel*, ii. 494.)

"The inner man Christ took our sins upon Him, and left the body, whereon He had laid the curse of God, hanging at the Cross as a curse of God. Thus He died, and in His death He spilt His blood, the blood of the holy man, into the essence of the external man, wherein death resided. But when this holy blood entered into death (with the external essence), then became death terrified at this holy life, and the wrath became terrified by the love, and went down into its own poison, as if killed or annihilated." (*Stiefel*, ii. 205.)

By means of this spiritual death the Lord was to sacrifice entirely to His celestial Father not only the human self-will (this having been already accomplished at the temptation), but also His holy love-will.[204]

"When the speaking Word of God in human quality arrested itself in the Redeemer, then the essentiality which had died in Adam, but became alive again in the Christ, called out together with the soul, 'My God! my God! why hast Thou forsaken me?' This means that the wrath of God had entered through the quality of the soul into the image of the divine essentiality, and it had absorbed within itself the image of God, because it was this image that was to bruise within the fiery soul the head of the wrath of God, and to change its fiery power into the eternal sun-life. As a candle dies in the burning, and as from this dying issues light and power, so out of the dying and death of Christ there was to arise the eternal divine sun in human quality. Thus there was to die in this case not only the selfhood of human quality, *i.e.*, the self-will of the soul relatively to (its desire to) live in the power of the fire, and to be lost in the image of love, but this very image of love had to enter itself into the wrath of death, so that all would sink down in death, and by means of death and perfect humility, and in the will and mercy of God, become raised again in paradisiacal substantiality, so that the Spirit of God might be all in all." (*Signature*, xi. 87.)

[204]Thus every one should sacrifice to God all of his actions, his thoughts, and will; he should not do anything out of his own power, but out of the power of God (after he once knows that power). As the physical body, except in a state of disease (such as spasms, epilepsy, &c.), does not perform any motions except such as originate in the will of the person, likewise the regenerated acts only as he is made to act by the God in him. Mortal and sinful man cannot perform anything really good by his own power; to attempt it would be a presumption and arrogance; for all that is good belongs to God; man is merely an instrument for divine power.

In consequence of this sacrifice of the whole of His will, the human soul-life of the Redeemer did not become annihilated, but it entered thereby entirely into the divine will.[205]

> "The humanity of Christ gave itself up as a sacrifice to the wrath of the Father, entering entirely into His fire-essence; but the love-spirit of God defeated the wrathful essence of the fire, so that it could not consume humanity (the human quality). It merely took away from humanity its self-will, and brought it again into the first universal will, wherefrom the will was (originally) given to man. Thus that same will came again into the will of the Father as into its first root (fountain or origin)." (*Mysterium*, xxxix. 24.)

> "The doctrine that Christ died a natural death in His human quality must not be understood as if meaning that His created soul had died, and still less that He had perished in His aspect as a divine being, or relatively to His celestial essentiality and celestial tincture. He only died relatively to His selfhood, *i.e.*, relatively to the will and regimen of the external world which ruled in man. He died relatively to the self-will and to the self-powers of the created self hood. All this He gave up entirely into the Father's hands as being the end of nature, the great mystery of the Father; but not so that it should be dead, but so that the Spirit of God should be therein all its life, and the divine regimen exist in the personality of Christ." (*Signature*, xii. 1.)

Neither did the external being of the Redeemer become lost by His corporeal death, but it entered thereby into its true and exalted substantiality.[206]

> "When Christ died He did not throw away the body which had been in His possession while upon the earth, or left it to be consumed by the four elements, thus keeping (or taking up) a body entirely foreign (to the terrestrial form); but He merely laid aside the suffering (the external consciousness) of this world, and clothed Himself in immortality, so that His body might live in divine power, and not in the spirit of this world." (*Three Principles*, xxv. 53.)

> "Christ assumed indeed earthly substance, but in His death—that is to say, as He overcame death—the divine being caused the earthly state to disappear and took away from it its supremacy. Not that Christ had laid aside something (which He did not), but so that the external being was conquered and, so to speak, consumed." (*Menschwerdung*, i. 8, 11.)

> "The true essentiality in Christ did not take away the earthly

---

[205]If the self-will is entirely sacrificed to the divine will in man, then does man's will not thereby become annihilated, but is itself rendered divine.

[206]However gratifying it may be for the curious seeker in history to know whether or when such an event has actually occurred in the history of the Jewish nation, such a historical belief would be of little benefit to him if he could not realise within his own inner consciousness that the death of his mortal nature cannot cause any loss to that which is immortal in him.

consciousness, but entered into the latter as its lord and conqueror. The true life was to be led first into death and the wrath of God. This took place on the Cross, on which occasion death became destroyed and the wrath imprisoned and extinguished by love, and thus conquered." (*Menschwerdung*, ix. 16.)

"When Jesus broke up death in (His) humanity and took away the sense of self, He did then not throw away the human quality wherein dwelt death and the wrath of God, but He now accepted them to the fullest extent; that is to say, He only now took the external realm within the interior one." (*Signature*, xi. 41.)

"The external active and feeling life, wherein the wrath of God was burning, died, but not in such a way that it would have become a nothing, but it descended into nothing; that is to say, in this case, into the will of God, into His acting and feeling. Thereby it became free of the will of the external world, which will is evil and good, and it lived no longer within the world and the constellations with the four elements, but after the nature of the Father and within the pure and divine element. Thus the true human life came to occupy again the position which had been lost by Adam, and entered again into Paradise." (*Signature*, xii. 5.)

The earthly being of the Redeemer was sanctified by His celestial blood, and thereby it was prepared for the resurrection.[207]

"When Christ poured out His celestial blood, then the fiery desire kindled in humanity became transformed into a love-desire, and out of the anguish of death there was born a joy and strength of divine power." (*Signature*, xi. 5.)

"When the Son of God poured out His holy blood in Christ, then did the poison of the wrath in Adam's flesh, soul, and spirit, which He took upon Himself, become sanctified and transformed into love. Thus the enmity ceased then and there, and God became *Immanuel*; that is to say, man with God and God with man. Then the flesh of Adam became tinctured and prepared for the resurrection."[208] (*Stiefel*, ii. 209.)

By the power of the glorification at which the Redeemer arrived through His entering into death He overcame the power of hell, so that now the life again issued from death.[209]

---

[207]The earthly body is those elements in the terrestrial man the ultimate expression of which is his visible form.
"There are two beings (natures) in man. The spirit-life is directed inwardly, and the natural life acts in an outward direction." (*Text*. v. 1.)

[208]The "flesh of Adam" is as invisible to us as the spiritual body of Christ. That which we see with our external eyes is merely an appearance.

[209]Whenever the light of Christ in the soul of man penetrates within the interior foundation of his fiery will, then is that will changed into sweet love, and the soul enters into freedom from the bondage of self.

"It is erroneous to suppose that the soul of Christ had left the body and had travelled down to hell, and that it had there, in divine power, attacked the devils and bound them with chains, and thus destroyed hell. It is rather to be understood that at the moment at which Christ laid off the kingdom of this world His soul entered into death and the wrath of God, and thus was the wrath reconciled in love. Thus the devils and all the godless souls in the wrath were imprisoned within themselves, and death was broken up; but the life sprang forth through death." (*Three Principles*, xxv. 76.)

"Death was wrestling with the external (life of) man, and thought that now the soul would have to remain in the *Turba;* but there was a stronger power within the soul, namely, the Word of God. This Word captured death and destroyed it, and extinguished the wrath. It was a great poison to hell when the light entered within it, and thus the Spirit of Christ imprisoned the devil, and led him out of the soul-fire into the darkness, and locked him up in the darkness, in wrathful harshness and bitterness." (*Forty Questions*, xxxvii. 13–15.)

"By the power of the celestial tincture God ignited the fire that had become dark within the essence of the soul, so that henceforth that fire began to burn in white, clear, and majestic power, in light and glory, and thus the wrath of God became extinguished in the essence of the soul and was made into love." (*Tilk.* ii. 259.)

"The soul of Christ came with the light of God into the wrath, and then the devils trembled; for the light imprisoned the wrath, so that it became a paradise, while the wrath remained in hell. The light closed up the principle of hell, so that no devil is permitted to show himself in the light. He is also blind relatively to it, and the light is his terror and shame." (*Three Principles*, xxv. 79.)

Thus, in consequence of the bodily death of Christ, the holy ones of olden times who had longed for His coming attained resurrection.[210]

"The holy ones, having put their faith into the Messiah, received now the pure element for a new body, according to the promise. For, as the promised hero entered through life into death, their souls clothed themselves in the body of Christ as in a new body, and lived in Him through His power. These were the holy fathers and prophets who in this world had been anointed in the power of the Word of God with the bruiser of the serpent's head, and who by its power had prophesied and performed miracles. They now became alive in the power of Christ." (*Three Principles*, xxiv. 52.)

"The fathers of the Jews had known Christ not in the flesh, but only in His prototype, and they had clothed themselves therein only in its

[210]If the purified soul of man enters into the divine fountain from which she originated, bringing with her the light which she has gathered unto herself during her terrestrial existence, then will this be like adding new fuel to the fire, and a new effulgence of light and glory will take place in the soul of the world.

power by means of the first incorporated covenant and word; but now they clothed themselves in His substance, for all those who had put their faith in Him, and had clothed themselves in the covenant in spirit, in these the covenant was then filled with celestial substantiality. Thus there were many who were raised with Him after His resurrection, and they caused themselves to be seen at Jerusalem, in testimony that they had been raised up in Christ." (*Grace*, x. 45.)

This conquest of hell and death was accompanied by certain phenomena upon the earth, indicating the approaching destruction of the whole terrestrial world.[211]

"As the prisons of the dark world were to be destroyed in the death of Christ, the earth trembled and the sun became darkened, which symbolised that, as now the eternal light had been born anew, the temporal light would have to cease to exist." (*Grace*, vii. 8.)

"When the earth received the blood of Christ she trembled and shook, for the wrath of God was now conquered in her, and there entered into her the living blood which had come from heaven out of the substantiality of God." (*Menschwerdung*, i. 10.)

"The wrath of the Father had to consume in death the life of Christ; but when the wrath had swallowed up the life in death, then the holy life of the deepest love of God moved in the death and wrath and swallowed up the wrath. Then the earth began to tremble, and the rocks burst and the tombs of the holy ones opened." (*Mysterium*, xxviii. 123.)

"After the Father had brought again the soul of the Redeemer, that had entered into His wrath, into love—that is to say, into the image from Paradise, which had disappeared—then the world trembled in the terror of death as with a terror of joy, and that joy entered into the dead bodies of those that had hoped for the coining of the Messiah, and awakened them to life. It was this very terror that tore the curtain in the Temple, namely, the veil of Moses, which hung before the clear face of God, so that man could not see God." (*Signature*, xi. 71.)

The body in which Christ Himself arose from the dead was paradisiacal and divine, and could not be apprehended by anything of an earthly nature; but as the terrestrial body was absorbed therein, therefore the Lord could make Himself visible to His disciples.[212]

---

[211]Likewise in each individual man will the terrestrial light disappear from his view when the Christ has arisen in him; for the Christ Himself is the Light, and surpasses the light of external nature. If that divine light arises in man, then will the celestial spirits that have been dormant in his soul arise and move and rejoice.

[212]Neither will any one's physical body, wherein the inner man is imprisoned as in a tomb, offer any obstacles for the prisoner to escape, after the latter has been raised from the darkness of ignorance into the light of spiritual self-knowledge. Then will the inner sight of the soul be opened and the rock be rolled away. Then may the inner man go out and visit his disciples.

"The body in which Christ became raised from the dead could not be stopped or arrested by rocks or stones. It passes through all things without breaking anything; it takes hold of this world, but this world cannot lay hold of it. Nothing can make it suffer, for in it is all the fulness of the Godhead." (*Three Principles*, xxv. 87.)

"There was no necessity for the removal of a stone to liberate the body of the Lord from the tomb. This took place merely to show to the Jews the folly of their imagining that they could withstand God, and also for the sake of the weak faith of the disciples, so that they might see that Christ had in truth been raised up." (*Three Principles*, xxv. 85.)

"Although Christ not always walked visibly among His disciples, nevertheless He showed Himself often visibly, tangibly, and substantially to them in the shape of the body which He had occupied while upon this earth, and which the new body had absorbed, but which it had the power to represent again." (*Three Principles*, xxiv. 97.)

The heaven wherein the Redeemer has entered after His resurrection is the fulness of divine power, by means of which He is Lord over the terrestrial world and over the world of hell.[213]

"The internal foundation of this world, whereof the four elements have originated, is heaven, and in this internal power Christ rules as true God and Man in the external world. When He says, 'To Me has been given all power in heaven and upon the earth,' and also, 'I am with you every day unto the end of the world;' and furthermore, if it is said of Him, 'He shall rule over His enemies until they are all made to be a footstool under His feet,' all this refers to His internal kingdom, because He rules within the internal and over and above the external and terrestrial, and likewise over the hellish world." (*Baptism*, ii. i, 29.)

Thus the Bible history of the life of Christ and the miracles which He performed, is a description of the processes taking place within the inner life of the regenerated. In Jesus Christ we behold the antitype of the one and only Redeemer of the world, as a whole, and of every separate individual. Every object or person we see in the world is nothing but a symbol of existing ideas; every event taking place in external life is the outcome of invisibly acting forces. The historical correctness of the occurrences described in the Bible may be questioned, but what they describe are facts known to those who have experienced them themselves. The truth of the religion of Christ does not depend on the verification of external historical events; for true Christianity is based neither upon a knowledge of cosmology nor upon history, but upon love.

[213]Man, having become one with the Christ in Humanity, will necessarily partake of His powers in Divinity. The will of the Father is then his own, and in the Son he rules as a Lord over the spiritual kingdom, and through the inner world over the external one.

"The innermost *ground* in man is Christ; but not according to man's human nature, but according to *His*, the divine quality in His celestial essence, which He has regenerated. The *second* ground is the soul, *i.e.*, eternal nature, wherein Christ (the light) becomes revealed; and the third *ground* is the external man, out of the *limus* of the earth with the stars and the four elements. In the first ground is the active life of divine love; in the second is the natural fire-life of the created soul, wherein God is called a fiery God; and in the third is the creation of all the qualities wherein Adam stood in the *temperature*, and which was objectified in the fall." (*Grace*, iv. 37.)

> "'Christ' means a penetrator; the act of taking away the power of the wrath; the illumination of the darkness by light; the transmutation (in the soul of man), by which the gladness of love rules over the lust of the fire in its wrathful aspect; the superiority of light over darkness." (*Signature*, vii. 3 2.)

To "love Christ" means simply to love the divine light of wisdom and truth, and is practised by being obedient to divine law.[214]

[214]"Why does the soul torment herself and strive in her own power and will, thus augmenting her torture? The more anxious she is, the greater will be her pain, and she acquires no rest. A dying plant does not begin to sprout and obtain sap by its own power, and likewise the soul cannot by her own power attain the kingdom of God. She ought to do nothing but abandon her own selfish will, then the evil qualities become weak, and her will returns to the one from which she came in the beginning. Here God will send His supreme love to meet her; that love which has been revealed in humanity, in Jesus Christ." (*Illumined Soul*, 46.)

Chapter XIII
Regeneration

"Art thou a master of Israel, and knowest not of those things?"
—JOHN iii. 10.

"Whoever will come after Me, let him deny himself, and take up his cross daily, and follow Me."—LUKE ix. 23.

No man can attain spiritual self-knowledge without being spiritual, because it is not intellectual man that knows the Spirit, but the divine Spirit that attains self-knowledge in man.

"Christ said, 'Unless you become like children, you will not see the kingdom of God.' And again He says (John iii.), 'Unless a person is born of the water and Spirit, he cannot enter into the kingdom of God; for that which is born from the flesh is flesh, and what is born from the Spirit is spirit.' It is clearly shown in the Bible that the carnal natural man does not conceive of the Spirit of God. That Spirit is to him a foolishness, and he cannot comprehend it."

"It is self-evident, and requires no further proof, that we are all made up of flesh and blood, and that we are mortal. Nevertheless, we are taught that we are temples of the Holy Spirit who dwells in us. We are also taught that Christ must take a form in us, and that He will give us His flesh as our nutriment and His blood for us to drink. He says that he who does not eat the flesh of the Son of Man will have no eternal life. Therefore we ought to seriously consider what kind of a man is within our own self similar to God and capable of becoming divine." (*Regeneration*, i.)

"For that which is made of mortal flesh will again return to earth. In it dwells the vanity of this world. It is desirous for that which is not of God, and it cannot be said to be a temple of the Holy Spirit. Much less can there take place a spiritual regeneration of this terrestrial flesh, because it dies and becomes dissolved, and is a dwelling for sins. But the true Christian is born out of Christ, and that which is regenerated is a temple of the Holy Spirit dwelling in us." (*Regeneration*, i.)

For the purpose of understanding the process of the spiritual regeneration of man it is useless to cling to a merely historical belief in a Christ supposed to have died for the purpose of paying our debts to an angry God, but it is necessary to eat of the flesh and drink of the blood of the living Christ within ourselves; that is to say that we must allow our soul to become filled with the divine substantiality of the body of Christ, and experience the paradisiacal power of Christ therein.

"To produce a true Christian it is not sufficient to he satisfied with a merely historical or scientific belief in a Son of God who is said to have once lived upon the earth. It is not that we are to be rewarded by some external God attributing righteousness to us on account of our confessing such a belief, but the recognition of divine truth must be born within us and received by us in a child-like manner. As the flesh is bound to die, so the life and the will of our sinful nature must die, and we must become like a child that knows nothing, but clings (instinctively) to the mother who gave it birth. And thus the will of the Christian must die to its own self-willing and self-assertion, and become like a child in Christ. Then, if the will and desire of the soul is directed only to its source, there will arise from the Spirit of Christ a new will and obedience in divine justice, out of the death of the self-will, and not the sinful will." (*Regeneration*, i.)

To form a correct conception of the regeneration of man, and of what kind of a being it is which is to be brought to life in us, we must learn to know what is eternity and time, light and darkness, good and evil, and especially the origin and the generation of man. We shall then find that man is of a threefold aspect. In one aspect he dwells continually in heaven, and is a member of the body of Christ; in another aspect he is subject to the powers of darkness, and in his third aspect he is made of mortal flesh. Nevertheless there are not three men in one human being, but he is only one.

It is nowhere stated that God is a temple of man, and that we can enter into Him with our human selfhood, however refined that selfhood may be. The spiritual regeneration of man is brought about by the divine power of God entering and becoming self-conscious in man, so that his whole being becomes filled with God as the darkness becomes filled with light.

"We behold the eternal world with its stars, and the four elements wherein man and all creatures live. This is not God, and is not called 'God.' God dwells therein, but the essence of the external world does not comprehend Him. Likewise the light shines into the darkness, and the darkness comprehendeth it not."

"God dwells in the world and fills everything; nevertheless He possesses nothing. The light dwells within the darkness, but does not own it; day dwells in night and night in the day, time in eternity and eternity in time; and so it is with man. He is himself time, and lives within it according to his external aspect, and likewise the external world is existing in time; but the inner man is eternity, and spiritual time and world, such as is created in light according to the love of God, and in darkness according to His wrath. His spirit lives in that principle which is manifest in him, either in darkness or in the light. Each of these dwells within itself; neither possesses the other; but if one enters within the other and desires to possess the other, then will the other lose its supremacy and power. If the light becomes manifest in the darkness, then the darkness ceases to be darkness; and if the darkness arises within the light, then the light and its power will be extinguished.

"The eternal darkness of the soul is the kingdom of hell; the eternal light in the soul is her heaven. Man, therefore, is created of, and lives in three worlds. One is the world of eternal darkness that arises from the centre of nature—eternal nature—wherein is born the fire as the eternal torment; the other world is the world of eternal light, wherein resides happiness and the Spirit of God. It is in this world of light wherein the Spirit of Christ assumes human substantiality. The third world wherein man lives, and from which he was generated, is the external visible world, with its four elements, and the visible stars." (*Regeneration*, i.)

Now the question may be asked, "By what means can man effect the process of his spiritual regeneration?" The answer is, that man, not being a god, can accomplish nothing whatever of that kind by his own will or power, and that it can only be accomplished by the unmerited grace of the god in him. No one can give unto himself anything which he does not possess; neither can any man attract unto himself by an exercise of his will the sunshine. All that man can do is to employ the powers which he has received from God for the purpose that there may be no impediment created by his self-will which might prevent the action of the Holy Spirit within his own soul. To accomplish this he must rise by the aid of the divine Spirit within himself above the inferior elements within his own nature, and thus surrender his whole self-will to God, an act which is expressed in the original meaning of the word "prayer."[215]

"Spiritual regeneration does not depend on learning and scientific knowledge; but there must be an intense and powerful earnest, a great hunger and thirst for the Spirit of Christ. Mere science is not faith; the latter is the intense hunger and thirst for that which I desire, so that it becomes formed into an image within me, and by grasping it in my imagination it becomes my own property. This hunger and desire moulds the substance of Christ, it being the celestial substantiality, into the weakened image, wherein the word of the power of God is the active life.

"If, then, the soul partakes of this celestial nutriment, she becomes kindled by the great love that dwells in the name Jesus. Then her

[215]In the German language the word *Gebet* (prayer) originates from *geben* (to give), and means, therefore, a gift or sacrifice to God. It does not imply the offering of selfish petitions or the asking for personal favours. However, if we give ourselves fully to God, and are accepted by Him, we then become, as it were, a part of God, and consequently a partaker of His divine powers. It would then be easy for us to grant our own desires, if in that divine state there could be room for personal desires of any kind.

anguish becomes converted into great joy and a real sun arises within her, while she becomes regenerated into another will. Then takes place the marriage of the Lamb, of which the mouth-Christians talk so much without understanding the meaning." (*Regeneration*, iv.)

"In the name of Jesus, God has opened a door for us to His ear, whereby we may hear God actually speak within us as in His mercy He speaks to us through this opened portal of thought. Again, the soul speaks through this door to God within herself, and during this inspeaking she is nourished, restored, illumined, and renewed by the outspeaking of God." (*Prayer*, xxxi.)

"If the soul is to receive actual advantage and fruition from prayer, then must her will turn away from all creatures and terrestrial things and stand pure before God. Let not the flesh with its desires co-operate (in prayer) so that earthly desires may not be introduced into the divine effect in the soul." (*Prayer*, xxxiv.)

"Every prayer which does not find and take (what it asks) is cold and insipid, and is obstructed by temporal terrestrial things; that is to say, the soul does then not approach God in purity. She does not want to sacrifice herself entirely to God, but clings to terrestrial loves which hold her imprisoned so that she cannot attain the kingdom of God." (*Prayer*, xviii.)

No man can truly pray in spirit and in truth by his own power, because only that which is divine can enter into relation with the Divine. True prayer is not a mere wishing or desiring, but an action within the power of the omnipotent God.

Prayer is the union with God effected by the sacrifice of the personal will. It is, therefore, the only "*Yoga* practice" worthy of serious attention.[216]

"The will necessary to accomplish prayer is far too weak as long as it is in our own powers that we pray, but if acted upon by divine power it becomes awakened, fiery, and full of desire. Within this desire God Himself is acting. Thus does man speak with God in truth, and God speaks in truth with the soul of man." (*Prayer*, xxix.)

"He who truly prays co-operates with God internally, while externally he produces good fruit." (*Prayer*, xxiv.)

"Mere word-prayer without exaltation of thought and divine desire is only an external thing, a mere repeating of words. Nothing pleases God except that which He does Himself." (*Prayer*, i. 2.)

Christ says (Matt. vii. 21): "Not all who say, Lord! Lord! will enter the

[216]True prayer is the bringing of will, thought, and word into one Δ by the power of the Spirit of God.

kingdom of heaven, but those who do the will of My Father in heaven." It would seem self-evident that no being inferior to the Father in heaven can possibly do the will of the Father, because no one can do the will of God unless he is in possession of God's will, and thus one with God. Therefore he who wants to pray truly or to practice "Yoga" must enter into heaven; that is to say, into the celestial state of will.

The new life which is accorded to man by means of his regeneration in the power of faith and prayer is not a mere spirit, but corporeal and substantial. The "body of the resurrection," even if it is invisible to mortal eyes, is far more durable and indestructible than any imaginable physical form.

> "While Christ eats the faith and the prayer of our soul, the human faith, together with the prayer and praise of God, become corporeal in the word of the power, and this new being is then one with the substance of the celestial corporeity of Christ, the eternal body of Christ." (*Mysterium*, lxx.)

> "The poor imprisoned soul, shut up within the darkness of death, is a hungering magical fire, which attracts from the incarnation of Christ the reopened substantiality of God, and out of this swallowing or nourishing she produces a body similar to Divinity. Thus, then, the poor soul will be clothed with a body of light, comparable to the fire in a burning wick." (*Letters*, xi. 21.)

> "The new man is not a mere spirit, but he lives in flesh and blood, comparable to gold in a rock, which is not merely spiritual, but has a body; nut only such a body as that of the gross rock, but a body which can stand the test of the fire." (*Menschwerdung*, i. 4.)

The creation of this new body is the beginning of the union of man with divine glory, but it is not the perfection of it. The process of regeneration, like that of physical generation, has its stages of development. Upon the baptism by "water" follows that of the "blood," and finally that of the "fire."

> "By means of the introduction of the divine will man becomes reunited to God and reborn in his emotional nature. He then begins to die relatively to the selfishness of the false desire (in him) and to be regenerated in new power. There is then still attracted to him the carnal quality, but in the spirit he walks with God, and thus there is born within the earthly man of flesh a new spiritual man with divine perceptions and with a divine will, killing day by day the lust of the flesh, and by divine power rendering the world—*i.e.*, the external life —heavenly, and causing heaven—*i.e.*, the inner spiritual world—to become visible in the external world, so that God becomes man and man God, until finally the tree reaches its perfection, when the external

197

shell will drop off, and it then stands there as a spiritual tree of life in the garden of God." (*Mysterium*, Supplement, viii.)

This imbibing of the "Elixir of Life" no man can accomplish by his own mortal power. All he can do is to render himself receptive for the divine power. The rest is done by the Spirit of God.

The new life of the regenerated is during his terrestrial existence continually exposed to great dangers, arising from three sources, namely, from the selfishness of human nature, from the devil (evil will), and from the desires of the mortal flesh and blood.

> "No one should imagine himself to be secure after having once obtained the crown of pearls, for he may lose it again. The soul is during her terrestrial life fettered by three fearful chains. First, by the severe wrath of God, the abyss and dark world, which is the centre of the created life of the soul, whose innermost root is desire. The second chain is the fiery longing of the devil for the soul, in consequence of which he tempts the soul and incessantly seeks to throw her from her rest in divine truth down into vanity—*i.e.*, into pride, avarice, envy, and anger; and these evil propensities he continually seeks to fan the fire in the soul, and thus the will of the soul is made to turn away from God and to enter into selfishness. But the third and most dangerous chain, to which the whole of the soul is tied, is the corruptible, vain, earthly, and mortal flesh and blood, which is full of evil desires and inclinations, together with the star region (astral plane), wherein, like in a great ocean, the soul is floating, and which causes her to become daily infected and inflamed in sin." (*Three Principles*, xxv. 7.)

There is a continual danger for the soul of sinking back into the acrid root of her existence, and at the same time she is continually exposed to the aggressions of the devil.

> "If a person is in the anxiety of enmity, and the sting of death and anger is moving in him, so as to render him avaricious, envious, angry, and irritable, he ought then not to remain in that evil essence, but stop to consider and draw (from the eternal fountain) another will, namely, the will to go out of malice and enter into the freedom of God, wherein is perpetual rest and peace. If then his anguish tastes the freedom, then will the torture of the anguish become terrified, and in this terror death will be broken up; for this terror is of great joy and consists in a kindling of the life of God. Thereby the branchlet of pearls appears, and this now stands in trembling joy, but also in great danger; for death and the torture of anguish are its root; as also the anguish in external nature has the quality that out of evil, *i.e.*, out of the anguish, the great life is born. Out of a manure, for instance, a beautiful green branch grows, it having, of course, a constitution, odour, and state (life) different from that which produced it." (*Menschwerdung*, xi. 8.)

"The poor soul is so much blinded as not even to recognise the heavy chains wherewith she is bound. The whole world is full of traps set by the devil for the purpose of capturing her. If the outer man could have his eyes (spiritually) opened he would be terrified. Whatever a man sees or touches, therein is a devil's trap, and if the Word of the Lord, having become human, were not occupying the middle, the devil would capture and devour all souls."[217] (*Menschwerdung*, xi. 6.)

"As long as earthly man lives the soul will be in continual danger, for the devil is at enmity with her, and shoots his rays with a false imagination into the spirit of the stars and elements, and he therewith reaches out after the soul-fire, and desires to poison it with an earthly and devilish desire. Then must the noble image (in the inner consciousness in man) stand up in defence; much fighting for the crownlet of the angels is then required, and there often arises doubt and unbelief within the old Adam." (*Menschwerdung*, xi. 6.)

"Even after the precious jewel is sown it does not immediately become a tree. Often the devil blows over it, and wishes to exterminate the mustard-seed. Many storms has the soul to suffer. Often she is deluded with sin, and everything seems to be against her. You must continually battle against the devil. Then will the pearl-tree grow like grass in storm and rain; but when it becomes big and brings forth flowers, you may then be sure of obtaining the fruit." (*Three Principles*, xxiv. 37.)

The new life of the Spirit unfolds itself within the innermost being, and the terrestrial man is only rarely pervaded by the divine luminosity.

"Not the mortal soul, but the inner (spiritual) soul from the eternal Word of God is to be married to Sophia. The external soul is wedded to the constellation (mental functions) and elements. This external soul only rarely obtains a glance at Sophia, for she has death and mortality within herself. After this time she is to be again transformed into the first image which God created in Adam." (*Mysterium*, lii. 13.)

"While the mortal house exists our soul does not dwell in the fountain of God, so as to apprehend that fountain in her selfhood. The sun shines through a glass and renders it luminous; nevertheless the glass does not become the sun. It merely remains (for a while) in the light and power of the sun, and the latter shines to and through its substance. Thus it is with the soul in her terrestrial state." (*Mysterium*, lii. 3.)

"As fire glows in hot iron, so are the rays of the Holy Spirit sometimes

[217]Here it may be useful to remark that if a person cannot perceive these dangers of the devil which are lurking in everything, it would be folly for him to imagine all sorts of dangers in his own fancy, whereby he would merely create for himself innumerable fears and perplexities, and become afraid of the world, instead of superior to it. The main paint for the seeker of divine enlightenment is, and remains, to put his "point of gravitation" into the divine self-reliance, and remember that he who has found his true dignity and manhood in God is superior to the devil, and there is nothing in the universe which could give him just cause for fear.

penetrating the other principle; namely, the new man penetrates the old one. But as iron, whether within or without the forge, always remains iron, likewise it is with the terrestrial man. He undoubtedly has to become a servant for the inner man, whenever the latter penetrates him with his glowing divine fire; and he is willing that this should be so as long as the glow of that fire is within him, but he cannot transform himself into the interior kingdom. 'The external flesh and blood,' says Christ, 'shall not inherit the kingdom of heaven.' It shall and must dissolve, like the husk of the kernel sown into a field." (*Stiefel*, i. 24.)

Only rarely, but especially in the moment of regeneration, there is within the human self the living sensation of a celestial existence.

"No one must ever think that the tree of the Christian faith can be seen or known in the kingdom of this world. External man does not recognise it, and even if it happens that the Holy Spirit manifests itself in the external mirror, so that the external life is glad and trembles for joy, and thinks that now it has received the esteemed guest, and that it would now believe, nevertheless there is no perfect duration therein; for the Spirit of God does not remain constantly within the terrestrial mind. It wants to have a clean vessel, and whenever it returns into its principle—this being the true image—then the external being becomes doubtful and full of fears." (*Menschwerdung*, cxi. 8.)

"The soul puts on her wreath; but it is again taken away from her and put aside. Thus it is with a crown with which a king has been crowned, and which is afterwards kept in the treasury. This is done to the soul because she is still surrounded by a house of sin; so that if she should fall again, her crown may not become soiled." (*Repentance*, i. 27.)

The first and greatest danger for the new-born being arises from pride; as is illustrated in the New Testament, for hardly is the new-born Saviour laid in the cradle, standing between the ox of self will and the ass of ignorance in the stable, represented by the animal constitution of man, when the king of pride (Herod) finds his kingdom endangered, and seeks to kill the child, which is to become the ruler in the new Jerusalem within the consciousness of man.[218]

"The enlightened children of God are threatened by a great danger; namely, in many of them who enjoyed the great sight of the holiness of God, wherein the triumph of life is attained, carnal reason mirrors itself therein and seeks to intrude its selfishness into the interior centre from whence the light shines. From this results miserable pride and self-conceit; and selfish reason,—being, moreover, nothing but a reflection of the eternal light,—fancies itself to be more than that. It thinks that it may now do as it pleases, and that, whatever it does, it is

[218]See "*Jehoshua, the Prophet of Nazareth.*"

the will of God doing it in it, and it believes itself to be a prophet. Nevertheless it enters nowhere except within its own self, and moves within its own desire, whereby the *centrum naturæ* soon begins to arise. Then the devil of flattery comes forward, and man becomes drunk with self-conceit, persuading himself that it is God who compels him to act as he does. Thus he ruins the good beginning, during which the light of God began to shine within nature, and then the light of God departs from him. There is then nothing left but the light of external nature within the creature, but self-assertion puts itself therein and fancies that it is the original light received from God."[219] (*Calmness*, i. 8.)

Within the human constitution the old terrestrial and the new celestial states are dwelling together, and this necessarily causes within the regenerated a continual battle during the term of his terrestrial life. This battle between the higher and the lower consciousness, between earthly desires and celestial joy, is experienced by every one, but it is especially marked in those in whom, on account of a higher degree of spirituality, the spiritual sensitiveness is more keen.

"Not in the terrestrial essence does God become manifest in us, but in the true image that became weakened in Adam; but the external thing clings to the internal, the inner man manifests the divine mystery, and the external one the external mystery or the mirror of wonders. From this results the battle in the new-born man. The new man wants to be lord, for he perceives the divine world; but the terrestrial man is opposed to him, and wants to rule also, for he perceives the external world." (*Forty Questions*, xvii. 14.)

"The cause of the antagonism between the flesh and the spirit can easily be found without much seeking, for the inner spirit has the body of God, born from the sweet essentiality, and the external spirit has the body of the fiery mirror of wrath, which continually seeks to awaken wrath; namely, the great wonders which are in the Arcanum in the sternness of the soul. The inner love-spirit protests and will not let the external spirit arise and fire the soul; because it would cause it to lose its own happiness and form, which would then be destroyed by the wrath." (*Forty Questions*, xvii. 14.)

"There are two kinds of will to be distinguished in the constitution of man. One arises within the lily and grows in the kingdom of God; the other sinks into the darkness of death and desires for the earth, she being its mother. This latter will continually battles against the lily, and the lily flies from its roughness. A sprout grows from the earth, and thus the substance of which it is formed flies from the earth and is

[219]The human intellect, in its relation to the divine spirit, may be compared to the moon that receives her light from the sun. In either case the former is merely a reflection, while in the latter rests the true light. Thus there are many who mistake the reflection for the true light and their own fancies for the wisdom of God, and from this arises that self-conceit which is never more repulsive than if found among those who boast of being the servants of God.

attracted towards the sunlight until it becomes a plant or a tree. So does the divine Sun draw the human lily, *i.e.*, the new man in his power, out of the substance of evil, until he finally becomes a tree in the kingdom of God. He then lets the evil tree or the husk wherein the new tree grew drop into the earth, its mother, for which that husk was longing." (*Menschwerdung*, xi. 8.)

Trees do not grow in the air, but require the dark soil and manure to take root and draw nutriment from the earth, and likewise the inner man requires the outer one for the purpose of gaining experience and self-knowledge.

"In the rough rock precious gold may be found growing, and the roughness of the rock aids it to grow, although the roughness is not like the gold. Likewise the terrestrial body must aid in generating Christ within itself, even though that body is not Christ, and never will be Christ in eternity." (*Grace*, viii. 94.)

"We are of an earthly nature, but we have also a celestial existence within the terrestrial one. During temporal life both are mixed with each other, but they do not act upon each other; each one is merely the dwelling of the other, as is the case with gold-bearing rock. The rock is not the gold, but merely its vehicle. The roughness of the rock is not that which produces gold, but this is done by the tincture of the sun acting therein."[220] (*Menschwerdung*, i. 14.)

In this battle between the terrestrial and celestial nature we need not be aggressive, but merely on the defence. This means that it is useless to resist evil or to combat it by remaining on the same level with it. We render ourselves free from the conflict by rising above the place of contention, and this rising is accomplished by surrendering ourselves to the Supreme; or, to express it in other words, we conquer the flesh by sacrificing ourselves to the eternal spirit in Christ.

"Adamic man may live in Paradise according to the inner element which is unfolded within his mind, provided he does not permit himself to be affected by malice and surrenders himself fully to the heart of God. Then will the virgin within the inner element receive him and illumine his heart, so that he may master the Adamic body." (*Three Principles*, xv. 20.)

---

[220]There are many "Christians," "Buddhists," &c., who imagine that they could attain the apex of perfection if they were only getting rid of their physical body. Some even go so far as to object to having a soul. Surely the Divinity *per se* does require neither a physical body nor a soul to be self-existent and eternal; but man requires all this to enable the light of Divinity to become revealed in him. Without that, man, even if he could continue to be, would be unconscious of his existence; a spirit without knowing or experiencing anything about it. Immortality is not attained by merely fancying oneself to be immortal; neither can there be much satisfaction for man to believe that God is immortal as long as he is godless himself. *Gautama* himself could not have become a "*Buddha*"—*i.e.*, an enlightened soul—if he had not been in possession of a soul which could be enlightened. This divine soul is the body of Christ.

"We are always exposed to temptations, but we can be victorious in Christ who has conquered, for His soul is our soul and His flesh is our flesh, provided that we trust in Him and surrender ourselves to Him entirely, as Christ surrendered Himself to His Father."[221] (*Forty Questions*, i. 10.)

Far easier is it to overcome the desire for evil than to destroy it after it has become embodied by being enacted.

"Desire is the introducing (of the will) into a thing, and from the desire results the formation of a corporeal being (in the astral plane). Therein is hidden the source of sin. It is far easier to ward off the desire than to destroy the body (formed by the act). The latter is far more difficult. Therefore it is advisable to turn away one's eyes from evil desire, so that the tincture (the life-principle) may not enter the essence and the mind be filled with that whereby the desire becomes substantial and which will require a (forcible) breaking up." (*Three Principles*, xx. 28.)

"It is far better to demolish the desire than to demolish afterwards the substance with great pains. If the free will already in the beginning (of a desire) destroys the desire, so that it does not become substantial, then is the physician (for the cure of that disease) already born, and there will not be needed such great earnestness as will be required by him who wants to come out of the company of the monsters which he has created, and who will have to destroy the being which he has brought into shape within his own soul."[222] (*Mysterium*, xxiv. 25.)

If men were realising their true nature as vehicles of the divine spirit, they would see the utter folly of their craving for that which is agreeable or useful for the material self alone, without benefiting the spirit. From a spiritual point of view, external pleasures which are not instructive are not merely worthless, but actually an impediment to the attainment of our permanent treasure; because in strengthening the ties which bind us to matter they loosen the link that connects us with heaven.

---

[221]The very same idea is expressed in the *Bhagavad Gita*, where man is advised to seek to realise that he is one with *Krishna*, and having realised it, he will be no longer a partaker, but merely a spectator, in the battle, which after all does not concern the Divinity in him, his own real self. No man can, however, identify himself by his own human power with Krishna or Christ; this always requires the presence and the power of Christ or Krishna Himself. In other words, it requires, as Boehme expresses it. "the *grace* of God, which, however, can be found within every person who ceases to desire evil." (*Mysterium*, lxi. 57.)

Boehme says: "No man can make himself a child of God, but he must throw himself entirely into a state of complete obedience to God. Then will God make him His child. He must be dead (to all sense of self), then will God in the Christ live in him." (*Tilk.* i. 398.)

"No man can by his own power raise himself into the light which is extinct within his will, but he may enter the ground that produces the light and wherein is hidden neither evil nor good, because he is himself that foundation (cause). If he then, in his imagination, sinks himself into the abyss, he is then already there, and in this abyss is his pearl (the celestial jewel)." (*Grace*, ii. 43.)

[222]This may be expressed in other words by saying that desire gives rise to the formation of a thought, and this thought is made alive by the will, and obtains substantiality and the right to live by being acted out. It is easier to avoid creating such an *Elemental* than to kill it after it has been created; because such a being is a part of our own self, and its destruction involves suffering.

203

"It is the greatest folly for man to crave for things which are not his own (but which are merely attractive to the being with which he is connected during his earthly career), and to introduce into his desire that which infects him with disease, and which even ultimately drives him away from God, excluding him in body and soul from his celestial state." (*Mysterium*, xxiv. 16.)

"He who wants to become a master over himself and a celestial citizen must not be a great sleeper, nor fill his abdomen with an abundance of food or drink, wherefrom the elements of the devil begin to qualify; but he must be temperate, sober, and wakeful, like a warrior before the enemy, for the wrath is continually against him, and he has enough to do to defend himself (without creating artificial obstacles)." (*Six Theosophical Points*, x. 23.)

"Over-eating and intoxication cause sin, because the pure will which emanates from the fire-life becomes imprisoned and drowned in desire, so that it is rendered impotent in the battle."[223] (*Six Theosophical Points*, cxi. 29.)

As the power of the inner man over the outer man increases, the former changes the qualities of the latter to a certain extent. Nevertheless the physical body cannot be completely changed into the spiritual body of Christ, it being far too gross for that purpose. As long as it exists in the physical world it will be burdened with physical substance.

"We must continually die in Christ and continually kill the man of sin within us, so that the new man may live; but we cannot entirely destroy the former; we can merely keep him imprisoned, and continually pour into his fiery essence water from the mildness of God." (*Stiefel*, i. 63.)

"The will, if it goes straight forward, is faith, and as such it can give the body another shape, according to the external spirit; for the inner man is the lord of the outer one; the latter has to obey the former, and the inner one can put the outer one into another figure, but not permanently." (*Forty Questions*, vi. 10.)

"If man enters into regeneration he may succeed in subjecting the external man to his power to such an extent that the latter must do that which he does not desire, because the former takes away the strength of the latter, and penetrates him; but as the gold dwells in a coarse rock, and nevertheless the coarseness of the rock does not become gold, so the earthly man does not become God." (*Stiefel*, i. 59.)

"The inner man continually kills the outer one by means of the love and sweetness of God, so that the external one cannot introduce into

---

[223]Here it may be remarked that it will hardly be sufficient to have merely a theoretical knowledge of the uselessness of material attractions to cure the desire for them. In this, as in all other cases, there can be no true self-knowledge except that which arises from practical experience.

the soul-fire his earthly poisonous desire, which is infected by the devil; but the external man cannot be entirely destroyed, for if this were to take place the kingdom of this world would depart from him entirely." (*Stiefel*, i. 51.)

"Even if Christ is born in us, nevertheless we cannot say, in speaking of ourselves as a whole, 'I am Christ,' for the external man is not Christ. We can only say honestly, 'I am in Christ, and Christ has become human in me.'" (*Stiefel*, i. 54.)

For the great majority of people the celestial inner man is either not perceived at all, or assumes a merely vague and nebulous appearance; but there are others who are aware of the divine qualities of the inner man, and who desire to enter into harmony with him, but they are often so constituted as to be powerfully attracted by the outer life, and they do not know how to overcome the external and sinful man of flesh.

"Sometimes a person is externally so badly constituted by the influence of the stars as to experience much trouble therefrom. Whenever he stops to consider, he then enters within himself and abstains from sin. Nevertheless he does not know how to get rid of the outer malicious man." (*Three Principles*, xx. 83.)

In external nature we see that the more the sunlight and rain favour a field the richer will be the vegetation growing thereon, not only in regard to wholesome plants, but also in regard to such as are noxious. Thus the power of the spiritual sun, acting within the soul of man, will cause the germs therein, whether good or evil, to sprout and grow. For this reason persons endowed with great spiritual power are sometimes inclined to evil practices, while there are others leading a blameless life merely because they have no power or virtue in them, neither for evil nor good.

"Many of the saints that were driven on by the Spirit of God went afterwards from that state of submission again into selfishness; namely, to their own reasoning and self-will." (*Calmness*, i. 34.)

During our terrestrial life it is not possible for us to become entirely rid of the old sinful Adam, but we should continually try to live above his plane; that means to say, we should maintain our point of gravitation in God.

"Man's life during his present existence is like a turning wheel, which suddenly turns uppermost what was below. It kindleth itself in every substance and defileth itself thereby; but it is purified in the water of meekness, wherein moves the heart of God, and out of that its fire-life

205

may evolve celestial substance." (*Six Mysterious Points*, ii. 13.)

"Our whole life ought to be a continual repentance, because it is also a continual chain of sin. Truly the noble lily-branch, newly born in Christ, does not sin; nevertheless the terrestrial man sins in body and soul, and seeks to spoil the noble flower."[224] (*Stiefel*, xi. 537.)

"A true Christian hates the will of the flesh and rejects it. He is continually his own accuser, and considers himself unworthy, and with his whole heart will he wish to enter into the mercy of God. He will never boast and say, 'I am a Christian;' but he will strive to enter into the mercy of God and desire His grace, so that he may become a true Christian. His whole life is a continual repentance, and he continually desires to grasp divine grace as that grace grasps him." (*Communion*, iv. 27.)

No Christian should contemplate his own holiness, or fancy himself to be better than others; but he should rather realise his own unworthiness, and regret the perverted state of himself and of humanity as a whole.

"No one should want to know his state of holiness while he lives in this world, but he should keep on drawing the sap of Christ from his own tree, and leave it to that tree to bring forth from him whatever branch or bough it may choose." (*Stiefel*, cxi. 345.)

"An earnest Christian does not wish to know his own sanctity; he sees only his imperfections, in which the devil battles against him. His imperfections are always before him, but his sanctity he does not know while he lives in this world. That sanctity is hidden by Christ at the foot of His Cross, so that the devil may not perceive it." (*Threefold Life*, xv.)

"A real Christian loves truth and justice, and hates hypocrisy." (*Communion*, iv. 228.)[225]

The new-born internal and spiritual life is benefited by trouble and suffering.

"To the pious, light arises out of darkness and day out of night. For them fortune results from misfortune, and out of the curse and malice of this world there grows for them a paradise. Paul says, To those who love God, all things are for the best.'" (*Mysterium*, lxvi.)

---

[224]True "repentance" does not consist in fancying oneself to be sorry on account of the consequences to be expected from sins committed in the past, or in worrying about what has been done and cannot be undone now, while perhaps the heart still craves to sin again; but it consists in a turning away from that which is sinful and evil, and in forming the firm resolution to sacrifice and surrender oneself, faults and all, to the immutable will of God. (Compare *True Repentance*, i.)

[225]No man can truly realise his own unworthiness so long as the light has not become active in him.

"Whenever God leads His children into trouble and anguish, they are then every time to produce a new branch on the tree of faith. Whenever the Spirit of God appears it always presents a new outgrowth, of which the noble image is exceedingly glad." (*Menschwerdung*, cxi. 8.)

The conditions by which man is surrounded during his terrestrial life may not permit the effect of his spiritual unfoldment to become fully manifest during that time, but at the time of the death of the physical body, when the obstacles presented by the flesh disappear, then will the inner man enjoy his perfections.

"The celestial kingdom in the saints is active and conscious within their faith, whereby their will surrenders itself to God; but the natural life is surrounded by flesh and blood, and is related to the contrarium in the wrath of God. Thus the soul is often in anguish when hell rushes upon her, and desires to manifest itself in her; but she sinks within the hope of divine grace, and stands like a beautiful rose among the thorns, until at the death of the body the kingdom of this world drops away from her. Only then, when there is nothing more to hinder it, will she become truly manifest in the love of God." (*Supersensual Life*, xxxix.)

The object of our life should be to die continually in regard to our human selfhood, and to live only in the love of God, labouring in His service. Thereby our activity will become blessed.[226]

"I am not rejoicing because I am living within my own sense of self, but because in my selfhood I am in the death of Christ and am dying perpetually, and I wish to die entirely in regard to my selfhood, and to leave it entirely in God, so as to be nothing whatever except an instrument of God, and know nothing any more about my (separate) self." (*Stiefel*, xi. 527.)

"Wherever self dwelleth not, there love has her dwelling. In the tranquillity at the bottom of the soul, where she dies as to her own selfhood, and where she does not will anything except what God wills (in her), there love resides. To the extent in which the self-will is dead within itself, to the same extent is the place occupied by love. In the place which formerly was the seat of self-will there is now nothing, and wherever there is nothing there the love of God is solely active." (*Supernatural Life*, xxviii.)

---

[226]We cannot labour in the service of God without dying to our human selfhood. To "labour in the service of God" does not mean that, for instance, "I, parson, or professor, or author So-and-so, in my human personality, considered as something separate and distinct from God, could with my human smartness render a service to some outside god, or please him, or advise him what to do;" but it is God Himself rendering the service to Himself through our instrumentality, provided that by rising above all conception of self and personality we become identified with Himself. For this reason all clerical assumption and pretence, by which is assumed an authority apart from that of the God to whom they profess to serve, is repulsive to the religious instinct of man.

"A true Christian knows himself to be a servant of God, whose duty it is to attend to the works of God properly. He is not his own property, and the terrestrial body which he inhabits is not his true home. He may seek and plant, cultivate, strive and act as he pleases, but he is always aware that he is doing it for God, and that he will have to render account for it. He should always remember that among these works he is a stranger, a guest, and a servant." (*Signature*, xv. 44.)

"He who hopes to perform something perfect and good, wherein he may rejoice eternally and enjoy it, let him come out of his egoism and self-will and enter into submission within the will of God. Even if the terrestrial desire for selfhood clings to him in his flesh and blood, if only the soul-will is not infected by that desire for self, then will that self not be able to produce anything; for the (inner) will of the soul, resting in submission to God, continually destroys the essence of the self-assertion, and thus the wrath of God cannot reach her. If the wrath should reach that essence, then the submitted will rises up in its power therein, and stands there in shape before God as a production of victory that will inherit the in fancy."[227] (*Calmness*, xi. 1.)

It is self-evident that no terrestrial possessions of any kind will benefit the spirit, but the acquisition of such possessions will not be an obstacle for us, provided that we possess them, and do not permit ourselves to be possessed by them.

"Dear soul, if you desire the light of God, and also the light of this world, if you desire to feed your body (and mind), and (at the same time) to seek for the mysteries of God, do as God Himself does. One of the eyes of your soul looks into eternity, the other one into nature. The latter goes on continually seeking in desiring and creating one mirror after another. Let that be so. It must be so, for God wills it. But the eye for eternity must not be turned (away from God) into desire; but by means of that eye you should seek to turn the other one towards you, and not let it turn away from you; *i.e.*, not let it turn away from the eye that looks into freedom. Put one will into that which you are doing, thinking that you are a servant in the vineyard of God; *i.e.*, into the Eternal. Sink your will every hour into humility before God; then will your image walk in humility with your will in the majesty of God, and be illumined perpetually by the triumphant light of God." (*Forty Questions*, xii. 28.)

All terrestrial fortunes or misfortunes with which we may possibly meet do not concern our real divine self, but merely the personality with which we are connected during our earthly life. This personality is given us for the purpose of gaining experience, be it good or evil, and

[227]If the saints or "adepts" are often addressed as "children," this is not a mere invented figure of speech, without any adequate cause, but has a deep signification; for no one can inherit the kingdom of heaven, *i.e.*, divine self-knowledge, unless he becomes like a child that of itself knows nothing in the realm of the spirit.

therefore we should always be satisfied and remain contented in God.

"Ultimately all things must be one and the same to man. He is to become one with fortune and misfortune, with poverty and riches, joy and sorrow, light and darkness, life and death. Man is then to himself nothing, for he is dead relatively to all things in his will. God is in all and through all, and nevertheless He is nothing in regard to all, and nothing can comprehend Him. Everything becomes manifest through Him, and He Himself is everything. Nevertheless he has nothing (objectively), because that which is before Him is nothing in His comprehension, for it does not comprehend Him. Likewise will this be the state of a person according to his submitted will if he entirely surrenders himself to God. Then will his will drop back into the unfathomable will of God, wherefrom it came in the beginning, and it will then be in the form of the unfathomable will, wherein God resides and wills." (*Mysterium*, lxvi.)

"The will, surrendered to God, says, 'Lord, if Thou wishest me to be imprisoned or in misery, I shall willingly be so. If Thou takest me to hell I will go with Thee, for Thou art in heaven. If I have only Thee, what should I care for either heaven or hell? Even if my body and soul were to perish, I shall remain in Thee and Thou in me. In possessing Thee, I have all that I want. Use me as Thou wilt." (*Mysterium*, lxvi.)

By conquering the terrestrial desire and entering into submission to Christ, we shall attain the internal power over external nature, first over our own and afterwards over "outside" nature, the latter being, after all, also within God, our own divine self.

"If you rule merely externally (by external means) over all creatures, you are then with your will in an animal quality, and your rule is of an external kind, dealing only with forms. Your desire will then be carried into the animal essence, which will infect and capture you, and you will receive animal qualities. But if you leave that which merely relates to forms, you will become superior to it, and able to rule over all creatures within the foundation wherefrom they have been created." (*Supersensual Life*, viii.)

"If you allow nothing to enter your desire, you will then be free from all things and possess power over all. You have then nothing within your receptivity, and are as nothing to all things, and all things will be nothing to you, in the same sense as God rules over all things and sees them all; but there is nothing that comprehends Him." (*Supersensual Life*, ix.)

"By your own power you cannot attain such a tranquillity that no creature can touch you. You must give yourself completely into the life of our Lord Jesus Christ, and surrender to Him all your own willing and desiring, so that you desire nothing without Him. Then will you be in this world and in its qualities, as far as your body is concerned. With your will you will be at the foot of the Cross of Christ, and with your will you will walk in heaven, at the goal from whence all creatures come, and to which they all return." (*Supersensual Life*, ix.)

The celestial body is formed by means of the terrestrial body. There is no regeneration after the body has died.

"The soul proper is nothing corporeal.; but the body in the *tincture* grows either celestial or infernal. It is not a tangible body in an external aspect, but a power-body; the body of God; the celestial body of Christ." (*Forty Questions*, vii. 18.)

"After this life there is no regeneration, for the four elements with their principles have departed." (*Threefold Life*, i. 1.)

Chapter XIV
Death and Eternal Life

"The mystic death is the beginning of eternal life."

MAN is a product of three worlds His spirit is of God, his soul from the constellation of the astral elements, his body from the elements of the terrestrial plane. In each of these aspects he partakes of the attributes of the principle from which he has originated. As a spirit he is, and has been, and will always be, immortal; and is even now in heaven, from which he has never departed. As a product of the astral plane, he is subject to the conditions existing therein, while his physical form must dissolve again into the elements to which it belongs. With whatever of these three states man identifies himself, that state will be his own.

"God willed to become manifest in all three principles, but the order did not remain as it was originally instituted. The middle went into the exterior, and the exterior into the middle. This is not the order of eternity, and therefore the external and the inner principles must become separated." (*Threefold Life*, xviii. 3.)

"The life which we receive in the body of our mother is merely from the power of the sun, the stars, and the elements, which not only organise the body of the child and endow it with life, but which also bring it to light and nourish and nurse it during the whole term of its life. They likewise distribute to it fortune and misfortune, and finally they cause it to die and to decompose." (*Three Principles*, xiv. 4.)

"Behold what you are. Dust of the earth; a corpse. Your life is subject to the stars and elements. It is they who rule you according to their qualities, and they endow you with talents and arts; but when their period and constellation under which you have been conceived and born is ended, then they will forsake you." (*Menschwerdung*, xi. 6.)

"The corporeal essences return to the earth; the elemental spirit, the air, returns to the air; the water and blood are received by the terrestrial water and earth, and there remains nothing of the external man. He has then ceased to exist. He had a beginning and he had an end." (*Threefold Life*, xviii. 8.)

"At death the four elements separate from the one element. Then the tincture, together with the shadow of that which constituted the man, goes into the ether and remains within the root of that element from which the four elements were born, and from which they emanated." (*Three Principles*, xix. 14.)

After the death of the physical form man remains still a being of twofold aspect; namely, as a celestial spirit, according to the divine principle in him (of which he may or may not be conscious); and secondly, as a supersensual, but nevertheless material being, according to his astral body. Each of these essences now gravitates to the plane to which it belongs according to its qualities. From this double but opposite tendency results the rupture or division of the soul and the judgment.

> "When a person in this world dies, he then comes before the angel who in his sword carries death and life, the love and the wrath of God. There his soul has to pass through the judgment at the portals of Paradise. If she has been captured by the wrath of God she will not be able to pass through the door, but if she is a child of the virgin and born of the seed of the (celestial) woman, she will then pass through. Then will the angel cut away from her nature that which has been generated by the serpent, and the soul will then serve God in His holy temple in Paradise, waiting there for the resurrection of her (celestial) body."[228] (*Mysterium*, xxv. 2.)

During his terrestrial existence man can remain consciously in the three worlds, and by the power of the will with which he is endowed penetrate into either one or the other; but after the separation of the soul from the body has taken place, he can continue to exist as an individuality only in one of these worlds, either within the realm of divine light or within the power of the fire; because together with his physical body he loses the power of self-government. He can then no longer follow his own will, but has to go where he gravitates.

> "There are three principles in the constitution of man, either of which he may unfold during his terrestrial existence; but after the body is disorganised, he then lives only in one principle and cannot evolve the other. In eternity he must remain in that state of consciousness which he has acquired here." (*Three Principles, Supplement,* x.)

> "There are not three separate souls in man, but only one. This soul stands in three principles; namely, the realm of the wrath, the realm of the love of God and the kingdom of this world. When the air of the external kingdom of this world deserts the soul, then will she become manifest in either the dark realm of fire or in the holy kingdom of light, which is the kingdom of the love-fire, the power of God. To whatever plane she has surrendered herself during her earthly existence, therein she remains after the external kingdom has departed from her."

[228]It will hardly be necessary to state that this is not to be taken in an external and superficial sense, as if the soul were waiting for the resurrection of that physical body which has then already been decomposed and passed into other organisms according to its constituting elements; but, like all other writings of occult nature, this has to be taken in an internal spiritual meaning, which we must seek to grasp with the spirit rather than with the sceptical brain. It refers to the unfoldment of the third principle, which remains latent in the soul during that state.

(*Mysterium*, xv. 24.)

During his terrestrial life man may live either in heaven or hell, or come out of one of these states and enter the other, because he can then govern his will by means of his intellect; but after the death of the body the function of the brain necessary for that purpose exists no longer, and then the soul is not able to change her will. She therefore becomes absorbed entirely into that principle which has obtained ruling power within her own nature. For this reason, it is of paramount importance for man to seek to unfold during his terrestrial life the love of God; *i.e.*, the appreciation of the ideal and the will to realise all that is noble and good within his soul, so that it will act as his guiding star in eternity.

"Man is in this world already in heaven or hell, wherever he corporeally may be. If his spirit is in harmony with God, he is then spiritually in heaven and his soul is in God. If he spiritually dwells in the wrath, he is then already in hell and in company of all the devils." (*Aurora*, xx. 86.)

"Here in the life of the soul is the balance. If she is evil, she can be reborn in love; but when the balance breaks and the angle has turned, then will she be in that principle which is prevailing in her." (*Forty Questions*, xxiii. 10.)

"During her terrestrial life the soul can change her will, but after the death of the body there remains nothing within her power by which she can change her will." (*Tilk.* i. 267.)

"Whatever the soul during her terrestrial life receives within her will, and wherewith she becomes entangled, that she will take in her will with her after the death of the body, and she can no more rid herself of it, because she has then nothing but that wherein she has entered, and which now constitutes her very self. But during terrestrial life she may destroy that wherein she has become entangled in her will." (*Threefold Life*, xii. 25.)

If during terrestrial life the will of the soul has become anti-Christian—that means to say, perverted into an evil spirituality—then will the evil nature of the soul likewise be perverted and anti-Christian, and this perverted essence will manifest itself in the other life as a shape and a power for evil.

"In so far as a person remains in a will foreign to his true nature, and does not want to be cured of it by entering into the holy Word, this foreign being will take substance in him and hold the celestial essence in subjection; so that the latter remains, as it were, imprisoned after death and cannot reach the kingdom of God, and from this results eternal death." (*Mysterium*, xxiv. 13.)

213

"Each one needs only to examine his own quality and see in what direction he is carried by his will. He will then know to what kingdom he belongs, and whether he is actually a man (in the image of God), as he fancies himself or pretends to be, or a creature of the dark world, an avaricious dog, a vain peacock, a lewd monkey, or a poisonous snake. If, then, the essence of the four elements departs from him at death, there will remain in him nothing but the internal poisonous and evil consciousness." (*Six Theosophical Points*, vii. 37.)

On account of the want of plasticity of the matter composing the physical body, the animal characteristics predominant in such a person become never fully expressed in his external appearance during his terrestrial life; but the soul is more plastic, and being likewise a product and expression of her internal character, she will after the death of the body assume the form of that animal or monster whose character is dominant in her.

"If the spirit remains unregenerated within its original principle, then will there appear at the rupture of the form such a creature as corresponds to the quality of the will (character) acquired during terrestrial life. If, for instance, during life you have the envious disposition of a dog, begrudging everything to everybody, then will this dog-character find its expression in a corresponding shape after the death of the body; for according to it the (animal) soul takes (assumes) her shape, and this kind of will remains with you in eternity, for the doors of the depths that lead to the light of God are then closed before you."[229] (*Three Principles*, xvi. 50.)

If the soul is devoid of the divine light, then will the four lower qualities of eternal nature become active in her and torment her in various ways.

"If you have not during your terrestrial life enlightened your soul, and the eternal spirit that has been given to you by supreme good, in the light of God, so that the spirit has become reborn in that light, in divine substantiality, then will the soul in the Mysterium return to the centre of nature, and enter into the quality of the anguish of the four lower forms of eternal nature. There she will then be in the company of all the devils, and be forced to devour that which she has stirred up." (*Menschwerdung*, xi. 6.)

"If the soul-fire has not become substantiated in the Spirit of God, nor

[229]There are not animals enough in the world to represent all the combinations of evil characters which may be formed within the soul of man; neither could such monstrous shapes exist in the physical plane, on account of anatomical and physiological laws; but in the hellish world, where the human element becomes mixed with the animal essence, all kinds of monsters, half human, half animal, may be found. The horrors of hell are, therefore, not mere inventions of poets and visionaries, but there is no reason why they should not actually exist. Certainly, from the point of view of the divine spirit, all forms are merely illusive, and as long as man is rooted within that spirit he may recognise them as such; but for the godless they are horrible realities, as real as the images of the terrestrial world appear to us.

sought for that substance in its desire, it is then a dark fire, burning in great anguish and terror, because there are in its constitution then only the four lower qualities of nature. If the will has nothing of the divine power of true humility, there can then be no entering of it within itself into the life by means of death; but the soul is then like a furiously turning wheel, seeking continually to rise and continually sinking down on the other side. There is in that state surely a kind of fire, but not a combustion, for there rules the severe harshness and bitterness. The bitterness seeks the fire and wants to increase it; but the acridity keeps it imprisoned, and thus it results in a terrible anxiety and resembles a turning wheel, turning perpetually around itself." (*Forty Questions*, xviii. 14.)

"The four forms of the original state of nature are the source of universal anguish. Each person feels that according to the quality of his *Turba*, one in one way and another in another. The avaricious soul, for instance, suffers from cold; the angry soul from heat; the envious soul experiences bitterness; the conceited is continually flying and dropping into an abyss." (*Forty Questions*, xviii. 21.)

Moreover, there is within the consciousness of the soul the memory of past deeds, misdeeds, and the reproaches of those whom she has injured, and as in that subjective condition all these subjective images are seen objectively, the soul lives in the miseries which she has created. In addition to this, the curses of the living (being projections of will) reach the soul and cause her to suffer.

"All sins are objective to the soul in her tincture. If she remembers the kingdom of heaven—which she, of course, does neither see nor know —she then sees the causes why she is suffering; for she has created these causes herself. There are within her tincture all the tears of those whom she has injured, and they are fiery, stinging, burning, and gnawing, and cause an eternal despair within the essences, and an inimical will towards God." (*Three Principles*, xix. 24.)

"There the master will have to render account to his servants, if he has, given them a bad example and caused them to enter the way of evil. Then will the poor soul cry out in despair against her master; for all this is objective before her in the tincture." (*Three Principles*, xxiv. 30.)

"If a godless person has left behind a great deal of falsehood and deceit, so that the tincture of hell is invoked over his tomb, then will that curse penetrate to his soul. This (curse) he will have to eat; for it is his food, sent to him by the living. To send such curses does not, however, belong to the children of God; for by cursing another, man casts seed into hell—into the wrath of God. Let every one beware, for he will reap that which he sows." (*Forty Questions*, xxiv. 4.)

During terrestrial life the voice of the conscience can be drowned in the turmoil of external life, and the recollection of evil deeds be driven away by allowing oneself to become immersed in sensual pleasures; but after death it does no longer depend on the will of the soul whether or not to remember the past, and her remorse is intensified to an enormous extent, by the absence of all external distractions. Moreover, the desire for gratifying her evil instincts still exists in her, but there are no means for such a gratification.

> "During terrestrial life the godless feels the presence of hell within his false conscience, but he does not understand it; for he still lives in earthly vanity, wherewith he amuses himself, and which causes him pleasure and lust. Moreover, his external life is in possession of the light of external nature, and his soul revels therein; so that the internal pain cannot become manifest. But when the body dies, the soul can no longer enjoy such protection and temporal pleasure. In addition to this, the external light will have been extinguished for her. Then will she be in an eternal craving after such vanity as she indulged in during her life on the earth; but she can attain nothing except her own false conceived will. She has now too little of that of which she formerly had too much, and with which she nevertheless was not satisfied. She would gladly commit still more evil, but has nothing whereby she can accomplish it, and thus she enacts all that within her own self." (*Supernatural Life*, xxxix.)

Now the godless soul is filled with her own infamy, and there is no room in her for the saving power of faith.

> "Man's own sins, his depravity and vices in rejecting God, are his hell-fire, which gnaws in him eternally. His mockeries are now before his eyes, and he does not dare to let even one good thought enter into his soul; for the good is to him like an angel, and on account of his great wickedness he cannot touch it with his soul, much less see it through her; but he must now eat his mockery, together with all his vices and sins for ever within himself, and he must despair eternally."[230] (*Three Principles*, xxiv. 29.)

> "The godless are free. There is nothing imprisoning them. They may go down as far as they like; there will everywhere be the abyss and the darkness, and they are always in the same place. The deeper they desire to go the deeper will they fall, and nevertheless they will arrive nowhere, because there is no bottom or end." (*Forty Questions*, xxxiv. 5.)

Every being can live only in that element to which it belongs. A fish suffers in the air and a man under water. Likewise the divine light of God is painful to the devils in hell, and appears to them in an angry

---

[230]The word "eternally" does not mean a succession of periods of time without any end, but a state in which there exists no conception of time.

aspect.

> "God also dwells in the abyss of the godless soul; but He is not recognisable to her in any other way than as a wrath, and this is the meaning where it is written—'With the saints Thou art holy, and with the perverted art Thou perverted.'" (*Mysterium*, lx. 44.)

> "The same eternally generating and speaking word speaks in heaven— *i.e.*, in the power of the light—as holy wisdom (delight); but in hell, in darkness, it manifests itself as the flames of torment." (*Mysterium*, lxi. 31.)

As the godless soul finds nowhere relief or aid, she ultimately surrenders herself fully to the devil; that means to say, to her own evil will.[231]

> "The soul is like a person dreaming of being in great anguish and torture, and that he is seeking for relief everywhere without being able to find it. He then despairs, and seeing no help he surrenders himself to his driver (to the interior impulse that is driving him on), that the latter may do with him as he chooses. Thus the abandoned soul falls into the power of the devil, where she can neither follow nor is permitted to follow her own inclinations; but whatever the devil does, she is compelled to do also. Thus she becomes an enemy of God, and would fain rise in pride and fire over the princely throne of the angels. While on earth and in her physical body she used to make a fool of herself, and now she remains a fool and a trickster, and whatever folly she has carried on in this life she now enacts it there. The same foolery is her treasure, and therein is, as Christ says, her heart and her will." (*Threefold Life*, xviii. 10.)

Nevertheless the devilish soul does not find full satisfaction in evil, for she trembles continually in fear of the judgment day, and the only gratification she finds is in her resistance to God, and in encouraging and supporting the evil deeds and inclinations of mankind.

> "The pain of the condemned (self-condemned) souls, which they suffer until the judgment day, is like that of an imprisoned convict who continually listens, and whenever something stirs thinks that the executioner is coming to submit him to justice and give him what he deserves. These souls have a perverted conscience, which tortures them; their sins are always before their eyes; they see all their injustice and frivolity, their conceit and the misery which they have caused, their scorn and arrogance, but now their self-confidence flies away." (*Forty*

[231] To the child of God, God is not anything objective, but exists within His own centre. Terrestrial man, in search of God or salvation, ultimately arrives, through disappointment and suffering, at the realisation that God, the true life and the truth, can be found for him not anywhere excepting within his own divine self. He then seeks for God within himself, and in finding Him he becomes identified with Him and is God. Likewise the godless soul, seeking for relief and comfort in external things or beings, ultimately returns within her own self, and finding no good within her, she necessarily identifies herself with her own evil will, and becomes a devil.

"The most depraved souls, however, are very daring. They deny God and curse Him, and are His worst enemies. They lie to themselves, saying that they are in the right, and they rebel against God, and want to rise above Him and perform miracles." (*Forty Questions*, xxii. 21.)

"The condemned soul enters magically into the godless essence and enjoys it, and she teaches persons in dreams how to perform all kinds of mischief, for she is serving the devil. If a wicked person (earnestly) desires something, the devil is willing to serve him, for he can act more easily through the soul of a human being than if he is left to himself." (*Forty Questions*, xxvi. 18.)

Thus we have now considered the fate of those unfortunate souls who have become self-conscious in evil; or, to express it in other words, whose spirituality has become, as it were, imprisoned within their lower qualities, and who are often spoken of as "black magicians" of varying degrees, from a simply malicious soul who performs villainous deeds for the mere sake of the enjoyment she hopes to experience from it, up to the devil incarnate, who has acquired occult knowledge and uses his spiritual powers for evil or selfish ends. But the condition of those who have during their terrestrial life found no internal pleasure in evil, but have fought against their evil desires, and striven to aid the good in them to conquer their evil propensities, is very different from the former when they depart from this world.

"If the inner will daily and every hour battles against the evil qualities with which it is afflicted, if it quenches them and does not permit them to take substance in it, while at the same time those evil qualities hinder the person, so that he cannot act always according to his good will, such a man may believe and know for certain that the fire of God is glowing in him and seeking to become light; and whenever the evil body with its evil conditions is broken up, so that it can no longer hinder the glowing spark from burning, then will the divine fire in its essence burst into a flame, and the divine image will be reconstituted according to the strongest quality which that person has introduced into his desire." (*Six Theosophical Points*, vii. 41.)

"If a person has a constant desire for God, and if his desire is so powerful as to enable him to break up and turn into mildness the evil essences whenever they begin to burn in him; if he can resign everything that in this world glitters and allures; if he can do good for evil; if he is powerful enough to give to the needy all that belongs to his externals, be it money or goods; and if he is ready willingly to desert everything for the sake of God, and to enter into a state of misery with the certain hope for the eternal; if in him arises divine power, so that he may awaken therein the kingdom of joy and taste God; such a person carries within himself the divine image with the celestial essence even during his terrestrial life, the image wherein Jesus is born of the virgin. He will not die eternally, but merely let the terrestrial kingdom pass away from him, it having been in this life to him an opposition and hindrance, wherewith God has (not filled but) merely covered him." (*Six Theosophical Points*, vii. 44.)

Such souls are during this terrestrial life, and still more after the death of the body, filled with the light and the power of God. This light moderates the action of the fiery will still active in them, the blessings of their good deeds surround them, the hope for still greater glorification is their life, and from the trouble and persecution which they have suffered there arises for them pure joy.

"The principle of the father wherein the soul has her basis is a burning fire, giving light, and in this light rests the noble image of God. This light moderates the burning fire by means of the substantiality of love, so as to render it beneficent for nature and life." (*Letters*, viii. 78.)

"Those earnest souls that have worked the wonders of God in His will at the foot of the Cross, having received the body of God, *i.e.*, of Christ, and who have walked therein in justice and truth, *all their doings also follow them* in their strong will and desire, and they experience inexpressible joy in the love and mercy of God, by which they are continually surrounded. The wonders of God are their nutriment; they are living in glory, power, strength, and majesty such as is beyond all description." (*Threefold Life*, xviii. 12.)

"The blessed souls are rendered happy by the works which they have performed while here, and those who have suffered much persecution for the sake of the truth will behold the wreath of victory which is to crown their new body on the judgment day. There takes place in them a continual uprising of joy whenever they contemplate the future. As their deeds have been varied, so is their hope. A day-labourer having gained much is glad of the reward. Thus it is there. A joyful consciousness abides in them. All the scorn to which they were submitted and all the accusations that have been falsely brought forward against them are to them a great honour of victory. Their frequent prayers, good thoughts, and good works in behalf of their neighbours are the nutriment which they take until the time when their (celestial) body will eat of the fruits of Paradise." (*Forty Questions*, xxii. 4.)

"He who aids the degraded blesses himself, for he wishes him everything good, and prays to God to bless him in body and soul. Thus his desire and blessing returns to the giver in the Mysterium and surrounds him, and follows him as a good work born in God. This is the treasure which man takes with him; his earthly treasures he will have to leave behind." (*Menschwerdung*, cxi. 4.)

There is no man without sin, and as he is followed to the other side of the grave by all of his works, his sins go with him, but if he has known how to obtain forgiveness for his sins, then his happiness will not be infringed upon by them.[232]

> "Man is followed by all of his works, and he has them eternally before his eyes and lives therein, unless he has out of his malice and falsehood been newly born by the blood of Jesus Christ. If so, he will then break through the earthly and hellish image and enter into an angelic one, and come into another kingdom, to which his imperfections cannot follow him, and thus will the image of God be restored out of the terrestrial and hellish form." (*Three Principles*, xvi. 47.)

The departed blessed souls trouble themselves neither about that which belongs to hell nor about terrestrial matters of any kind. Their existence resembles that of a man enjoying a happy dream.

> "The rest of the soul is like that of one who rests in a sweet sleep." (*Forty Questions*, xxix. 1.)

> "Those happy souls that are resting in Abraham's bosom, in Christ— *i.e.*, in the heavenly essentiality (Devachan)—cannot be disturbed by anybody, unless they should wish it themselves, in case that they were very favourably inclined towards some particular soul in harmony with their own. They do not trouble themselves about terrestrial things, unless it be for the glorification of God. In that case they will be indefatigable in revealing things in a magical way." (*Forty Questions*, xxvi. 22.)

In regard to the intercourse between mortals and that class of spirits Boehme says in a letter:—

> "You are asking questions of things which I cannot know, because for that purpose I would have to be myself within the departed soul, and the spirit of that soul would have to be my own; but as we are all having one body and one spirit in Christ, therefore all of us may see in Christ out of one spirit and enjoy His knowledge. Thus our soul is in relationship with the souls of the dead. They cannot come to us, but we may penetrate unto them." (*Forty Questions*, xxv. 1.)

Fully sanctified souls are in possession of an enormous amount of self-knowledge; others have less.

---

[232]This "forgiving of sin" has a meaning very different from that which is commonly accepted. Nobody can forgive the sins of another man; the sinner himself must free himself of his sins.
"Sin is like a shell, out of which the new man grows, and he then throws the shell away. This is called 'forgiveness,' because God (in man) gives that which is sinful away." (*Menschwerdung*, xi. 10.)
"Nobody can forgive sins except Christ in man. Whenever Christ lives in man, there is the absolution." (*Grace*, xiii. 11.)

"The soul which in this body has entered into the new birth and penetrated to God through the doors of the depth has great wisdom and knowledge, even as regards the heavens; for she has come from the womb of the virgin, wherein have been unfolded the eternal miracles of God, and the splendour of the Holy Trinity shines out of her. But we err if we attribute great wisdom to a soul that has hardly escaped from the clutches of the devil, after having left a world wherein she cared nothing about divine wisdom, but merely followed her own desires." (*Three Principles*, xix. 61.)

It is an absurdity to believe that the departed souls of God, the saints, could petition God in regard to our necessities, or argue the case with Him, or that they could put into motion the eternal and infinite mercy of God.

"The departed souls do not petition God on our behalf. Why should they do so? Our salvation does not depend on their begging, but on our entering. If any one puts his will into God, then will God help him. His arms are outstretched by day and night for the purpose of aiding man. Should then a soul be so presumptuous as to make out of God an over-severe Judge, unwilling to receive a converted sinner?" (*Forty Questions*, xxvi. 23.)

It is explainable that the souls of deceased saints have performed what is called "miracles;" but this did not take place after the manner in which it is commonly believed, but by a conjunction of the faith (will) of the living with the faith of the departed.

"We do not deny that (as it is taught by Popery) great departed saints have appeared to many persons and performed miracles. This is true, although it is now denied by many; but it belongs to a different A B C (to another department of occult science) than is known to those who affirm it, or to those who deny." (*Forty Questions*, xix. 63.)

"The reason why our forefathers have sometimes appeared after death in some wonderful manner is to be found in the faith of the living; for faith is a power that may move mountains. The faith of these living persons was still good and pure, and they did not worship their bellies or adore earthly show. Therefore their faith penetrated into heaven; *i.e.*, into the one element, to the saints. Thus one faith grasped the other; for the saints also were reacting upon that strong faith, especially those saints who while upon the earth had converted many to God. Thus some wonderful works have been accomplished by invoking their memory." (*Three Principles*, xviii. 80.)

"One faith grasps the other. The faith of the living caught that of the saints, and the faith performed the miracle. Faith can overthrow

mountains. It could destroy the world, if God were so to direct it."[233]
(*Forty Questions*, xxvi.)

In the above we have considered two different classes of human spirits or souls; namely, those in whom the principle of darkness and evil has become manifest, and who ultimately become identified with that principle which is called "the devil," and we have also investigated the fate that awaits those in whom the principle of light, or good, becomes manifest; but there is to be met a vast number of souls in whom the division of good and evil, within the fourth form of eternal nature has not yet taken place, and who are in that state which is called *Kama loca* in the East and *Purgatory* in the West, although the meaning commonly attached to these terms is not quite identical.

> "The souls in which doubt and faith are mixed have their basis neither in heaven nor in hell, but they stand in the middle of the portal, where fire and light become separated from each other. They are held by the Turba. Many a soul is held there for a considerable time; the wrath, however, cannot devour the little spark of faith which the soul possesses, and has ultimately to release her. What (suffering) this implies, I leave those to experience who remain wilfully in sin to the end, and then wish to be saved." (*Forty Questions*, xxiv. 5.)

> "It is not possible to describe what kind of a purgatory such a soul will have to pass through before, by means of her little spark (of love), she can enter (into eternal life). The world would not believe such a description; the world is too clever, and likewise too blind, to understand it. People cling for ever to the letter. I wish to God that no one would have to pass through that experience; I would then gladly keep still and say nothing about it." (*Forty Questions*, xviii.)

A soul from which the higher principles have entirely departed will, of course, suffer nothing, because she has no (spiritual) intelligence. Such an entity is merely an astral corpse, which is no more affected by the destructive influence of the astral elements than the unconscious physical body by its own decomposition; but if there is still any spiritual intelligence left in that astral form, it will then have to pass through a painful and forcible separation.

> "Many a soul will, after taking leave of this world, have to remain for a considerable time in purgatory, if she has stained herself with gross sins, and if she has never truly entered into regeneration, but merely tasted of it to a certain extent, as is sometimes the case with persons that are here loaded with temporal honours and power, in which case personal claims being substituted for justice, malice, but not wisdom, is

---

[233]If there is nobody living to-day able to perform a miracle by the power of faith, this does not disprove that the true living faith is a spiritual power, capable of manifesting all the qualities that are claimed for it, but it is, rather, suggestive of the degraded state of the present generation.

the judge. When the hour of death approaches and the conscience awakens, such a soul trembles in great fear of hell, and would like to be saved; but there is only very little of the saving power of faith within her, while before her is nothing but injustice and falsehood, earthly lust, and the tears and sighs of the down-trodden. Her desire turns to a certain extent towards God, but the sins she committed are in her way, and there arises in her a great doubt and unrest. Many a soul then clings to the saving power as it were by a thin thread. When, then, death actually takes place, and separates the soul from the body, the poor soul will then cling to that thread and refuse to let go her hold of it, but all her essences are still deeply immersed in the wrath of God; she is tortured by her gross sins, and the thread of faith (the umbilical cord) of the new-born being is very feeble.[234] Therefore when the bridegroom says 'Come!' the poor soul answers, 'I cannot; my lamp is not yet ready;' but she clings to the thread and puts her imagination into the heart of God, and thus she becomes ultimately redeemed by the suffering of the Christ (in her) from the pool of putrefaction; *i.e.*, from her fearful sins that are burning in the wrath of God and wherein she is immersed." (*Three Principles*, xix. 41.)

A soul that has gathered her divinity around herself like a garment of light and cut loose from all earthly attractions will have no desire to return to the earth and takes no interest in terrestrial affairs, which in fact she has forgotten, like a person who forgets his external circumstances after he goes to sleep; but a soul still held captive by the terrestrial essence or state may reappear among mortals in her sidereal (astral) body for the purpose Of seeking gratification for some personal wish. Such souls sometimes return for the purpose of asking the living to aid them with prayer.

"When a person dies the external body becomes decomposed and returns to that of which it has been formed, but the soul born from eternal nature, and having been introduced into the Adamic essence by the Spirit of God, cannot die; for she has not originated in time, but from the eternal generation. If the soul has introduced her will into temporal things, she has then conceived of the quality of those things in her desire, and holds to them magically, as if she were possessing them corporeally. Of course she cannot keep the elementary (physical) body, but she may retain her sidereal body until it leas been consumed by the constellation (the astral elements). Thus it happens sometimes that persons after death are seen in their houses, in their own body, but that body is cold, dead, and stiff, and the soul-spirit attracts it only by means of the astral spirit, until the (physical) body is decomposed." (*Letters*, xxii. 8.)

"Souls that have not yet reached heaven have still the human state, with its deeds, clinging to them, and therefore many a soul of that kind

---

[234]Such souls are called "*sutratma's*" (thread souls) in Eastern books.

223

returns in her sidereal form and haunts her house, and is seen in human form. She may then ask for this or that, and think to be able to obtain the blessing of the saints for her rest (by means of the prayers she asks), and she may likewise concern herself about children or friends. All this, however, does not last any longer than until her astral spirit has been consumed, and then she will enter into rest. After that all leer sorrow and trouble is over, and she has then no more knowledge of it; only that she sees it in the wonders, in the *magia* (of the spirit)." (*Forty Questions*, xxvi. 8.)

"Christ says, 'Wherever your treasure is, there is your heart.' Thus it has often happened that unfortunate souls have reappeared in their community and asked for help by way of prayer, and that they fancied that in this way they might find relief. Out of such facts the doctrine of the purgatory has originated." (*Threefold Life*, xii. 24.)

As a matter of course, no dead soul can be made alive by prayer, neither can mere lip-prayer or any empty ceremony aid the soul in freeing herself from the bonds of matter, but the living may aid the "dead," and especially the dying, by means of true prayer; *i.e.*, by an exercise of the spiritual will (divine aspiration) in them. Thus prayer may aid them to combat the powers of darkness, provided that the prayer of those persons is earnest and full of faith.

"We acknowledge that the community of Christ has great power in redeeming a soul, provided that they do their work earnestly, as it used to be done among the primitive Christians, when there were still saintly persons and saintly priests in existence. They surely did succeed, but not those who assert that they carry the keys and could let souls out of purgatory according to their pleasure and according to the amount of money received for it. For such persons, it would be better if they were never given any money, so that they would not cling to it with their desire." (*Forty Questions*, xxiv. 12.)

"The prayer of the living for the dead may be useful in so far as those who pray are truly Christians (in their hearts), and in a state of regeneration. If the poor soul has not become entirely brutalised into a worm or an animal, but if she still enters into God with her desire, and is therefore still connected with Him by the thread of regeneration, and if the soul-spirit of those who pray, together with the poor soul herself, turns in fervent love, towards God, then will the former aid the latter to wrestle with the elements of darkness and to burst the chains of the devil. This is especially possible at the time of the separation of the spirit from the body, and eminently so in the case of parents, children, or blood relatives; for among those who are related with each other by blood the tinctures enter easier into the necessary harmony (co-vibration), and then the spirit is more willing to enter into the battle, and there is then more facility of conquering than if only strangers are present. All this is, however, useless unless these persons are themselves in the state of regeneration, for one devil cannot destroy another devil. If the soul of the dying is entirely separated from that which links her to Christ, and if she reaches not by her own efforts for the thread, then will the prayers of the others avail nothing." (*Three Principles*, xix. 55.)[235]

---

[235]The bond that connects the soul with the divine state is the power of spiritual love. If at the time of death there is only a thread of that power strong enough to attract the soul to the Divinity, then will the soul tear herself loose from her sinful self and enter into heaven; and therefore it is written that the sins of the woman (the soul) were forgiven, because she had loved much. An ignorant man, having the love of God in his heart, will gain eternal life according to the degree of his love and enlightenment; but he who has much enlightenment, but without any love, is a child of the devil.

"The ways of God are different from the ways of man. That which man loves, therein God hides Himself." (*Myster. Magn.*, lvii, 17.)

Conclusion

"For a long time efforts have been made to transform a whore into a virgin, but thereby her whoredom has only been ornamented and increased. If this whore is to perish, then all the sects will have to perish, together with the animal whereupon she rides, for they are all only images of the whore." (*Myster. Magn.*, xxxvi. 69.)

"Extra Ecclesiam nulla salus."

HE who has grasped the meaning of the writings of Jacob Boehme, of which the foregoing pages are merely a condensed review or summary (written for the purpose of encouraging the study of his works) will not ask for a corroboration of the truth of his doctrines by man-made authorities, but he will find that corroboration in Christ. On the other hand, he who is not able to open his own eyes to the perception of eternal truth, and to see the divine light by the power of that divine light within himself, will always be in doubt, no matter how many books he reads. Thus the perplexed "freethinker," imagining that he can find divine wisdom somewhere else except in wisdom itself, and the benighted "sectarian," who seeks for Christ in some external Church, outside of Christ, are like the blind, stumbling about in the dark, seeking for the truth in external things, in books and authorities, but not in the truth itself. They may read one book to-day, and if it is according to their taste, imagine it to be true; and to-morrow perhaps they will get hold of some other book in which contrary assertions are presented, and if they appear more plausible to them than those of the first, they will reject the former and swear to the truth of the latter, until at some future day perhaps still another book is accepted by them, still more plausible than the rest.

> "I say it openly and publicly, that all that is patched together out of fancies and opinions, wherein a person has not divine self-knowledge, but from which he merely draws conclusions, is nothing but Babel, and not wisdom; for the work has to be done, not by seeming and fancy, but by self-knowledge in the Holy Spirit." (*Epistl.* xi. 39.)

> "Of this we complain about Babel, that they are so blind, and have so little knowledge of God. They have thrown away *Magia* and philosophy, and accepted the Antichrist. Now they are devoid of understanding. They have a science, but no real knowledge. They have broken the mirror and are looking through spectacles." (*Forty Questions*, xxi. 16.)

What, then, it is asked, is poor humanity to believe? Is there no way by which they may determine what is true and what false? Are they to accept the doctrines of the "Christian" Churches or "esoteric Buddhism," or some Eastern theology, or the doctrines of those that are called "theosophists;" or shall they reject everything, read nothing, and care for nothing except their temporal comforts?

To this we would answer, that there is no salvation anywhere except in the Christ; that is to say, in eternal truth itself. No one can actually know what is and what is not true as long as the truth is not alive and conscious within himself. No one can know divine wisdom unless he is a god. It is said that we may test all things and keep that which is best; but to be able to judge of what is best in the end we have to be ourselves in intimate connection with the Best; *i.e.*, we must be in possession of God. We cannot judge between wisdom or folly if we are not wise; we cannot know what is really good if we depart from the foundation of eternal Good.

> "The spirit of this world does not know its own self, unless it be that another light shines into that spirit—a light wherein the mind may rest and know its own self." (*Threefold Life*, v. 28.)

> "The touchstone of the Christian is his love towards God and mankind." (*Threefold Life*, xiii. 42)

> "Learn to know the guide from the inner world and also the guide from the outer world, so that ye may know the magic school of both worlds. Then will your mind be free from delusions, for in delusion there is no perfection. The spirit must be capable of grasping the mystery. The Spirit of God must be the guide in man's desire. Without that man will be merely in the external mystery, in the external heaven of the constellation, which also frequently strongly kindles and drives the human soul; but he has not the divine *magic* schooling, such as exists only in a simple and childlike mind." (*Epistl.* xi. 62.)

> "The external guide works and shines merely in the mirror; but the inner one lights up the essential being, and this it could not do unless guided by the Spirit of God. Therefore he who knows the celestial school is with God, and will be a *Magus*, without doing much effort, if he is held by God and driven on by the Holy Spirit." (Epistl. xi. 62.)

No one, except he who lives in the light and in whom the light is a living reality, can know or perceive light. To him who is and has always been immersed in darkness every theory about the nature of light is nothing more than a theory. This is true alike in regard to the external sunlight as it is in regard to the light of the spirit. The external light of the sun is the cause of all external life, activity in all terrestrial beings, and the spiritual divine light is the life of the soul. The realm of that light is the only true and infallible, but unknown, Church of Christ, wherein alone salvation can be found, and there is no other Church possessing the power of redeeming mankind, because that "Church" is not a system wherein the qualities of the light are described, but the light itself, and only the light can overcome the darkness; the darkness cannot redeem itself. That light can only be found in itself, but not in the darkness, where it has not become manifest.[1]

The "true Church of Christ" means the spiritual and divine aspect of humanity as a whole, and to whatever denomination, "Christian" or "unchristian," a person may belong externally, if he has found the true light of the Christ, *i.e.*, his own conscience, within himself, then is he a member of the true Church of Christ, and a "member of the inner circle," an "initiate" and "adept;" but if he has not found the Christ within himself, then all his titles and pretensions are worthless and ridiculous.

This light is the *Atma-Buddhi*, eternally shining into the *Manas* (mind). It is the light of Buddha, because without that light *Gautama* could not have become a "*Buddha*," *i.e.*, "enlightened." It is the light of *Jesus of Nazareth*, for without that light the germ of divinity that sleeps within the peaceful corner, the mystic "*Bethlehem*" within the soul of man, that child could not become *Christ*. It is the light of every human being, for it is the centre and the sun of his own eternal life, the fountain of all his knowledge, for only in that light rests the recognition of eternal truth.

> "The will of God is open to every man, by whatever name the man may be called. . . . Of what use are creeds and opinions to him who has attained self-knowledge? Opinions are not the Spirit of Christ that gives life, but the Spirit of Christ gives testimony to our spirit that we are children of God. He is in us, and we do not need to seek for Him in opinions." (*Threefold Life*, xi. 82.)

> "You need not hunt for any place or locality to find the Holy Ghost; for as the sun rises and shines until it sets, so the Christ shines into all places and hidden corners from the beginning of His humanity unto eternity. The community of Christ is everywhere and in all countries, wherever men and women avoid sin and enter into the will of God." (*Threefold Life*, xi. 88.)

---

[1] "Abel is the fundamental church representing God. The church of Cain is to be converted through Abel. Therefore God has not rejected the church of Cain in so far as not to be willing to receive any member thereof; but the true church is like a lamb among the wolves on account of the wolfish natures of the members usually composing that church." (*Three Principles*, xx. 89.)

"How blind are those who imagine that they are not permitted to touch the great mystery, and that this could only be done by man-made priests. Wherever true Christians are assembled, there is the temple of God." "You are all on good terms with the church, but no one is willing to enter the temple of Christ. Nevertheless there is no other salvation than to enter out of death into life. Unless you do so you will for ever remain in darkness." (*Threefold Life*, xi. 81.)

Humanity resembles a tree, of which Christ is the trunk, the individual souls the branches, and the ever-changing personalities that successively appear upon the earth are the leaves. Within the trunk all are one. The branches differ in their shapes; some are big, others small, and grow bigger from year to year. But the leaves drop off in the autumn and grow again in the spring; they may rustle and stir in contrary directions when the wind blows, they may have separate and opposite interests to fight for, but the tree remains one. The tree may live without the individual leaves, but the leaves cannot continue to exist without the tree. Only within the trunk of the tree, and not in any separate association of leaves, can we find the source of our life and our origin and know our true nature. Therefore Boehme is continually advising us to strive for that trunk of our tree of life, and for that fountain of eternal light and life. He who seeks in Boehme's book for information to gratify his curiosity is usually disappointed, because Boehme does not profess to teach anything outside of Christ, or to supply us with any knowledge which we may not find within ourselves, if we seek like him within the interior fountain. He even protests against wanting to know anything that is not in Christ, and says that such things as cannot be found in Christ are worthless and vain.

"Christ" means the Way and the Truth; it means *Eternal Life* for humanity and for every individual. No one would ever think of seeking for the source of his own life anywhere except within his own inner soul, for the universal life awaits him only in so far as it is active within himself.

Nevertheless this is exactly that which the inhabitants of Babel are not willing to see.[2] They seek for God everywhere except within the Divinity that is dormant within themselves. They dream of some God in the sky whom they expect to come and to save them, while they neglect to save themselves. They seek for information from books, but never listen to the voice of that Word by whose power the All was created, and which speaks within their own hearts.

This want of understanding in regard to the true Redeemer of mankind is the cause of all social troubles with which mankind is at present afflicted, because they cannot see that all true salvation must come from within and not from without, and that merely external reforms are of little value as long as the selfishness of man, which is the root of all evils, is not reformed within.

The fact that the sacred name of Christ has been and is continually

[2]Every one thinks he does not belong to Babel, but Babel is as big as the world.

misunderstood, misapplied, and prostituted by "Christians" and "anti-Christians," by bigots and rationalists, does not change the truth of His being the spiritual light of the world, and the spiritual light within the soul of every individual being, man, woman, or child. To seek for the Christ within one's self (not in dreams and visions), but within one's own inner consciousness, and to practise the power of clinging to Him, exclusively of other thoughts and desires, a practice which requires the continual exercise of repelling all that is vulgar and low, is the only "practical occultism" worthy of any attention.

All the accusations brought forth, either justly or unjustly, against the Christian Churches, all the vilifications and maledictions hurled against Church authorities, have never had as much effect upon the true Church of Christ as a breath of air would upon a leaf, for while the external Church, with its desire for temporal power and authority, will for ever remain the great courtezane, riding upon the beast created by her pride and selfishness, the spiritual Church of Christ rests in eternal tranquillity safely in God. This Church is inaccessible to aggressions of any kind from external sources, because it is divine, internal, and invisible. All the faults for which the "Christian Church" has been blamed, all the innocent blood that she has spilled in the abused name of Christ, all the curses which those Churches have loaded themselves with by their misdeeds, have nothing to do with the true Church of Christ, they belong to the devil parading under the garb of a saint. The history of bigotry is not the history of what ought to be properly called the Christian Church; it is the history of human ignorance, villainy, and superstition. Such corruption has nothing to do with true Christianity, any more than a wart upon a man's body has to do with the man's intelligence. Sects and sectarians are not the Church, the external body of Christ. They are the necessary effects of unnatural causes, and as such they must exist until the mental and spiritual darkness of the world is dissolved by the light of the Truth, which is, and always will be, the only Redeemer of man. When this light once penetrates into all the depths of the soul, then will the darkness cease to exist, and as man will thereby come into possession of real self-knowledge, there will be nothing that he does not know, for man himself will then be the Truth, the Christ; the All having been swallowed up by the Christ in Him who is the Lord[3] of all. Therefore

---

[3] "A thing which is a unity, having only one will, does not fight against itself; but if there are many different kinds of will in one thing, each of them then wants to go its own way. If one will is the *Lord* over the others, having them entirely in his power, then does the complex of the thing constitute only one being, for the many wills are obedient to their lord. Thus life is a cause of trouble, for it exists in many different wills, each essence having a will of its own which may be put into action. Thus the life of man is its own enemy, one form fights the other, and this is the case not only in man, but in all creatures; it be then, that the forms of life obtain a mild, lovely Master, to whose power they must obey. He can break their self-will and

Boehme says:—

> "The Man-Christ (man having become Christ by Christ becoming man) is Lord over all, and comprehends within Himself the whole of divine existence. There is then no other place where we can recognise God except within the substance of Christ (in us), because in Him resides substantially the fulness of Divinity." (*Questions*, i. 153.)

> "All that God the Father is, and all that is in Him, will then appear within *me* (in man) as a form, an image of the essence of the divine world. All colours, powers, and virtues of His eternal wisdom will be manifest in *me* as His true image. *I* shall myself be the manifestation of the spiritual divine world and an instrument for the Spirit of God, wherein He plays with Himself. I shall be His stringed instrument and celestial harp, and not only "I," but all my co-members in the gloriously constructed stringed instrument of God." (*Signature*, xii.)

This means that when the Divine Light (the *Atma-Buddhi* or "Christ" in humanity) becomes fully manifested within the mind (*Manas*) in man, then will the man (*Manas*) be illumined by it, and be itself that Light, *Atma-Buddhi Manas* or Christ. Thus, when man enters the true Church, *i.e.*, the spiritual realm of divine light of wisdom, then will that light of divine wisdom penetrate him, and man, having become all "mind," will be rendered self-luminous and self-knowing thereby. All that prevents man from entering into that state is his selfish will and egoism, and therefore when man, relatively to his own selfish will (constituting his own terrestrial self), has become entirely helpless, as if nailed to a cross, and if his selfish will has died upon that cross, then will take place his glorious resurrection as a divine being, even as the very Christ Himself. Then will his former illusion, whereby he imagined himself to be an isolated being and a thing separate from the rest of humanity, have passed away, and he will recognise the God in him, and himself as that God, living in the Light that pervades the All, and being himself the All, and with arms outstretched upon the cross of life, drawing to his heart every human being by the power of divine love.

This divine love is neither a chimera nor a dream, nor the belief in it a superstition, but it is the most substantial reality; for it is the very essence of that of which the world has been created. Its beauty can be perceived by man in everything by means of what is beautiful in himself, and it is tangible to the soul touched by it. It is not confined in gross material bodies, but superior to everything. It is self-existent and

power. This *Lord* is the light of life, the master over all the qualities. He can tame them all, and they love to submit to him, for the light gives them mildness and power. They give their will to the life-light, and it endows them with mildness." (*Six Points*, iv. 4.)

232

free, and causes the soul,, the light, to arise out of the dark fiery will, comparable to a beautiful plant growing out of the dark soil. It is not an unconscious mechanical force or attraction, but divine will and self-consciousness, in other words, the Spirit of God.

The realm of this divine love-light is the only true church, outside of which no salvation can be found, neither by scientific acquisitions nor by anything that is inferior to divine love. The true divine self of every human being is a member and an inhabitant of that church, and he who severs his connection with it throws away his own life.

Science says that each thing has an *aura* of unknown extent wherein the qualities of that thing are revealed, and the same truth may perhaps be more correctly expressed by saying that each thing and each being is a part of an individual power of unknown size, possessing certain qualities, and having evolved a form or organism, wherein some of these qualities have become manifest. Thus our visible material bodies are only a manifestation of a part of the true man living in the kingdom of light. The real man is an inhabitant of heaven, it is merely his shadow which walks in mortal form upon the earth.

Not to identify ourselves with the shadow, but to attain the knowledge of our celestial self, is the object of this terrestrial life.

This recognition of one's own divine self no mortal being can attain by his or her own power, because only that which is immortal in man can recognise itself as being immortal. Without the presence of eternal truth that truth cannot be recognised, nor can, in the absence of light, the darkness illumine itself.

It is therefore not sinful man, the shadow, that can know the true light, the Christ; but Christ recognising His own divine image in man. Thus Christ lives in the sanctuary of man, and all that is capable in man of recognising the Christ in him, lives in the Christ; but if man has attained that state in the Christ, he will then cease to be merely a man, but free of the illusion of self, he will know himself to be God. He will then no longer desire to attain, or to become something, but rest in his own divine self-consciousness, knowing his shadowy self to be nothing but a delusion, and his divine self All in the Christ.

Appendix

"THE soul originates from three principles; she lives therefore in a threefold anguish, and is held by three ties. The first tie links her to eternity and reaches within the abyss of hell (the fiery will); the second is the kingdom of heaven; the third is the region of the stars with the elements. The third kingdom is not eternal, but has a certain period of existence; nevertheless it is this kingdom that causes the man to grow up, endowing him with manners and will, and desires relating to good and to evil. It gives him beauty, riches and honours, and makes him a terrestrial god. It is with him unto the end of his time, and then it departs and as it aided him to obtain life, so it aids him in death, and cuts him loose from the astral soul.

"First the four elements break away from the one element, and thus the activity in the third principle ceases; and this is the most terrible thing, that the four elements are broken up within themselves. Then the *tincture* with the shadow (of what was man) enters into the other, and with this the shadow remains in the root of the element from which the four elements were born, and from which they issued. This breaking up alone is the suffering and the pain; it is the destruction of the sensitive house of the soul.

"But if the essences of the soul in the first principle have been so much attached to the ways of this world that they have desired only for the lust of the latter, for temporal honour, power, and pomp; the will, the soul, *i.e.*, the essences out of the first principle, still retain the astral essences as their most precious treasure, and desire to dwell therein; but as these essences are now deprived of their mother, the four elements, they become gradually consumed in the essences of the first principle.

"Then will the soul in her astral garment, floating within the doors of the depth, experience great uneasiness owing to her earthly state, and by the power that belongs to her astral constitution she may reappear in the shape of her former corporeal body, asking for this or for that, such as has been her desire before she passed away, and seeking to obtain rest; and she may also go about haunting places and trying to manifest her presence at night, according to her sidereal spirit, making noises of various kinds.

"That with which she has clothed herself during life, this will be her garment. If it is luxury, lust, ambition, riches, malevolence, anger, lies, or the illusions of the world, then will the strong power of the essences out of the first principle hold on to these things by means of the sidereal spirit, and render it active according to the astral quality. The

235

sidereal spirit restlessly clings to that for which it desires; as is said by Christ, 'Where your treasure is, there is your heart.' Therefore it often happens that the ghosts of dead persons are seen going about in great unrest. That with which the soul has clothed herself here in the body (in her will and thought), that constitutes her anguish, and according to her anguish will be her shape and form in the astral state, until this state and anguish is consumed. Her eternal dwelling-place is the deep abyss without end or number, and the works which she performed here are embodied in the forms in her tincture, and follow her.

"There is no light neither from this world nor from God, but the ignition of her own fire is her light, it being the terrible flash of her wrath and inimical. The kind of the anguish of such souls differs according to the quality of that with which the soul has burdened herself. For such a soul there is no help; she cannot enter into the light of God; and even if St. Peter had left a thousand keys upon the earth, neither of them would unlock the door, for she has severed the bond that connected her with Divinity." (See *Three Principles*, xix. and foll.)

ASCETICISM.

"It is written that it is very difficult for a rich man to enter into the kingdom of heaven. This does not refer to the possession of wealth, but to one's vain and avaricious life; for while man grows fat, God is forgotten. None ought to imagine that he is blessed because he is poor. If he is an unbeliever and godless, he is then in the kingdom of the devil, in spite of his poverty. Neither ought the rich man throw away his money or give it to the spendthrift, thinking thereby to gain eternal bliss. The kingdom of God is in truth, justice, and love towards the needy. It condemns none who properly uses that which he has. You must not lay down your sceptre and go into a corner and lament. This is only hypocrisy. You can be of service to the law of justice and to the kingdom of God better if you keep your sceptre and protect the oppressed and weak, and work for right and justice; not according to your avarice, but in the love and fear of God." (*Principles*, xxv. 74.)

ASTRAL SPIRIT.

"All that we think and do and desire in our external being is the work of the spirit of this world acting within our constitution; for the body is nothing but the instrument of that spirit wherewith it works, and, like all other instruments that are born of the spirit of this world, it will ultimately break and be decomposed. Therefore no man shall despise or condemn another man if the latter has not the same qualifications as he; for the natural heaven (the constellation) builds up each man according to the nature of the ruling influences. It gives to every person his or her ways and manners and shape, and also his desires and instincts, and this cannot be taken away from the external man as long as the external heaven does not break up his animal constitution. But if the external man does *not* do that which the spirit of the external world

236

desires in him, but is forced to depart from that which is false and illusive; then such a power does not come from the external heaven, but from the new-born man within, he being from eternity, and battling with the earthly man; and often he gains a victory over the latter." (*Three Principles*, xxv. 6.)

ATONEMENT.

"If you wish to follow the path (of light), you must use great earnest. It must not be mere talk or pretence, while the heart is far away; for in this way you will attain nothing. You must gather together your whole mind, with all your senses and reason, into one single will, if you wish to become reformed, and to come out of your abominations. You must put your sense into God, into His charity, with full confidence and assurance, and then you will attain it. And if the devil in you says, 'It cannot be; you are too great a sinner;' let not this terrify you; for he is a liar and the father of doubt.

"There are not more than two kingdoms moving within you. One is the kingdom of God, wherein is Christ, desiring you; the other is the kingdom of hell, wherein is the devil, and he desires you also. Then will the poor soul have to battle, for she is in the middle. Christ offers to her the new robe, and the devil the cloth of sins; and whenever you have a good thought or desire for God, and wish to enter into the true atonement (becoming one with the Divine), that thought is most certainly not from yourself, but from the love of God, and the noble virgin is calling to you to come, and not to desist in your efforts. But if on this way you are met by your great sins, that seek to detain you like mountains, so that you can find no peace in your heart; then is this most surely the work of the devil, who causes you to think that God is not willing to listen to you. Let not in such moments anything detain or terrify you; for the devil is your enemy. It is written that if your sins were as red as blood, if you truly repent, they will become as white as snow." (*Principles*, xxiv. 34.)

"Thus the precious jewel is sown; but remember well, it does not immediately grow into a tree. Often will the devil brush over it and seek to uproot the mustard-seed; the soul will often have to weather heavy storms, and be covered with the shadows of her sins. But if you constantly battle against the powers of evil, then will the tree grow and blossom, and you will obtain the fruit." (Comp. *Three Principles*, xxiv. 37.)

THE CROSS.

The cross with the image of a dying person nailed thereon is the symbol of regeneration and initiation. It reminds the true follower of Christ that he must pass through the mystic death and become regenerated in the spirit before he can enter into the glory of eternal life. The cross represents terrestrial life, and the crown of thorns the sufferings of the soul within the elementary body, but also the victory of the spirit over the elements of darkness. The body is naked, to indicate that the candidate for immortality must divest himself of all desires for terrestrial things. The figure is nailed to the cross, which symbolises the death and surrender of the self-will, and that it should not attempt to accomplish anything by its own power, but merely serve as an instrument wherein the Divine will is executed. Above the head are inscribed the letters:

I. N. R. J.

whose most important meaning is:

IN NOBIS REGNAT JESUS.
(Within ourselves reigns Jesus.)

But the signification of this inscription can be practically known only to those who have actually died relatively to the world of desires, and risen above the temptation for personal existence; or, to express it in other words, those who have become alive in Christ, and in whom thus the kingdom of Jesus (the holy love-will issuing from the heart of God) has been established.

To the cynic, sophist, and fool this symbol will be incomprehensible, and in the hands of the bigot and hypocrite it is a token of his disgrace, and a testimonial of his own godlessness and self-condemnation.

"The external world or the external life is not a valley of suffering for those who enjoy it, but only for those who know of a higher life. The animal enjoys animal life; the intellect the intellectual realm; but he who has entered into regeneration recognises his terrestrial existence as a burden and prison. With this recognition he takes upon himself the Cross of Christ." (*Epistles*, ii. 34.)

DEATH.

"The holy and heavenly man, hidden in the monstrous (external) man, is as much in heaven as God, and heaven is in him, and the heart or light of God is begotten and born in him. Thus is God in him and he in God. God is nearer to him than his bestial body.

"The animal body is not his own native country, wherein he is at home; the true man, regenerated and new-born in Christ, is not in this world, but in the paradise of God; and although he is in the body, nevertheless he is in God. And although the animal body dies, nevertheless nothing happens to the new man, but he comes forth out of the contrary will and torment-house into his native country. There needs to be no removing to any distance or place, whither he may have to go, that it might be better with him, for God is everywhere revealed in him." (*The Epistles*, xxv. 13.)

DOUBT.

"The nothing wherein the devil resides. Doubt is the negation of that faith which is God. It is the outcome of selfishness and of that blindness which causes man not to recognise the possession of what he already has." (See *Threefold Life*, xiv. 41.)

GOD.

"God is eternal unity, the unmeasurable one good, having nothing before or after it that could possibly endow it with something or move it. It is without any inclinations or qualities, without any beginning in time, within itself only one. It is purity itself, without any contact; requiring neither place nor locality for its dwelling, being at once outside of and within the world. Into its depth no thought can penetrate, neither can its greatness be expressed in numbers, for it is infinity itself. All that can be counted or measured is natural or figurative, but the unity of God cannot be defined. It is everything, and has been recognised as good, and is called 'good,' because it is eternal mildness and beneficence within the sensitivity of nature and creature, the sweetest love. For the unity in its aspect as good issues out of itself, introducing itself into willing and moving. There the unity lives and penetrates the willing or moving, and the willing and moving experiences the mildness of the unity. This is the foundation of love in the unity, of which Moses says, 'The Lord our God is an holy God, and there is no other besides Him.'" (*Theos.* quest. i. 1.)

HUMILITY.

"God is the centre of man, but he resides only within himself, unless the spirit of man becomes one spirit with him; in which case he will become manifest in human nature, in soul, mind and desire, whereby he becomes perceptible to the inner senses of man. The will sends the senses into God, and God impresses the senses and becomes one being with them. Then the senses carry the power of God to the will, and the will receives them joyfully but tremblingly; for it recognises itself as being unworthy knowing that it comes from an unsteady dwelling. Thus it receives that power by sinking down before God and out of its triumph arises a sweet humility. This is the true essence of God, and this conceived essence within the will is the celestial body, and is called the true and just faith, which the will has received in the power of God. It sinks within the mind and resides in the fire of the soul." (*Menschw.* x. 8.)

JESUS CHRIST.

"In the fifth quality the glory and majesty of God becomes manifest as the light of love. It is written that God resides in a light into which none can enter. This means that no created being has ever been born out of the central fire of love, for it is the most holy fire, and even God Himself in His Trinity. Out of this holy fire has emanated the JAH, a ray of the sensitive unity. This is the dear name of JESUS, redeeming the poor soul from the wrath-fire, and in taking up human nature, giving itself up to the central fire of God in the soul, in the wrath of God within the soul; kindling her again with the love-fire, and uniting her with God." (*Theos.* quest. iii. 25.)

"CHRIST is he that is regenerated of human quality; the mother of regeneration, the anointed one." (See *Stief,* 19.)[1]

MAN, TERRESTRIAL AND CELESTIAL.

"The virgin says: I have something against you. I have raised you up from among the thorns. When you were a wild animal, I have configured in you my own image. But the wild animal is among the thorns: this I will not take unto my bosom. You are still living within your wild animal. When the world takes that animal, because it belongs to it, then will I take you. Thus each one will take its own belongings. Why do you therefore love so much that wild animal which causes to you nothing but sorrow? You cannot take it with you. It does not belong to you, but to the world. Let the world use it as it may, but remain you with me. It will be only a little while; then will your animal break, and you will be rid of it, and remain with me. How will you then rejoice, if you think of that animal, which afflicted you day and night, and of which you are then free. As a flower grows up out of the earth, so do you rise up out of your wild animal. You say, 'I am your animal; you are born in me.' Listen, my animal! I am greater than you. When you was to become, I was your constructor. My essences are out of the root of eternity; but you are of this world. You will break; but I remain eternally in my power. Therefore I am far nobler than you. You live in the wrath; but I will put my fearful wrath into the light, into eternal joy. My works are in power, while yours remain as shadows. When I am once rid of you, I will then never accept you again as my animal; but (I take) my new body which I am regenerating within the deepest root of the holy element." (*Principles*, xxi. 69.)

NATURE.

"Lift up your mind in the spirit, and see that the whole of nature, with all the powers therein, with its depth, width, and height, heaven and earth, and all that is therein and above the heavens, is the body of God, and the powers of the stars are the arteries in the natural body of God in this world." (*Aurora*, ii. 16.)

---

[1]Jesus represents the Logos and Christ the Karana sharira in Eastern terminology.

"Nature is not God, no more than the body of a man is man. Nature is the echo and image of eternal nature, made manifest by the power of the Word." (*Tabulæ Principiæ*, li.)

PATH.

"Neither in the sky, nor upon the earth, or among the stars or the elements, can we find any way by which we may enter into rest. We behold merely the entrance into life, and next to that its end, when our body will be borne back to the earth and all our works, labour, and sciences, and glory will be inherited by another, who also troubles himself for a while with such things, and then follows us (into death). This continues from the beginning of the world unto its end. During our misery we can never know where our spirit remains while the body breaks and becomes a corpse, unless we are new-born out of this world; so that although we live in this world in our body, nevertheless we dwell in our soul and spirit in another eternal, perfect, and new life. Therein a new man will be found in our spirit and soul, and therein shall and will he live eternally. Only in this new form will we learn to know what we are and where our true home is." (*Principles*, xxii. 5.)

PLANETS.

The seven planets refer not only to certain visible stars, but to the seven qualities of eternal nature, namely—

1. ♄ *Saturn*—Astringency; darkness.

2. ♃ *Jupiter*—The active desire within the astringency.

3. ♂ *Mars*—The fiery strength.

4. ☉ *Sun*—The light of nature.

5. ♀ *Venus*—The beginning of substantiality.

6. ☿ *Mercury*—Life; sound; the *verbum fiat.*

7. ☾ *Luna*—Moon; corporeity.

"If the first three qualities have their superiority in the dark principle, then will the other qualities be dormant in their centres; and all the seven are then evil, as follows:—

1. *Saturn*—Avarice.

2. *Jupiter*—Cunning.

3. *Mars*—Anger.

4. *Sun*—Pride.

5. *Venus*—Lewdness.

6. *Mercury*—Envy.

7. *Luna*—The flesh.

"If the three first qualities have their superiority in the principle of light and are born out of the dark centre, then will they have in them the nature of light. They will then all the seven be good, as follows:—

1. *Saturn*—Charity.

2. *Jupiter*—Wisdom.

3. *Mars*—Meekness.

4. *Sol*—Humility.

5. *Venus*—Chastity.

6. *Mercury*—Beneficence.

7. *Luna*—The substantiality of the body of Christ."

PRINCIPLE.

"A principle (beginning) is nothing else but a new birth, a new life. There is only one principle in which is eternal life, namely, the eternal divinity, and this would not become manifest if God had not created within himself creatures, such as men and angels, who know the indissoluble band, and how the birth of eternal light in God takes place." (*Principles*, v. 6.)

"God had no other material out of which to create anything, except his own essence. But God is a spirit, intangible, and having neither beginning nor end. His depth and greatness is everything. A spirit does nothing except that it rises, and stirs, and moves, and gives birth to its own self. In its birth there are especially three forms—bitterness, astringency, and heat; but in these three forms there is neither a first, nor a second, nor a third; but they are all three only one, and each one gives birth to the other and to the third." (*Principles*, l. 3.)

SEX.

"The male is the head, and has in him the upper regiment with the tincture of the fire, and in his tincture he has the soul that desires for *Venus* as its corporeal matrix. The soul longs to have spirit and body, and this has the matrix of woman. But the lower regiment is the female

242

one, and her regiment stands in the *Moon;* for the *Sun* gives the heart, and *Venus* the *tincture,* not of a fiery, but of a watery kind. The spirit furnishes the air, and its tincture is not in the heat.

"The female desires the male, and the *Moon* longs for the *Sun;* for she is of a material nature, and desires a celestial heart. Thus the female *matrix* desires for the heart of man and for his *tincture* the soul; for the soul is eternal good. Thus exists sexual desire among all creatures, and they wish to mingle with each other. The body does not understand this, neither is it understood by the air-spirit; but the two *tinctures,* the male and the female ones, know it well." (*Threefold Life,* ix. 106.)

SOPHIA.

"The fiery soul, pure as clear gold, and tested in the fire of God, is the husband of the noble *Sophia,* for she is the *tincture* of the light. If the tincture of the fire is perfectly pure, then will Sophia be united with it, and thus *Adam* receives again the most noble bride that was taken away from him during his sleep, and will take her into his arms. This is neither a man nor a woman, but a branch on the *pearl-tree* standing in God's paradise. But how the bride receives her groom in his clear and bright fire-quality, and how she gives him the kiss of love, this will be understood only by him who has been at the marriage of the Lamb. To all others it will be a mystery." (*Mysterium Magnum,* xxv. 14.)

SUBSTANTIALITY.

"If you boast of being a Christian, why do you then not believe Christ's words when he said, 'I am with you even to the end of the world;' and furthermore, that he will give us his body for food and his blood to drink? You say, 'Christ has gone to heaven; how then could he be in this world?' Perhaps you agree that he is present with us in his Holy Spirit. But what would become of the new-born man in you if he were fed only by spirit, this being merely food for the soul? Each life eats of its own mother. The soul is spirit, and eats spiritual food; the new-born man eats of the pure element, and the external man of the outcome of the four elements.

"What will it benefit the (ethereal) body if the soul eats of the pure divinity? for you know that the soul and the body are not one and the same thing. The soul is spirit, and needs spiritual food. Or do you think that you can feed the new man with earthly food? If so, you are then still far from the kingdom of God." (*Principles,* xxiii. 6.)

SULPHUR, SALT, AND MERCURY.

"The word *Sul* means and is the soul of a thing; for in the word *Sulphur* it is the oil or the light, which is born from the syllable *Phur.* It is the beauty or goodness of a thing; its love or best beloved. In a creature it is the intelligence and sense, and it is the spirit born from the syllable *Phur*. The word or syllable *Phur* is *Prima Materia*, entering into the third principle within itself, the Macrocosm wherefrom the elemental (terrestrial) kingdom or essence is born; but in the first principle it is the essence of the innermost generation, wherefrom God the Father from eternity gives birth to his Son. In man it is also the light born from the sidereal spirit within the other centre in the Microcosm, but in the *Spiraculum* it is a soul-spirit in the inner centre. It is the light of God, which alone possesses that soul which is in the love of God, for it is kindled and breathed upon by the Holy Spirit." (*Three Principles*, ii. 7.)

"*Sal* is *Prima Materia*, astringency. In the strong astringency arises the bitterness; for in the powerful attraction arises the uneasiness of the spirit. For instance, if a person becomes angry, his spirit attracts that which causes him to become embittered and trembling; and if he does not resist and put it down, then the fire of wrath becomes kindled in him, so as to make him burn in malice. Then in his mind and soul this becomes substantial and a being." (*Three Principles*, i. 9.)

"*Mercury*, an astringent bitter fire—sulphur—water; the most terrible of all states; but you must not imagine it to be a *Materia* or a tangible thing; it is spirit and the source of the first beginning of nature." (*Three Principles*, i. 10.)

"It comprehends all the four qualities wherein arises the life; but it has its beginning not in the centre, like Phur, but according to the fire-flash within the terror of the dark quality." (*Threefold Life*, ii. 42.)

WORD.

"The whole power of the Father speaks out of all the qualities the WORD, *i.e.*, the Son of God. The same word, or the same sound, spoken by the Father issues out of the *Salniter*, or the powers of the Father, and out of the Father's *Mercurius* or sound. Thus the Father speaks the word out of himself, and the same sound is the glory of all his powers; and after it is spoken out, it is no longer contained within the powers of the Father, but sounds and rings in the whole of the Father in all powers. This power outspoken by the Father has such a strength that the sound of the word immediately and rapidly penetrates through the whole depth of the Father, and this strength is the Holy Spirit; for the outspoken word remains as a glory or majestic command before the king; but the sound, issuing through the word, executes the command of the Father which he has spoken out through the word, and in this is the birth of the Holy Trinity. The same takes place in an angel or man. The power in the whole of his body has all the qualities as in God the Father." (*Auror*. vi. 2.)

"In the spirit of the word is to be understood the whole of Divinity, with all its powers and effects, and with its whole essence; its uprising, penetrating, and changing; the whole action and the whole generation." (*Auror.* xix. 72.)

"Thus every creature has its own centre for its out-speaking, or the sound of the formed word within itself, both the eternal and temporal beings; the unreasoning ones as well as man; for the first *Ens* has been spoken out of the sound of God, by wisdom, out of her centre into the fire and light, and has been formed into the *fiat*, and entered into 'compaction.' The *Ens* is out of the eternal, but the *compaction* is out of the temporal; and therefore in everything there is something eternal hidden in time." (*Mysterium Magnum*, xxii. 2.)

"In that quality in which each word in the human voice in the act of outspeaking forms and manifests itself, either in the love of God, as in the holy *Ens*, or in the wrath of God; in the same quality will it be taken up again therein after it has been spoken out. The false word becomes infected by the devil, and sealed up for (future) detriment, and is received within the *Mysterium* of the wrath, as in the quality of the dark world. Each thing returns with its *Ens* to that wherefrom it has originated." (*Mysterium Magnum*, xxii. 6.)

The word is near to thee, even within thy heart and lips, and God himself is the word which is in thy heart and lips." (*Three Principles*, iv. 10.)

Made in the USA
Middletown, DE
31 July 2024